FEB 0 9 1997

Barry Goldwater

THE OKLAHOMA WESTERN BIOGRAPHIES
RICHARD ETULAIN, GENERAL EDITOR

A recent portrait. Goldwater's association with the Smoki is reflected in the tattoo on his hand. Barry Goldwater Photograph Collection, courtesy of the Arizona Historical Foundation

Barry Goldwater

Native Arizonan

By Peter Iverson

UNIVERSITY OF OKLAHOMA PRESS : NORMAN AND LONDON

Also by Peter Iverson

The Navajos: A Critical Bibliography (Bloomington, Ind., 1976)
The Navajo Nation (Westport, Conn., 1981; Albuquerque, 1983)
Carlos Montezuma and the Changing World of American Indians (Albuquerque, 1982; 1984)
(ed.) *The Plains Indians of the Twentieth Century* (Norman, 1985; 1986)
The Navajos (New York, 1990)
(ed., with Albert L. Hurtado) *Major Problems in American Indian History* (Lexington, Mass., 1994)
When Indians Became Cowboys: Native Peoples and Cattle Ranching in the American West (Norman, 1994; 1997)

Library of Congress Cataloging-in-Publication Data
Iverson, Peter.
    Barry Goldwater : native Arizonan / by Peter Iverson.
        p.   cm. — (The Oklahoma western biographies : v. 15)
    Includes bibliographical references and index.
    ISBN 0-8061-2958-1 (alk. paper)
        1. Goldwater, Barry M. (Barry Morris), 1909–   . 2. Legislators—
United States—Biography. 3. Arizona—Politics and government—1951–
4. United States. Congress. Senate—Biography. 5. United States—Poli-
tics and government—1945–1989. 6. Hopi Indians—Arizona. 7. Navajo
Indians—Arizona. I. Title. II. Series.
E748.G64I94   1997
973.92'092—dc21
[B]   97-2996
                                                                                            CIP

Barry Goldwater: Native Arizonan is Volume 15 in *The Oklahoma Western Biographies.*

The paper in this book meets the guidelines for permanence and durability of the Committee on Production Guidelines for Book Longevity for the Council on Library Resources, Inc.⊚

1   2   3   4   5   6   7   8   9   10

To Erika, Jens, Scott, Tim, and Laurie

Contents

List of Illustrations   ix
List of Maps   x
Series Editor's Preface   xi
Preface   xiii

1. Growing Up with the Country   3
2. Seeing Arizona   20
3. Aviation, the Military, and Electronics   47
4. Entering Politics   66
5. Gaining the Nomination, Losing the Race   92
6. Returning to the Senate   128
7. Native Arizonans   151
8. Building Arizona   189
9. Coming Home   221

Sources   243
Index   251

Illustrations

Barry Goldwater   *frontispiece*
Josephine Goldwater   8
Baron Goldwater with children   10
Barry Goldwater in youth   13
At Green River, Utah   33
Welcome to Arizona   34
Taking care of laundry   36
Charlie Potato, Navajo   44
Peggy G in Greenland   53
Barry Goldwater, pilot   55
Phoenix City Council   71
With Howard Pyle   74
Campaign rally at Phoenix College   117
Election day cartoon   124
With Hugh Scott and John Rhodes   137
Peggy Goldwater   141
Barry Goldwater, Smoki   166
With Billy Wilson   171
Monument Valley   173
With Kachinas   176
Camelback Mountain   207
Grand Canyon   212
With model airplanes   225
At home   230

Maps

Arizona   2
Grand Canyon   30

Series Editor's Preface

STORIES of heroes and heroines have intrigued many generations of listeners and readers. Americans, like people everywhere, have been captivated by the lives of military, political, and religious figures and of intrepid explorers, pioneers, and rebels.

The Oklahoma Western Biographies series endeavors to build on this fascination with biography and to link it with another subject of abiding interest to Americans: the frontier of the American West. Although volumes in the series carry no notes, they are prepared by leading scholars, are soundly researched, and include a brief listing of sources used. Each volume is a lively synthesis based on thorough examination of pertinent primary and secondary sources.

Above all, the Oklahoma Western Biographies series aims at two goals: to provide readable life stories of significant westerners and to show how their lives illuminate a notable topic, an influential movement, or a series of important events in the history and culture of the American West.

Peter Iverson clearly achieves these goals in his smoothly written and well-organized biography of Barry Goldwater. Iverson's Goldwater is a lively, opinionated, honest, straightforward man, mostly conservative but obviously open to a variety of people and ideas. Like earlier biographers, Iverson shows how Goldwater the politician reflects important trends in national politics. But the author moves beyond other biographers in demonstrating the important links among national, regional, and state happenings that Goldwater's career has provided.

In addition, Iverson adeptly places Goldwater in important contexts of the twentieth-century American West. For example, the author elucidates the Arizona senator's central roles in issues such as water politics, federal policies in the West, and bittersweet urban growth. Moreover, Iverson is balanced in handling these complex topics. In several instances he admits to disagreeing with Goldwater, but those disagreements are always handled fairly.

Overall, Peter Iverson provides an illuminating biography of a major figure in recent western history. Already well known for his distinguished studies of twentieth-century western social and economic history, Iverson has now produced another valuable volume in this new life story of Barry Goldwater. His book is a superb example of what writers in this series aim for: to provide a readable, well-researched biography of a significant westerner whose life illuminates major events and ideas of the American West.

RICHARD W. ETULAIN

University of New Mexico

Preface

MANY writers have attempted to tell the story of Barry Goldwater. Almost all have told a familiar tale, emphasizing in particular Goldwater's candidacy for the presidency in 1964 and in general his role in the evolution of the Republican party. Most older Americans who recall Goldwater do so in the context of the 1960s. They remember him, as they do the era, with either great enthusiasm or utter disdain. Whether we speak of the perspectives of authors or the public, we observe usually a simplistic portrait, one without complexity, with limited understanding of personal background, and with no evolution over time. This is not to suggest, of course, that some of the primary dimensions of Goldwater's image are without foundation. Goldwater was, indeed, a conservative. He believed in individual initiative, free enterprise, and a limited role for the federal government in regard to domestic issues. Goldwater remained consistent in his perspective, even though it meant alienating others who might want the government to push more strongly for civil rights, for example, or to limit choices in regard to birth control. His participation in World War II strongly influenced his views on the role the United States should play in world affairs. He adhered to an outlook common to his generation: the nation must invest deeply in defense and must intervene internationally where American interests appeared threatened. This conclusion dictated a militant anticommunist stance.

Goldwater should be understood, however, in the context not only of prevailing ideology and of time but also of place. He is, above all, a native Arizonan. His life and career reflect in many ways the evolution of Arizona in the twentieth century. Born in Phoenix in 1909, three years before Arizona became a state, he mirrored in his world view the country in which he grew up. His interest in the diverse cultural and geographical terrain of Arizona encouraged him to represent it in his photography. He perceived the need to exploit the natural beauty of Arizona to boost national and international interest and investment in the state. An early fascination with aviation allowed him to see that terrain from a different perspective and later affected his participation in World War II. Aviation, the military, and electronics all proved central to the development of Arizona during and after the war; Goldwater's involvement in such spheres and his commitment to building and developing his city and his state inspired him to enter politics, first as a Phoenix City Council representative and then as a United States senator. His outspoken views, rooted in southwestern experience and heritage, fueled his rapid rise to national prominence. His involvement with Native American communities came naturally from early exposure to different ways of life; his lack of engagement with the small African American population in Arizona hindered his understanding of the civil rights movement. His very success in promoting the explosive growth of the Salt River valley and Arizona ultimately inspired some second thoughts about the potential or actual cost of that growth. In his later years, Goldwater occasionally experienced what one observer aptly has termed "native's remorse" for the dilemmas posed by demands upon the land and sky of Arizona. Through a long, active, and colorful career, Goldwater spoke from the heart. If he occasionally spoke too soon, not always realizing the full impact of an off-the-cuff remark, he maintained an old-fashioned honesty which endeared him eventually to many Americans of all political persuasions. Goldwater became an Arizona patriarch— free, as always, to speak his mind, expressing his opinions in a candid, unpretentious style.

I attempt here a western biography, in keeping with this series published by the University of Oklahoma Press. I acknowledge that the national and international aspects of Goldwater's career must be analyzed, but I am determined not to rehearse them at great length. Readers who wish a highly detailed account of Senator Goldwater's views or actions about some particular concern that I choose not to recount here can consult many other published sources. Rather I wish to emphasize a critical part of this man's experience far less known and understood, even within the Southwest. I see Goldwater as a symbol of Arizona in this century; in this book, I try to link his life with the evolution of America's forty-eighth state. Because relatively few historians have paid serious attention to Arizona in the twentieth century, this biography affords the opportunity to suggest significant aspects of that fascinating and often paradoxical story. *Barry Goldwater* is presented in essentially chronological order, with each chapter centering on themes which overlap in time. Chapter 1 traces his family heritage, his childhood, and his coming of age. "Seeing Arizona" concerns his photography and his personal discovery of the Grand Canyon; both linked with the expansion of *Arizona Highways* as a publication which brought particular images of Arizona to people all over the world and which played no small part in attracting people and businesses to move to the Southwest. Chapter 3 relates Goldwater's participation in aviation and the military and demonstrates how these two components, combined with electronics, proved central to the transformation of Arizona during and after World War II. The next three chapters focus on Goldwater's political career, emphasizing his campaigns and perspectives as city councilman, senator, presidential candidate, and then, once again, senator. His political career, including his run for the White House and his part in the final days of the Nixon presidency, is brought forth in the context of his background as an Arizonan. Goldwater's involvement in vital issues relating to the Southwest, both as a senator and as a public citizen, are discussed more fully in chapters 7 and 8. "Native Arizonans" considers the meaning of the term *native* and concentrates on Goldwater's association with American Indian affairs, using primarily his association with the Navajos and the Hopis to illustrate that engagement. This chapter also contrasts Goldwater's immersion into American Indian matters with his far more limited association with the state's Mexican American and African American communities. Chapter 8 selects several examples of the complications inherent in building Arizona and examines how Goldwater's own choices illustrated some of the problems that stemmed, almost inevitably, from the state's rapid growth. In an epilogue I delineate the end of Goldwater's active political career but as well his continuing participation in the remarkable maelstrom that Arizona politics reliably engenders. Through this account I try to present a more complicated and more even-handed analysis of a man, his time, and his place.

My interest in Barry Goldwater is tied directly to my own life experience as well as my research. My mother's parents taught in Indian schools in Navajo and Hopi country in the 1930s and early 1940s, and their stories, combined with those of their children, inaugurated my enduring fascination with the peoples and landscapes of northern Arizona. My residence in Arizona, beginning with a three-year sojourn on the Navajo Nation from 1969 to 1972, resumed in 1975 to 1976, and continued since 1986, acquainted me with different stages of Goldwater's career as well as questions Arizonans have confronted about the nature of their society and the direction of their future. This is a book, then, not only about a man but also about his native state, which has become my home.

In 1964, as a sophomore at Carleton College, I enrolled in a course offered but once every four years. Our class analyzed the forthcoming presidential election, and our main assignment asked us to predict the result, with our grade hinging to a significant degree on the accuracy of our prognostications. In 1960 the task had been a harrowing one. However, the contest between Lyndon Johnson and Barry Goldwater dashed any hopes the instructor had for grading on a curve. Weeks before election day, the outcome seemed obvious, and the voters in November did not surprise us. At that time one had to be twenty-one to vote—a situation Goldwater later helped to alter—and I did not participate directly in that election. But had I been given the franchise, despite my misgivings about the character of Lyndon Johnson, I would have voted for Johnson rather than Goldwater. As a high school student I had heard Jack Kennedy speak in 1960 and had been enthusiastic about his candidacy for president. Since the completion of my graduate studies in 1975, I have lived in the arid West and have followed the advice given to Montana farmers: vote Democratic in a drought and Republican when it rains. In southern Wyoming and in southern Arizona there never seems to be sufficient precipitation. So Barry Goldwater's politics have not been mine, but working on this biography has allowed me to see him, as well as the time and place in which he has lived, in a more thorough way.

I began to think about this book soon after I returned to live in Arizona in 1986. When Goldwater spoke to my classes in western history at Arizona State University, his stories and the response of my students to his presence convinced me that at some point I wanted to attempt a concise, interpretive biography. In 1989, I organized a forum, titled "Continuity and Change in Arizona since World War II," to which Senator Goldwater, Phoenix attorney Frank Snell, Salt River Project manager Jack Pfister, and Arizona historian and lifelong friend of Goldwater, Lester "Budge" Ruffner, were invited. Budge presided over a wonderful morning of reminiscences, jokes, and musings. A summer research grant in 1990 and sabbatical leave in the fall of 1992 at Arizona State University allowed me to devote more time to this project.

Doris Berry, the personal secretary of Senator Goldwater, kindly arranged for me to obtain a personal interview. Although this interview, eventually conducted in November 1995, had to be postponed and did not occur until I had reached a very late stage in my writing, the opportunity to visit the Goldwater home and to ask particular questions was most welcome. I thank Ms. Berry and Mr. Goldwater for their hospitality to me on this occasion. In a related sense, I would like to acknowledge the untiring assistance offered by people associated with the Arizona Historical Foundation, where the Goldwater papers are housed. The foundation, founded by Goldwater, has played a vital role in the preservation of Arizona's heritage. Former director Dick Lynch and staff member Susie Sato helped me get started with this project, and current director Evelyn Cooper, curator Ed Oetting, and several staff members, particularly James Allen and Jenny Armendt, helped me finish it.

Archivists Pat Etter and Chris Marin of the Department of Manuscripts and Special Collections at the Hayden Library of Arizona State University assisted me in sifting through various holdings. Graduate assistants AnCita Benally, Paul Hietter, and Paivi Hoikkala helped find materials during early stages of my research. Faculty, students, and staff in the history department at Arizona State University have made Tempe a good place for me to be during the past decade. I would like to add a special note of thanks to the graduate students with whom I work; their imagination, dedication, and enthusiasm mean a great deal to me.

Thanks as well to Jack Pfister, now a member of the Arizona State University community, for his encouragement and insights. I would also like to acknowledge the willingness of Gary Avey, Hugh Harelson, Richard Hart, Jonathan Marshall, Elsa Mulhern, Bob Reveles, and Barton Wright to speak to me about particular dimensions of Goldwater's career. Thank you to Carol Cooperrider, of Albuquerque, New Mexico, for contributing the two maps in this book. John Drayton, editor-in-chief of the University of Oklahoma Press, and Dick Etulain, editor of the Oklahoma Western Biographies series, have been patient and supportive and have offered valuable counsel. My wife, Kaaren, my best friend and most constructive critic, has listened and responded to this study as it evolved, and her suggestions have made this a much better book. Adelaide Iverson, Erika Iverson, Jack Pfister, Frank Szasz, Bob Trennert, Phil VanderMeer, and readers for the University of Oklahoma Press also read the manuscript, gave me the benefit of their counsel, and improved the final result.

As always, I close by expressing gratitude to members of my family. My father died in 1994, but his example as a teacher and his courage in the face of adversity remain with me. My mother got me interested in politics about the time I learned to walk. Her participation in the League of Women Voters and her reading each day of every last word of the *New York Times* exemplify her understanding of government. My brothers David and Paul, and their families, and my aunt Alice and uncle Harry, have given me more than they know. Violet and Joe Gonsoulin, David and Becky Gonsoulin, Diane and Dick Ellis, and Mark and Terry Gonsoulin have offered affection, laughter, catfish, and another view of American politics. Kaaren, thank you, again. This book is for Erika, Jens, Scott, Tim and Laurie.

PETER IVERSON

Tempe, Arizona

Barry Goldwater

Arizona

CHAPTER I

Growing Up with the Country

HIS is an American story. His father's parents left Eastern Europe to seek a better life, free from persecution. Although his grandparents did not know great financial success, they and their relatives built a foundation for the next generation. His father became a prosperous businessman, and that prosperity opened all the doors in a small town to him and his siblings. He grew up believing that his home state and his country should be, as he once phrased it, a "haven for people who seek an outlet for initiative and a reward for work." He grew up knowing that frontiers changed and challenges remained, that what he deemed progress offered the key to opportunity for all. In the life and career of Barry Morris Goldwater, one sees a deeply rooted respect for yesterday and optimism for tomorrow. In the lives of his family he perceived lessons for himself and for others. Born on the first day of the first month in the first decade of this century, he became a man who never lost his faith in the future.

Barry Goldwater's grandfather, Michel Goldwasser, fled from Poland, moved to England, altered his name to Michael Goldwater, and migrated to America in 1852 along with his brother, Joseph. By traveling in steerage, they had enough money to make the long journey to New York City. From there they decided to move on, by way of Nicaragua, to San Francisco. About one hundred miles to the east lay Sonora, one of the many mining towns dotting the Sierra Nevada foothills. Lacking the funds to pursue their first choice of enterprise, starting a store, they made the same, obvious business decision of countless frontier entrepreneurs: they opened a saloon.

3

By the spring of 1854 the business had done well enough to allow Mike Goldwater to send for his wife, Sarah, and their two English-born children, Caroline and Morris; they were accompanied by Sarah's sister, Esther, and her son, Marcus. Fortunately, the quintet made the trip as passengers in a second-class cabin rather than in steerage.

Sonora, California, represented more than a slight transition from London, and Sarah Nathan Goldwater frowned at her new surroundings. Her continuing resentment toward her brother-in-law's role in convincing Mike to come to America led eventually to Joe's departure for other parts of California. Sarah announced herself ready to depart for San Francisco, where she gave birth on July 15, 1857, to Samuel Goldwater, her second child born in the United States (following Elizabeth's arrival in 1855). Sarah remained there, with Mike visiting from time to time; Henry Goldwater was born a year later on July 27, 1858.

The Sonoran economy had not lived up to Mike Goldwater's initial expectations. He joined Joe, who by this time had moved to a town that appeared to have a promising future. In Los Angeles, whose population had swollen by the end of the 1850s to all of four thousand people, the brothers attempted a fresh start. By declaring bankruptcy, Mike escaped the burden of past debts, but as the new decade began, about all he could claim as an asset was his family, including daughter Leonora, or "Annie," born in 1860. Although Sarah had rejoined Mike Goldwater that year in Los Angeles, she did not exactly perceive her latest residence as a proper place to live.

And so, in the best American tradition, Mike Goldwater moved again, this time across the Colorado River to Gila City, a bustling mining town in southwestern Arizona. It looked like a good prospect for business. Sarah Goldwater waited in Los Angeles, where she gave birth to the final two of the couple's children. Brothers Ben, born on March 23, 1862, and Baron, born on May 8, 1866, joined the Goldwater clan. Mike Goldwater tried La Paz, another mining town, at the end of 1862 or the beginning of 1863. He worked initially at Bernard Cohn's store, soon joined Cohn as a partner, and then started to expand his business interests. By the end of the 1860s, as La Paz declined, the new community of Ehrenberg beckoned. On September 18, 1869, "J. Goldwater and Bro." opened its doors as "wholesale dealers in clothing, dry-goods, boots, shoes, grain, groceries, provisions, etc." Within three years the reunited brothers had started a second store in another little town that, like Los Angeles, looked as if it might grow: Phoenix. They put young Morris Goldwater in charge of this latest enterprise.

Morris Goldwater had an aptitude for business and a penchant for politics. It is not surprising that he became a model for and major influence upon his nephew, Barry Goldwater. He came to Arizona as he entered his twenties. By twenty-two he had run, as a Democrat, for a place in the territorial assembly. Unsuccessful, he nonetheless made a creditable showing in his first foray into the political arena. Morris Goldwater looked forward to other opportunities in expanding Arizona territory.

Given the number of business establishments already situated in Phoenix, the store there barely held its own, and the Ehrenberg store fared little better. The obvious choice for another fresh start loomed in the territorial capital of Prescott. At year's end in 1876, the family tried again. It kept open the Ehrenberg store, closed the one in Phoenix, and invested in a new business in Prescott. This time the venture worked. Determined to fit into the bustling town, the Goldwaters joined various local organizations, including the Masons. Without the presence of a sizable Jewish community, the Goldwaters' Jewish faith began to become more of a memory than a part of daily life.

Morris Goldwater was elected mayor of Prescott in 1878 and worked with his father to plan for a bigger and better Goldwater store in the town, following the decision of Mike and Joe Goldwater once again to go their separate ways. This concern, now called "M. Goldwater & Son," threw open its doors in May 1880. Morris proceeded to become a central figure in the history of Prescott and figured prominently in the early political development of Arizona. He served in the legislature, on the county board of supervisors, as mayor of Prescott, as vice president of the Arizona constitutional convention in 1910, and as president of the senate in the second Arizona state legislature in 1914. In addition to his initial year in office, Morris Goldwater was mayor of Prescott from 1894 to 1897, 1905 to 1913, and 1919 to 1927. He drank his share of whiskey, earned a reputation for blunt speaking, and enjoyed a good political argument.

Baron Goldwater did not share the political ambitions of his older brother, but he had his own dreams—ones that revolved around business rather than government. The Goldwater family legend holds that Baron defeated Mike in a game of casino in 1894, with the stakes being another try at the Phoenix market. By 1896, M. Goldwater & Bros. had inaugurated its Phoenix store at 18 and 20 North First Avenue. It carried the slogan Morris had fashioned: "The Best Always."

This new "dry goods emporium," so labeled by the *Phoenix Gazette,* represented a departure from earlier Goldwater stores. It catered to women. And under the direction of Baron Goldwater, the store emerged as a smashing success. It outgrew the confines of the First Avenue building and by January 1899 had made the transition to 134 East Washington Street. Baron resided at 128 East Adams Street and commuted a long block to work. He awaited the new century with confidence.

The new century, however, also marked a transition between generations. Mike Goldwater, who had returned to Sarah and San Francisco following his retirement from the Ehrenberg store, died in April 1903 at the age of eighty-three. Although Morris Goldwater married Sarah Shivers Foster, known universally as Sallie, in 1906, his wife was forty-seven at the time of the wedding, and the couple had no children. The other remaining Goldwater in Arizona, Baron, had also not seemed a particularly good prospect for matrimony. Yet the arrival of Josephine Williams in 1903 doomed his chances for remaining a bachelor.

A native of Bowen, Illinois, Josephine (or "Jo") Williams grew up on a farm west of Omaha. She attended the Illinois

Training School for nurses in Chicago and began work as a nurse in the city before she contracted tuberculosis. In her mid-twenties, she hoped the dry climate of Arizona might save her. And Arizona obviously agreed with her; she lived to be ninety-four. She took the Santa Fe train from Chicago to Ash Fork, where she planned to transfer to the local that would carry her to Phoenix. The absence of a ticket she had ordered in Ash Fork deterred her only momentarily. She had come this far. If she had to walk the 125 miles south to Phoenix, why, she would do just that. A passing freight train saved her from the hike. Jo Williams accepted the offer of a free ride in the caboose and soon reached her destination.

Within three years of this somewhat inauspicious entrance, she had become engaged to be married to Baron Goldwater, by now one of the leading businessmen in Phoenix. Married in the Saint Paul's Episcopal Church in Prescott on New Year's Day, 1907, Jo and Baron Goldwater traveled by train to New York City for their honeymoon. After an initial residence at 818 North Second Street, they moved to 710 North Central Avenue, where two years to the day later, on January 1, 1909, their first child was born. They named him Barry, his father's nickname, and attached Morris as a middle name. Robert Williams Goldwater followed on July 4, 1910, with Carolyn Goldwater completing the trio on August 13, 1912. The three children thus spanned three and one-half years. Josephine Goldwater had her hands full.

In 1989, Barry Goldwater told a group of Arizona State University students: "My mother was a breed of cat you don't see too often. She taught us how to hunt, to fish, and to camp and drove us to Santa Monica, California, in the summers." He added, "My father couldn't drive a car or a nail and never shot a gun." On another occasion he observed: "He had a motto: never do anything you can pay somebody else to do." So, "Mun," as her son always called her, had the primary role in raising the three children, who were brought up in the Episcopal Church. Baron Goldwater devoted himself to his business but invested relatively little time in his rambunctious

Josephine Goldwater. She helped her children learn about the beauty of Arizona. "Mun" taught her older son how to shoot a photograph—and a rifle. Barry Goldwater Photograph Collection, courtesy of the Arizona Historical Foundation

children. He enjoyed wandering over to the Arizona Club to play cards, and he liked to dress well. However, as Goldwater recalled in 1995, his father "was never too enthusiastic about the valley." He could not imagine that it would develop past a certain point. "He told me," Goldwater noted, "that the land north of the Arizona Canal would never be worth more than fifty cents an acre."

Mun introduced her children to the world beyond the small town of Phoenix. Through camping trips and other excursions she helped kindle from their earliest memory a love of the outdoors and a curiosity about the wonders in the extraordinary country encompassed within Arizona's borders. Mun encouraged Barry to take his first photographs, imparted the importance of patriotism, reminded him that all Arizonans, regardless of color or creed, merited respect, and imparted a kind of can-do spirit of confidence that served him well.

En route to Japan in 1967, Barry Goldwater thought about his mother and penned a tribute. He considered her eyes:

> Sometimes they questioned, as only knowing eyes can question, was I being honest with her? More than anything else in this world, honor and truth guided her life. Was I doing my best? I remember her eyes as she helped with our schoolwork, as she taught us to respect and love our flag, as she shared through them her great love of the wondrous mountains and rivers and forests and deserts we call Arizona. I will all my life see the challenging twinkle in her eyes as she said through them, "do as well" after a good bird shot or the sinking of a long putt or yes, the winning of a poker pot.

A convert to the beauty of Arizona, she made sure that her children, native Arizonans, appreciated its unique grandeur. Barry Goldwater grew up appreciating his surroundings for what they offered rather than lamenting what they may have lacked, either in terms of particular vegetation or the trappings of a more urbane environment. He saw the land with a native's eyes rather than through the spectacles of a transplant from afar.

Baron Goldwater with his three children (*left to right:* Robert, Carolyn, and Barry), 1915. Baron Goldwater preferred the comforts of town to the uncertainties of camping. Barry Goldwater Photograph Collection, courtesy of the Arizona Historical Foundation

The Goldwater children hardly felt deprived. To the contrary, they relished the freedom of growing up in a small town in an age when kids still had the run of the place and parents did not worry about their safety. Central Avenue, then known as Center Street, the spine of the community, had yet to be paved. Horses and carriages carried people up and down the street before the dominance of the automobile. Young Barry watched the men walking to work in the morning. "On the way home at night," he recalled, "they would stop in wherever they felt like it, have a drink and then go on, and some of my most pleasant memories of my most youthful days were those in my home when people who were not yet prominent or very prominent people, including men in politics and even governors and future governors would drop in." He added: "On the sideboard in the dining room was always a bottle or two of something to drink; they would pour themselves a drink, talk to me or talk to my father or mother if they were there and then go out the door and go home."

Even in Goldwater's childhood, the automobile began to change this leisurely scene. In 1913, five years after the introduction of the Model T, Phoenix boasted ten automobile dealerships. One of the first customers had been Baron Goldwater, who, his son recalled, purchased a Chalmers. It was the second sale of an automobile in the community. The elite of the city continued to cluster along North Central Avenue, but the automobile inevitably began to prompt a slow but steady dispersal of Phoenix's population. The city limits had increased to 3.2 square miles, with the boundaries as far west as Twenty-Third Avenue and as far east as Sixteenth Street, as far north as McDowell and as far south as Yavapai. The car inspired a bridge over Central Avenue across the Salt River, completed in 1911. The Phoenix population almost tripled in the decade, ballooning from 11,134 in 1910 to 29,053 in 1920.

Goldwater and his pals formed what they called the Center Street Gang, again reflecting a time when "our gang" had a different connotation. Local kids, including Harry Rosenzweig, joined. Rosenzweig became a life-long close friend and an important adviser and confidant in Goldwater's political career. Another childhood buddy, Paul Fannin, went on to serve as both governor and U.S. senator. The group rode their bikes out to Riverside Park on South Central Avenue at the Salt River to spend the day swimming and diving. They had track meets, baseball and football games, boxing matches, and bicycle races. From the perspective of a child growing up in Phoenix in the second decade of the twentieth century, it became clear that life offered adventure, excitement, and promise and that one ought to spend as much of it as possible outside.

The only significant time Goldwater spent indoors during the day involved school. There his performance appeared consistent. He remained an indifferent student, despite admonitions from parents and teachers. Goldwater absorbed lessons, but often more about life than about his subjects. He credited his sixth-grade teacher, Mabel H. Lathan, with helping him learn "a great love for consistency and integrity," even if, as he wrote her in 1963, he may have been "the worst student you ever had in the sixth grade." When a journalist asked him about his failings in 1986, Goldwater responded, "Oh, God, how much time do we have?" But he began by saying: "I was a very bad student." Journalist and historian Bert Fireman, who helped Goldwater establish the Arizona Historical Foundation in 1959, once chortled: "You told me that you were lousy in Latin yet they said at Phoenix Union High School that Latin was your best subject. I now have a transcript of your high school grades. You were both right!"

Although elected president of the freshman class at the high school, Goldwater earned a reputation for being a less than diligent student and for having a knack of getting into trouble. When the school principal informed Baron Goldwater that his eldest son had done so poorly in his work that he might not be able to return for his sophomore year, Baron decided enough was enough. He informed the startled and chagrined Barry that he would have to transfer to the Staunton Military Academy in Virginia. Since he had a business trip lined up to New York, Baron Goldwater would accompany his

Barry Goldwater in his youth. Barry Goldwater Photograph Collection, courtesy of the Arizona Historical Foundation

son to Virginia on the train. Maybe the strict surroundings of
Staunton might pound some sense, discipline, and academic
ambition into his eldest child.

In 1924, at the age of fifteen, Barry Goldwater enrolled at
Staunton. The years, Goldwater later said, offered "a compass
for me." The military school generally fulfilled his father's
hopes and expectations. Barry Goldwater never rose above
being an average student, yet he graduated in 1928 having garnered an award for being the best all-around cadet in his class.
Along the way he also developed a great appreciation and affection for the world of the military, emotions he would always
carry with him. Inspired by the trappings of the school and by
his own success within this kind of place, he eventually dreamed
of going to West Point. However, his mother insisted he come
home. She missed him, and her husband's health worried her.
So Barry Goldwater headed south of the Gila River rather than
to the Hudson, becoming a student at the University of Arizona instead of the United States Military Academy; in a life
overflowing with achievements and happy memories, his
inability to go to West Point remained one of the few clear
disappointments.

Mun's premonitions had been correct, however. Within a
year after Barry Goldwater returned to Arizona, his father died
of a heart attack. As the oldest son, Goldwater believed he had
little choice about what to do next. He dropped out of college
and came home to work in the family business. Again, the decision rankled in his memory, for he always felt shortchanged
in regard to his intellectual foundations. In the halls of Congress he later encountered men who had graduated from the
nation's best colleges and universities, who had received the
benefit of training in the country's best law schools. With
them he tackled problems confronting the nation—dilemmas
deeply rooted in history or mirroring the complex workings
of the economy. Of course he followed his mother's admoni-
tion and did his best, but the idea gnawed at him that completing his undergraduate studies would have better prepared

him for such tasks. Goldwater termed leaving the university "the biggest mistake of my life."

Returning to the family business did not mean beginning life at the top. Barry Goldwater started as a salesman in the piece-goods department at fifteen dollars a week, because Sam Wilson, who followed Baron Goldwater as the head of the store, wisely told the young man he had better know something about the day-to-day world of the business. Goldwater displayed talent as a salesman, and by the time Wilson moved on in 1937, Baron's son had proven himself ready to be president of the operation. He had already tried out a number of ideas, some of them more inspired than others, and demonstrated his knack for promotion. The most publicized example came with "Antsy Pants," boxer shorts with red ants emblazoned on them, that sold faster and to more people around the country than one can imagine. *Women's Wear Daily* told its readers in 1939: "Keep your eyes on Barry Goldwater, the 30-year-old Arizona retailer who did not know that 'you can't sit in the middle of a desert and sell original exclusive fashions to women in the metropolitan centers of the world.'" By decade's end Goldwater's had achieved great success through sales by direct mail and a few small advertisements in national magazines. "Purely Southwestern" fashions, the industry publication noted, created by and for Goldwater's for national distribution, had evoked tremendous interest from throughout the country.

Barry Goldwater would be the first to argue that his greatest success in the 1930s occurred not in his business but in his personal life. He had liked the idea of having participated in the first wedding held in Arizona after it had become a state; at the age of three he had served as the ring bearer for Joe Melczer's wedding. Goldwater later insisted he could remember the event "with quite a bit of vividness," noting that the wedding party had dallied outside of the Women's Club at Fillmore and First Avenue until the telegram came certifying that President William Howard Taft had signed the bill for statehood. Now, a little more than three decades later, he had his own wedding to ponder.

On September 22, 1934, Barry Goldwater married Margaret Johnson of Muncie, Indiana, in Muncie's Grace Episcopal Church. The *Muncie Sunday Star* described the wedding as "one of the most brilliant and fashionable nuptial events ever recorded in the social annals of the city." They had met, appropriately enough, in Goldwater's in Phoenix, when Peggy accompanied her mother into the store. Peggy's parents spent some of the winter in the Phoenix area; her father, Ray Johnson, was president of the Warner Gear Company.

Peggy Goldwater may have come from a family of means, but she had not been shielded from the concerns and problems facing less prosperous people. She had studied art in New York and had worked as a volunteer at a women's infirmary. Peggy Goldwater later recalled: "There were so many babies born to impoverished mothers. . . . They realized they could not cope with these babies emotionally, mentally, or physically. New offspring meant spreading meager resources thinner and thinner among parents and the existing brood." She could not forget what she had observed: "To the young girl I was then, it seemed an injustice and a terrible tragedy for a little baby to come into the world unloved, unwanted, and with no chance for health, dignity, and self-fulfillment."

After she had become a resident of Phoenix, Peggy Goldwater vowed to do something about this ongoing dilemma. Thus she helped start Planned Parenthood in Phoenix in the late 1930s. Initially the group offered but one service; it fit married mothers with diaphragms. However, for 1930s Phoenix, any initiative of this kind made the participants, she remembered, feel "somewhat bold and daring." In the context of the era, the organization hardly earned universal applause, and members of the group sometimes felt embarrassed about their activity. Yet, she said, "any embarrassment we may have felt was overbalanced by the conviction that we were doing something about the demoralizing and dehumanizing effects of unplanned parenthood." Peggy was a shy person who never sought the limelight, so she had to have some conviction to assume her role in Planned Parenthood. But she did, and there is no indication that her husband attempted to dissuade her.

The Goldwaters had the means, of course, to support their children and wanted them. Their first child, Joanne, named after her two grandmothers, shared her father's birthday, arriving on January 1, 1936. Barry, Jr., was born July 15, 1938. Michael, named after his great-grandfather, followed in 1940. Peggy (known in the family as Peggy, Jr.) was born in 1944. Although Barry Goldwater remembered his father's relative absence, the standard roles for husbands and wives had not changed markedly, and Peggy Goldwater assumed, just as her mother-in-law had, the major share of day-to-day parenting. World War II took Goldwater away from his young children, and then his election to the Senate in 1952 and his subsequent rise to national political prominence meant many absences from the household. For a man of his time, Goldwater did more than many; he showered his children and later his grandchildren with letters; he tried to find ways to let them know they remained in his thoughts when he was far from home. Like many men of his generation, even so, he shook his head in his later years and acknowledged what he had missed.

The newly married Goldwaters spent their first years together in a Phoenix community that continued to grow, despite the difficulties inherent in the Depression era. The 1940 census recorded a growth in the city's population by 17,065 over the decade to a total of 65,414. Although Chandler and Tempe showed little change, Glendale grew by 1,190 to 4,855 and Mesa expanded from 3,711 to 7,224. The federal government invested in the area through various public works projects. Sky Harbor Airport, Encanto Park, Papago Park, South Mountain Park, North Phoenix High School, Phoenix College, the Pueblo Grande Museum, and the Phoenix Municipal Stadium all benefited from federal investment. The government put a lot of people to work and cushioned to some extent the overall impact of the downturn in the regional and national economy. For someone raised on the gospel of individualism, self-sufficiency, and pioneer determination, this degree of federal intervention, however, did not appear to be an entirely welcome phenomenon.

Goldwater and other business leaders in the city and the state chafed at the degree of dependency they perceived and sought means to bolster the state economy to lessen reliance upon the federal presence. Such an attitude on the part of many conservative westerners has been criticized as contradictory at best and hypocritical at worst by many observers, who have pointed out the extent to which supposedly self-reliant westerners have gorged willingly at the public trough. The development of water resources glared as the most impressive example but hardly offered the only case in point. If the New Deal would not last forever—an eventuality both anticipated and desired by more conservative southwesterners—then states such as Arizona would have to find some means to supplement and, ideally, replace contemporary reliance on dollars from the District of Columbia.

What could Arizona count on, regardless of economic climate? The answer was, indeed, its weather. The Salt River valley did not seem to be a particularly alluring label for the Phoenix area. How about, a local advertising agency suggested, the Valley of the Sun? This inspiration in 1934 quickly became a new slogan for the nascent tourism industry. Goldwater himself in 1940 contended, "The natural thing to which to turn was the capitalization of our climate, our natural beauties, and the romance of our desert." The kind of advertising Goldwater had used to bolster the fortunes of his store could be employed to bolster the fortunes of his community. And it had a ripple effect, he concluded: "The stimulus from the injection of these tourist dollars into the veins of our economic being have been felt by every person doing business in this area. The farmer has sold more produce. The hotels have filled more rooms. The merchants have sold more goods. It is easy to see, therefore, why businessmen are so unanimously enthusiastic about the continuance and enlargement of a proper advertising program."

As the grip of the Depression eased, the possibilities appeared almost limitless. Goldwater numbered among those who realized at an early date that in the beauty of the state lay a key to building the kind of state he wished so desperately to materialize. For Arizona to grow up, its land, its sky, would be central to an elusive but achievable future. He could see it. And by the end of the 1930s, in fact, he had already started to work with others to do something about sharing with the world what Arizona had to offer.

CHAPTER 2

Seeing Arizona

AS Senator Albert Beveridge of Indiana prepared in 1902 for a journey to the Southwest, he anticipated what he would witness. He succeeded entirely in restraining his enthusiasm. Arizona and New Mexico were another world from the comfortable and developed environment of the Midwest. Chairman of the Senate Committee on the Territories at the turn of the twentieth century, Beveridge had the responsibility of reviewing the possibility of these territories' becoming full-fledged states. New Mexico, however, seemed to him to be too Hispanic; Arizona also appeared to be tainted by the presence of Mexican Americans and outlaws. Moreover, Arizona's population was too small, its economy too undeveloped, its landscape a desert. Beveridge's dismissal of Arizona's promise, his denial of Arizona's worth, symbolized the kind of attitude against which Barry Goldwater and his peers struggled for much of the twentieth century.

Beveridge embarked upon his trip by railroad to the Southwest, ostensibly to find out on a firsthand basis about New Mexico and Arizona. To the zealous boosters of Arizona statehood, the tour looked like little more than an opportunity to confirm the senator's suspicions. Like the reluctant American tourist who travels to a foreign land saying he will not like the experience and has his expectations fulfilled, Beveridge saw what he anticipated in a whirlwind visit. In ninety-six hours in Arizona, Beveridge's party spent but two nights in hotels. The *Coconino Sun* suggested that the senator and his colleagues may not have been open to new perspectives:

Out in the West, the wild, wild West, the private car of
   the Senators flew
And the farther they went the thicker the dust
On the polished pane of the window grew.
"I'll brush it off," said the Porter man.
Said the Dignified Senators, "Nay let it be.
If the glass were clear and the glass were clean,
There are many things which we might see."

After his hasty departure from the territory, Beveridge
wrote to an acquaintance that at present "Arizona is a mining
camp." His committee noted a growing percentage of people
it called "American," but expressed its dismay at the considerable number of Indians and "Mexicans." Prostitution, gam-
bling, drinking, and illiteracy prevailed. Without additional
water storage projects, agricultural development could not be
accomplished; mining could not be depended upon as a solid
base for long-term economic growth.

Passage of the Reclamation Act in the year of Beveridge's
visit, however, helped create the Salt River Project and, in turn,
the construction of the Roosevelt Dam. On March 18, 1911,
former president Theodore Roosevelt participated in the
dam's dedication. The dam would allow the Salt River valley
population and economy to expand. In less than a year, President William Howard Taft signed the bill authorizing Arizona to become the nation's forty-eighth state. Arizona entered the union on February 14, 1912.

Admission did not erase the negative images Beveridge and
countless other Americans held of Arizona. Nonetheless,
tourism promised to improve that image as well as buttress
the local economy. The advent of the Santa Fe Railway and the
efforts of the Fred Harvey Company succeeded early in the
century in luring more travelers to Arizona. The Harvey
Houses, the Harvey Detours, and the construction of El Tovar
and the Bright Angel Trail at the Grand Canyon all encouraged people to make the journey. Arizona was becoming "the
Grand Canyon State."

For larger numbers of people to see Arizona, automobile

tourism offered convenience, flexibility, and, at times, unanticipated adventure. The Arizona Good Roads Association, headquartered in Prescott, published in 1913 a tour book designed to promote travel by car and general development in the state. The volume presented what it called the first book of road maps and touring information ever published in Arizona. "Engineers from the Office of Roads, at Washington and other highly qualified experts agree," it began, "that Arizona has not only the best natural roads in the Union, but that here are to be found accessible deposits of the best natural road materials known." In other words, few roads were truly improved, let alone paved, but help was on the way.

A program of road construction carried out by the state and the counties promised to reduce the difficulties the book admitted could be "encountered in the remote sections." And Arizona hospitality would welcome the traveler, wherever he or she might venture. The guide featured the Grand Canyon on its cover and included, its cover stated, "photos of roads, landmarks, towns, points of interest and detailed information on every part of THE WONDERLAND." County boards of supervisors, towns, and commercial interests underwrote the nearly nine thousand dollars it cost to publish the volume, so the descriptions occasionally included a bit of editorial license. Florence's air was "so dry and pure as to render the creation and propagation of disease germs impossible." Bowie, "a wide awake town," emerged as "a busy place." The summers in Mesa were "balmy," with "temperatures sometimes high in July and August." However, given the dryness, the heat was "at no time oppressive" and sunstrokes were "unknown."

Within the pages one can discern the contours of a conscious economic strategy. Hotels, gas stations, restaurants, and other enterprises are poised to capitalize on the proximity of mountains, monuments, and other scenic attractions, including the Navajos and Hopis. Trader J. L. Hubbell of Ganado stood ready to assist and guide the tourist in Navajo and Hopi country. Verkamp's store at the south rim of the Grand Canyon welcomed travelers to come in to see "Navajo Squaws weaving blankets and Navajo Bucks making silverware." In a comparably offensive tone, Navajo County advertised the Hopi snake dance and the Hopi villages as "the famous Moqui villages noted the world over for their peculiar locations as well as the conducting of the strangest, most peculiar and spectacular religious ceremony ever held by any known race of people."

Arizona Highways provided the next logical step from the guide. Inaugurated in 1921 as a modest newsletter, it began to be transformed in 1925—a year before the completion of Route 66—by the highway department into an up-to-date version of the earlier Good Roads book, offering information about the latest road conditions and black-and-white photographs of Arizona scenery. The arrival of Raymond Carlson in 1938 as the sixth editor signaled a new stage in the development of the magazine. He turned out to be, said *Native Peoples* publisher and former *Arizona Highways* editor Gary Avey in 1996, "the right guy put in the job for all the wrong reasons, as a political payoff for working in the Arizona governor's campaign." From Miami, Arizona, Carlson had earned membership in Phi Beta Kappa during his sojourn at Stanford University, where he studied Romance languages. Carlson had worked in Miami on the town newspaper, the *Silver Belt*. At the time of his appointment, *Arizona Highways* still included engineering reports and minutes from the state highway commission meetings. Carlson wanted to move the journal from discussions of road construction to a focus on travel and tourism. Through better photography and improved writing, *Arizona Highways* could lure both tourists and settlers to Arizona. Carlson had some definite ideas about what he wanted to do, even if, according to Avey, he "didn't really know anything about visuals and art." Fortunately, Carlson found in Avey's father, George, a person who "was great with visuals" and thus an ideal person to become art editor. George Avey had grown up in Mesa and attended the University of California in Berkeley. A quiet complement to the more boisterous Carlson, he shared his colleague's love of Arizona. The two men labored in three

adobe rooms by the railroad tracks in back of the state highway department's wrecked equipment yard. The floors featured linoleum over dirt. In such less than glamorous surroundings, they began to transform the magazine. And the
providential, if hesitant, visit by a photographer to Carlson's
office a month after he took the job confirmed the direction
the new editor wanted to take.

An immigrant from Germany, now residing in Santa Barbara,
California, Josef Muench had spied a copy of *Arizona Highways* during a stay in the state. Muench knocked on Carlson's
door and proceeded to show the editor a box of fifty eight-by-
ten black-and-white photographs he had taken from throughout Arizona. Muench remembered: "He went through the
prints, all 50 of them, turning them over one at a time. Finally,
he said, 'This is what I want to bring this magazine to. Can I
keep these?'" All fifty found their way into the pages or onto
the covers of *Arizona Highways*. The cover helped boost the
circulation of a magazine then printing only about thirty-
four hundred copies of each issue. Within six months after
Carlson's assumption of the editorship, the first full-color
cover photograph appeared; the July 1938 issue featured a striking panorama of Oak Creek Canyon. Norman G. Wallace, an
engineer for the state highway department, had the honor of
the photo credit.

Carlson promptly turned to recruit other photographers
and writers to contribute to *Arizona Highways*, especially those
photographers whose work featured the stunning beauty of
the Colorado Plateau region, the site not only of the Grand
Canyon but also of Monument Valley, Canyon de Chelly, and
other remarkable places as well. Chuck Abbott (first contribution in 1947), Ansel Adams (1946), Wayne Davis (1948), Carlos
Elmer (1940), Esther Henderson (1938), Hubert Lowman
(1942), Ray Manley (1943), Herb McLaughlin (1946), and
Joseph McGibbeny (1946) numbered among those who helped
build the magazine, along with another photographer Gary
Avey described as "a hard core Arizonan," Barry Goldwater.
Avey added: "In Muench's photographs, the people were in-

cidental," but in much of Goldwater's best work the people were centrally important.

Goldwater traced his initial interest in photography to the same person who introduced him to Arizona. His mother took an ordinary box camera along to take snapshots of various family outings. In due course she let Barry use it. He soon realized that the camera captured images of nature as well as memories of excursions. The camera became an ally, a means to show others why he believed, as he later phrased it, "that God got about 114,000 square miles out of heaven and let it fall down here in Arizona."

His interest in photography increased when he took his first flying lessons. From the vantage point of an airplane he saw the Salt River valley in a different way. And so when he flew over Phoenix he began to take pictures of what he witnessed. Almost inadvertently, he had started his role as an amateur historian of Arizona. Indeed, his commitment to photography increased because of his lifelong interest in the history of Arizona. Given his mother's and uncle's affection for the state, he began to collect books and other materials about its heritage. After he returned from his brief stint at the University of Arizona, Goldwater started to put together what became, in his judgment, "probably the biggest private library in Arizona and northern Mexico."

During an era when public libraries had limited holdings, students began to come by and ask to use the Goldwater library on Arizona. Every so often, Goldwater remembered, "they'd say, 'Have you ever seen Pipe Springs?' I'd say, 'Yeah, I've been there.' They'd say, 'Do you have a picture of it?' And, I'd say, 'No.'" That, in turn, gave him an idea: "So, I started going around the state taking pictures of out of the way, seldom visited places."

In order to begin to do a better job of it, he needed a better camera and he needed instructions. Peggy Goldwater provided the camera, an Eastman 2¼-inch reflex camera, as a Christmas present in 1934. Tom Bates, a Phoenix portrait photographer, taught Goldwater something about using a darkroom and "about light substances and the different modes of photography you could get into, if you wanted to." Goldwater added, "The rest of it has been sort of copycat."

That characteristic modesty should not disguise the quality of the cats he copied. In particular, Ansel Adams and Edward Weston, two of the most outstanding photographers ever to work in the American West, offered models to emulate. Goldwater knew Adams personally, happening to run into him in northern Arizona en route to Rainbow Bridge. Over the course of a friendship that spanned half a century, Adams passed along some ideas about photography, and Goldwater reciprocated by relating some of his knowledge about his home country. The two remained in touch over the years, and Adams wrote a foreword for *Barry Goldwater and the Southwest*, a collection of Goldwater's photographs published in 1976. Adams remembered meeting at the head of the Rainbow Bridge trail "a young man who was obviously pursuing photography, as I was and with obvious fervor." Goldwater admired both Adams and Weston, but Adams's instructor, Weston, ranked as his favorite photographer because of his "pure" style. "He didn't try to dummy it up or gloss it up or fuss it up," Goldwater once told historian Evelyn Cooper. "It was just the picture as he saw it."

Such a straightforward approach became a kind of credo for Goldwater's photography. To be sure, it meant more than just taking a snapshot. Bates had started him thinking about how labor in the darkroom and light itself affected the final result. Peggy Goldwater did more than buy her husband a camera; she also had attended the Grand Central Art School in Manhattan and knew about composition. She accompanied him on many of his early photographic excursions. As he took photographs and later as he worked in the darkroom, she made suggestions about how to proceed.

Goldwater's penchant for tinkering soon came into play as well. A photograph of him published in the Phoenix newspaper probably in the late 1930s shows him with what is described as "a time-lapse device constructed by Mr. Goldwater for use in flower photography." The caption explains: "The device turns on photographic lights, causes the camera to expose one movie frame, turns off the lights, and repeats the process at predetermined intervals." This procedure permitted Goldwater to capture the full sequence of blossoms of a cactus that bloomed only at night. A gasoline generator provided power for photographs taken in the desert.

In 1940, Goldwater embarked upon a journey that marked a turning point in his life. The pioneering river runner, Norman Nevills of Mexican Hat, Utah, sought a small group to join him for a most promising adventure. He wanted to re-create the famous voyage of John Wesley Powell through the Grand Canyon. Nevills's hardy band put in on June 20, 1940, at Green River, Wyoming. Slightly more than two months later they ended their trip, on August 22, at Lake Mead. Barry Goldwater sought the opportunity to join the crew. He drove up to Mexican Hat, Utah, and spoke with Nevills. "He said, OK, but it will cost you six hundred dollars. I said OK, but my wife raised hell." Nonetheless, Goldwater met the group at Green River, Utah, and experienced the remainder of the expedition—through Labyrinth Canyon, Cataract Canyon, and Glen Canyon, past Lee's Ferry, into Marble Canyon, and then into the Grand Canyon itself.

Goldwater later commemorated the trip in a book he entitled *Delightful Journey*. At the time he made the voyage, however, long before the river had been dammed upstream and its flow regulated, the journey certainly could prove to be other than pleasant. Just a few years before, Glen and Bessie Hyde had lost their lives in an ill-fated attempt to make their way through the Grand Canyon more rapidly than any previous party. In 1938, Nevills had taken passengers on the first commercial trip on this route. By re-creating the Powell voyage, he could achieve something special and earn considerable publicity in the process. Although the three wooden boats he put in for the trip represented something of an improvement over his initial boat, constructed from his mother's horse trough, they were a far cry from the more buoyant rafts that floated

the river after World War II. At least, unlike Powell, he took
along enough food to last the party for the entire trip. Goldwater remembered color-coded cans—yellow for soup, red for
meat. Of course the group deliberately painted some of the
cans the wrong color just to irritate Nevills; "It drove him
nuts," Goldwater said, smiling at the recollection.

Making the expedition fulfilled a "long smoldering desire."
He left Peggy on vacation in San Diego and boarded an American Airlines flight to Phoenix. Goldwater rationalized that,
sure, they would miss each other, but he would be back soon,
and now he could get this trip "out of my system forever." At
least that is what he wrote in the beginning of the diary he
kept along the way, perhaps half believing the words. Asked in
1995 whether, in fact, his wife actually believed him on this
score, Goldwater responded: "Oh, she never believed anything
I said." Running the Colorado became another Goldwater
family tradition as well as another opportunity for photography. In the summer of 1995, Anna Goldwater, Michael's daughter, worked on developing photographs from one of those
outings. "Here is my grandmother," she chuckled. "She looks
just like she came from the beauty parlor. And here is my
grandfather, looking like a derelict." Goldwater delighted in
later years in introducing and reacquainting relatives and
friends with the majesty of the river. It created islands of time
away from the demands of everyday life and, to be sure, it produced more good stories, like the time Michael challenged
him to shave using peanut butter. His father immediately accepted the challenge and assured one and all that it allowed
for a pretty good shave—if you didn't mind smelling like
peanuts for some time afterward.

Peanut butter and sleep lay in the future as Goldwater left
Phoenix at 3:15 in the morning, following a desultory pass at
department store business for an hour and a change of clothes.
His friend, Bill Saufley, and Saufley's fiancee, Opal, accompanied him on the drive northward. In those days before Interstate 17, they took the traditional triangular route—east to
Wickenburg, up the Yarnell hill to Prescott, and "through a

glorious sunrise over Mingus Mountain." Goldwater scribbled that night: "Here I was, starting out to do something that has held a fascination for me ever since I first heard of the Colorado River, and of the Powells, the Dellenbaughs, the Kolbs, and the other men who have tried running this strange river, the same river that intrigued my forefathers eighty years ago— the same river on which their successes and their failures occurred as often as this fickle river changed its course." He and Saufley alternated driving, Goldwater tired but too excited to sleep. They paused for breakfast at the Cameron trading post, north of Flagstaff, visiting with the owners, the Richardsons, before continuing. At Tuba City they turned back to the northeast, paused to chat with another old Arizona denizen, John Wetherill of Kayenta, then headed north to Monument Valley on the Arizona-Utah border. In Mexican Hat they added Norman Nevills's mother as a passenger; she guided them through country the Arizonans had never seen before: Snake Canyon, Bluff, and Monticello up to Green River. Even Goldwater had to admit southern Utah had its share of spectacular sights. "Things that I had suspected existed outside of Arizona but never really believed, unreeled before me like a panorama," he noted, with the grudging, hesitant praise that Arizonans reserve for southern Utah—somewhat in the slightly annoyed tone Montanans save for Yellowstone Park in Wyoming, muttering in the same breath that this kind of terrain ought to belong to them.

The adventure began on July 10. Goldwater joined a group of eight. Nevills and Thomas Delbert Reed had made the trip two years before. Nevills's wife, Doris, Mildred Baker, Hugh Carson Cutler, Charles W. Larabee, and John Silas Southworth, along with Goldwater, tackled the challenge for the first time. Of Doris and Norman Nevills, Goldwater recalled, she "was the real river rat." On only fourteen previous occasions had the run through the Grand Canyon been achieved; Goldwater considered himself to be the seventy-third person to ever accomplish the feat. The rough water arrived soon after the Green joined the Colorado. As it had to boats on previous

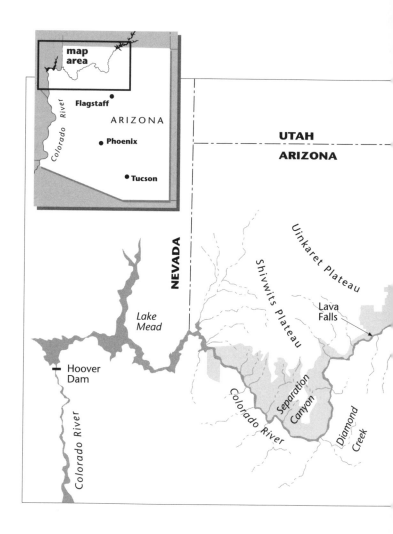

The Grand Canyon

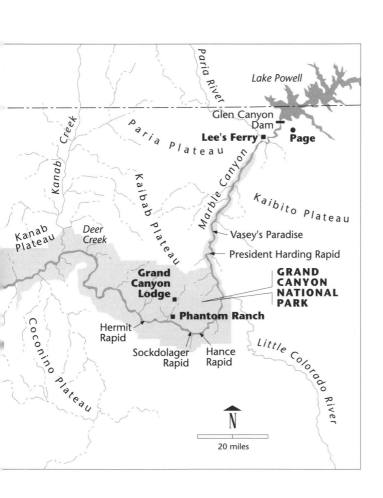

Lake Powell

Paria River

Glen Canyon
Dam

Lee's Ferry ■   ● Page

Paria Plateau

Kanab Creek

Marble Canyon

Kaibab Plateau

Kaibito Plateau

Vasey's Paradise

President Harding Rapid

Kanab Plateau

Deer Creek

Grand Canyon Lodge ■

GRAND CANYON NATIONAL PARK

■ Phantom Ranch

Hermit Rapid

Sockdolager Rapid

Hance Rapid

Little Colorado River

Coconino Plateau

N

20 miles

expeditions, Cataract Canyon exacted its toll. On the sixth day out of Green River, Utah, one of the three boats, the *Joan,* got caught in the rocks, which tore a hole in the left side of the bow; the bottom of the boat suffered a tear, and an oar broke. Del Reed and Hugh Cutler were rescued after a two-and-three-quarter-hour struggle in late afternoon.

They continued south, the temperatures consistently soaring past 100 degrees. At camp 13, Goldwater jotted: "Weather: Hot as hell, 110 degrees; no shade." Goldwater's knees troubled him. He watched for inscriptions from past travelers, musing about those who had gone before. Echo Camp at Rainbow Bridge provided a break on days nineteen through twenty-two. Goldwater reveled at the sight and, perhaps inspired by his surroundings, reached new culinary heights. He mixed roast beef cooked in jerky gravy with asparagus. "The resulting dish was the most terrible shade of purple I have ever seen," he noted, "but it tasted good, and when we finished not a bite was left in the pan."

In the Glen Canyon area they stopped in late morning at the Crossing of the Fathers, where Padre Escalante had walked in 1776. After a two-hour hike in midday to gain a better sense of Escalante's route, they shoved on, entering, Goldwater recorded, "my beloved Arizona" at 4:20 in the afternoon. As he knew he would, he "noticed immediately a more bracing quality in the air, a clearer, bluer sky, a more buoyant note in the song of the birds, a snap and sparkle in the air that only Arizona has." He added, "I said to myself, without reference to a map, that we were now *home.*" Goldwater chiseled on the wall of Warm Creek Canyon an inscription which he filled in with white lead:

ARIZONA
WELCOMES
YOU

The next day, camp 24, they arrived at another historic landmark: Lee's Ferry. Always conscious of the historical significance of his surroundings, Goldwater recalled the site's

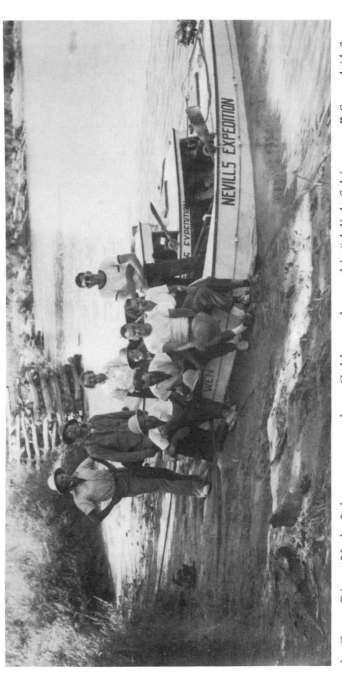

At Green River, Utah, July 10, 1940, where Goldwater began his "delightful journey." Seated (*left to right*): Norm Nevills, Del Reed, Ann Rosner, Barry Goldwater, Doris Nevills. Standing (*left to right*): Hugh Cutler, Charles Larabee, Mildred Baker, and John Southworth. Barry Goldwater Photograph Collection, courtesy of the Arizona Historical Foundation

Goldwater paints a sign welcoming travelers to his native state,
1940. Barry Goldwater Photograph Collection, courtesy of
the Arizona Historical Foundation

past. He remembered the Mormon pioneers who had employed the route through this spot as they migrated to Arizona. And he thought of John Doyle Lee, who fled here to the mouth of the Paria following the infamous Mountain Meadows Massacre in 1857. Lee remained here until 1874, establishing a ferry to move travelers across the river. Lee's Ferry had gained additional significance in the 1920s, as the place marking the division between the upper and lower basins of the Colorado River, where the flow of the river had been measured through the years and the evidence used to allocate water among the thirsty states of the region. All who cared about water in the West marked this spot.

Lee's Ferry also had become the point where voyagers in the twentieth century began a new map. It was mile zero, the official starting place on the way toward the Grand Canyon. The group paused before continuing on, and Goldwater took the opportunity to leave the river and drive with Larabee and Southworth to Gap, thirty-nine miles away. There he called and spoke with Peggy, Bill Saufley, and brother Bob. He assured one and all that the trip was already a success. The lining had been restored to his stomach; he now "sweat water instead of Old Taylor." The following day, Goldwater set out to photograph Navajos from the area engaged in traditional activities of herding and weaving. In the afternoon he lent a hand to Bill Brown at the service station in Navajo Springs. Goldwater hit upon the importance of steering newly arrived tourists in the right direction: "I proved to myself that tourists could be persuaded to stay in the state. Six people spent at least one day in Arizona because someone took a little time, while filling their gas tanks or washing their windshields, to tell them of interesting places nearby to see. Why, I wonder, isn't there more of this? The tourists are hungry for information, and we are hungry for their business—let's both satisfy our hungers."

Right after noon on August 4, with the food packed and canteens filled, the Nevills party continued, passing under the steel bridge on Highway 89 six miles south of Lee's Ferry and

Goldwater takes care of his laundry, 1940. Barry Goldwater
Photograph Collection, courtesy of the Arizona Historical
Foundation

entering Marble Canyon, which Goldwater immediately labeled "the most beautiful canyon I have ever seen." They
stopped to bathe and wash their clothes the following day at
Vasey's Paradise.

   Late in the afternoon Goldwater took a turn at the oars,
rowing through the comparatively calm President Harding
Rapid between miles 43 and 44. The rapid had gained its name
in 1923 when the Geological Survey party learned at this site
of the president's death. Perhaps he heard the joke still being
retold in 1995, although as a good Republican he did not

bother to repeat it in his journal, that it wasn't much of a rapid, but then Harding wasn't much of a president. Instead, Goldwater worried aloud that "the magic of photography" might not be able to capture the "indescribably beautiful" red sandstone walls.

On August 8 the Nevills group said goodbye to Marble Canyon and entered the Grand Canyon itself. As he did when he crossed the Arizona state line, Goldwater wanted to notice an immediate change in the environment. "The air seems to be charged with an aura of bigness," he believed; "buttes tower, walls are higher, promise of beauty lies everywhere, and we are all happy to know that we are now on the bottom of the world's greatest hole." He had so often stood on the rim and yearned for this day. Now it had finally arrived.

At nightfall of the following day they reached Phantom Ranch. Goldwater allotted one word for the weather: "Phew!" The low water of the river had reduced the power of the first of the famous rapids, Hance and Sockdolager, but had increased the chances for damage to the boats. Hance carved a hole in the *Wen;* the boat "was leaking badly" when the group stopped for lunch. After the hole had been patched, Sockdolager proved kind, and Phantom Ranch allowed for two days of loafing, phone calls home, and time to admire what Goldwater termed "the handiwork of God." One hundred fifty miles of the river remained. Refreshed, and steadily more experienced and confident, Goldwater and company, save Ann Rosner, who chose to leave the group at this point, began to look toward the end of the adventure.

They had come this far without major mishap. The journal began to lecture any available listeners about the four ways to deal with a rapid: "run it, line it, portage it, or cuss it and walk out of the canyon." After no problems on the morning of August 13 with fabled Hermit Falls, Goldwater recorded: "I may be wrong but it seems to me that if one keeps one's eyes open and exercises caution, these rapids involve nothing more than a little fast work and the possibility of a good dunking."

Maybe such words invite trouble. Maybe the number of days

encouraged problems. Perhaps difficulty for Goldwater came with the location, even if Nixon Rock just south of Tuna Creek Rapid had yet to acquire its name. In any event, Hugh Cutler's boat had a hole ripped in it, then the *Wen* caught on a rock, and as Goldwater scrambled out to push, the boat suddenly moved on, leaving him to grab on to a rock to which he clung in the face of the current. Cutler's boat proceeded to hit the very same rock that had impaled the *Wen* and tipped on its side. Through some feverish efforts by all concerned and the use of a stern line and a bow line, everyone made it to safety. Already tired by a night during which no one had slept well because of a steady wind, they were now exhausted. Even worse: under the forward hatch of the Cutler boat lay all of Goldwater's exposed and unexposed film. Miraculously, although the boat had taken on a lot of water, the film had escaped undamaged.

Nor did the remainder of the trip turn out to be uneventful. They experienced a number of mishaps, including "a near catastrophe" soon after a stop for lunch at Deer Creek Falls at mile 136. The Nevills' boat almost capsized in an unmarked rapid, and Doris Nevills flew into the water. But, not too much the worse for wear, she and the rest carried on to spend the night seven miles downriver at Kanab Creek. Goldwater that night permitted himself "the most gratifying of experiences—toying with memory." He remembered hunting and time with friends on the North Rim, playing poker at a lodge at night, the beauty and bustle of the South Rim, "and all of the happy days of my life, and I am not surprised that they are legion." And he concluded that life had dealt with him gently and kindly. Goldwater thought of family: "my mother, whom I would have had in mind had I been the one to name Bright Angel, then my father, then Carolyn and Bob, and now Peggy with her trio of blessings." He possessed "a full and happy past, a future more rosy than our sunset tonight, and a present more clear and sparkling than the sky that now becomes my blanket."

A week later they concluded the trip, with an extra day

thrown in at Diamond Creek to rest. They made the final miles in leisurely fashion, Goldwater starting to daydream about his bedroom at home, free of sand and bugs "carrying knives, sabers, and broken bottles"; tired of blowing up his air mattress, he mumbled in his journal that "sleeping in the open is one of the most overrated opportunities of camping." The group posed cheerfully at the plaque at the head of Lake Mead in Separation Canyon, where so many years before the ill-fated trio of Seneca Howland, O. G. Howland, and William H. Dunn had departed the Powell expedition, only to have death await them in nearby terrain. The now-bearded Goldwater stood in the back row of the assembled party, whose faces all seemed to say: "Yes! We did it!"

As the group on August 22 crossed Lake Mead for Boulder Dam, Goldwater marveled at the power of the dam and its success in harnessing the water of the river "to be used as man wants it." He had, he knew, and he wrote to this effect, closed a chapter of his life. He expressed jubilation for having shared the route of Powell, Dellenbaugh, and Kolb and "for having seen more of my beloved Arizona." This journey, he observed, would be "stored forever behind the dam of my memory" and would "remain forever a part of me and my life." In 1995 he stated without hesitation: "I enjoyed it as much as anything I ever did."

The lessons Goldwater drew from the weeks on the river he applied to particular issues he later faced as a politician representing Arizona. He had a new understanding of the power of nature and the utility of channeling it for the benefit of human civilization. He appreciated anew the importance of preserving as much as possible the country through which he had just passed. There would be times in his political career that such lessons conflicted, or appeared to conflict. Perhaps, above all, Goldwater knew even more fully the beauty of the Colorado Plateau—the country that kept calling him back, that really became in a direct sense his second home. This broad region, basically encompassing the Grand Canyon and its adjacent lands along with the territory now occupied by the Navajos and Hopis, had a particular power, a certain majesty. Although Goldwater had come to love every last square mile of Arizona, somehow this part of it towered above the rest in his heart and his imagination.

Fortunately for posterity he had recorded what he had witnessed not only on paper but also on film. Others had photographed the Grand Canyon. Brothers Emory and Ellsworth Kolb had run the river as early as 1912 and made a career out of their studio on the South Rim, where for six decades countless thousands of tourists watched the black-and-white film of their successful undertaking. The Kolb film had been mandatory viewing for prospective runners of the Colorado. It no doubt influenced Goldwater, who did not need much encouragement, to photograph his own experience. What he might not have anticipated, however, was the enormous public demand that greeted the color movie that Goldwater had put together, complete with melodramatic narration and music to accompany the remarkable footage. Part adventure story and part geology lesson, the film gave audiences a vivid sense of the rapids and the challenges of running the river. He showed the film first at the Heard Museum, again to another sold-out house, in the spacious Phoenix Union High School auditorium, later at the Orpheum Theatre in downtown Phoenix, and eventually throughout Arizona. If the film did not cause him to go into state politics, as he later averred, at least it did not exactly harm his chances for political success, for it unmistakably branded him as a man who loved Arizona and who had experienced some of its grandeur in a way that prompted admiration.

By the time he had completed his delightful journey, his photographs had begun to be featured in the pages of *Arizona Highways*. On hand for the opening of the Apache Brewery in Phoenix, Goldwater happened to bump into Raymond Carlson; the two proceeded to drink beer "like it was going out of style." In due course they got to talking about photography. Carlson asked him if he happened to have a good photograph of Coal Mine Canyon, near Tuba City. Goldwater did. He sent it to Carlson's office, and it was published in 1939.

Thus began a long and mutually beneficial association. Carlson served as editor of *Arizona Highways* for more than three decades. During his tenure the magazine became recognized as clearly the preeminent one of its kind, emulated but never duplicated by a host of other state travel journals. Goldwater's work continued to be featured during and after Carlson's editorship, even though his political career largely eliminated the time he could devote to the pastime. By the 1990s nearly three hundred of his photographs had been included in *Arizona Highways*. Hugh Harelson, who from 1982 to 1995 served as the magazine's publisher (as the top position was now termed), noted that his predecessor had been wise to turn to Goldwater. Goldwater supplied him not only with good photographs of the state's Indian citizens, but also with valuable political support over the decades, safeguarding the publication from bureaucratic interference or potential raids on its coffers from the state government and helping it maintain a nonprofit mailing permit, which freed it from dependence on outside advertising. He took great pride in his work in the magazine, Harelson observed, and he continued to follow the publication, sending notes and comments about it during Harelson's tenure as publisher.

One of Goldwater's favorite memories involving Carlson and the magazine concerned a particular idea Carlson conceived for a good photograph shortly after the close of World War II. Goldwater had obtained part-ownership in the Rainbow Lodge, located at the head of the trail down to Rainbow Bridge. Although he never operated the lodge on his own, he enjoyed flying there and spending what time he could in that beautiful spot, leading an occasional pack trip for those few tourists who wished to make the fourteen-mile trek down to Rainbow Bridge. Carlson had an inspiration. In late February 1946 he asked Goldwater to take a photograph of Navajo girls herding their sheep in the snow.

Goldwater listened, nodded, and objected. "Ray," he said, "that's a great picture, but it doesn't snow up here at this time of the year." Informing Carlson he would have to wait until

the following winter, Goldwater flew up to the lodge a couple
of weeks later, woke up one morning, "and, by God, it had
snowed." He had spotted two Navajo girls recently about
three miles away with their sheep. Goldwater raced to get
dressed, grabbed his camera, and scurried down to see if he
could locate the girls and their sheep. There they were. He
took the photograph, in color, and it became the cover in 1946
of the first all-color issue of the magazine.

As a relatively young man, then, Goldwater came to know
Navajo and Hopi country and became sufficiently acquainted
with individuals from those communities that they permitted
him to take their photographs. Goldwater's association with
the Indians of Arizona will be discussed in much greater length
in a later chapter, but it is useful now to emphasize the degree
to which Navajo and Hopi lands had become "Indian country" for him and that in turn, the images from their particular
reservations, with the Grand Canyon, had become quintessen-
tial Arizona. When one thinks about the dominant images of
the state, from the pages of *Arizona Highways* or from any
other source, one immediately calls to mind Monument Valley,
Canyon de Chelly, the San Francisco Peaks, a Hopi village, a
Navajo with his or her sheep, Hopi pottery, Navajo weaving,
Hopi and Navajo silver work. There are, of course, other
beautiful places in the state that are emblematic of Arizona,
but even those—Sedona and Oak Creek Canyon, for example—often are variations on a Colorado Plateau theme. Goldwater, Josef Muench, and other photographers regularly featured in *Arizona Highways* thus played a central role in the
process of establishing that visual identity for a new state. The
"real" Arizona early on could not be found among the tall
buildings lining Central Avenue in Phoenix or even in the
"old pueblo" of Tucson, nor could it be perceived along the
wide streets of Snowflake or even among the Victorian homes
of Prescott, as pleasing as those sights might be to certain people. *Arizona Highways* seemed less likely to display on its cover
downtown Bisbee or even the splendor of autumn in the
White Mountains. Rather, again and again, the magazine and

thus its readers returned to the Arizona north of old Route 66 and the Santa Fe Railroad and from the Grand Canyon and Marble Canyon eastward to the New Mexico line.

Years later, in 1978, Rand McNally published *Arizona,* a splendid anthology of the photographs of David Muench, Josef's son. Goldwater penned the accompanying text. The book is divided into six sections in the following order: Indian country, canyon country, high country, valley of the sun, desert country, and the old West. The order is no more accidental than the distribution; "Indian country" is allocated the largest amount of space in the volume. And "Indian country" for Muench and Goldwater is almost exclusively Navajo country: Monument Valley, Canyon de Chelly, the Lukachukais.

In such collections of Goldwater's photographs as *Arizona Portraits* and *People and Places* it is this country and its people that not merely stand out, but truly dominate the pages. Perhaps Goldwater's best-known image is that of Charlie Potato, a Navajo man Goldwater met at an arts and crafts fair in Winslow in 1939.

Goldwater looked at him and said, "That's a good face." So he asked him if he could take his picture. That more or less became the Goldwater method of operation—asking respectfully, knowing that he might be turned down, and with no great master plan. He told Evelyn Cooper: "I didn't care about recording their lives. If they invited me in their homes, I would go in, but I would not use a camera in a home." As Cooper observed, most of the Goldwater photographs of Indians divided into three categories: children, old people, and artists. When queried about this seeming preference, Goldwater acknowledged that he loved old people and children and he had not thought about artists. Perhaps as much as anything those photographs of weavers and potters reflect the place of art in the Indian world and the likelihood, especially in the 1930s and 1940s, that an older woman would be engaged in such work. Although Goldwater never saw himself as a cultural anthropologist, inevitably his photographs recorded a transitional era, particularly among the Navajos. For the Diné, as

Charlie Potato, Navajo, 1939. Photograph by Barry Goldwater. This is the most famous of Goldwater's portraits of Indian individuals. Barry Goldwater Photograph Collection, courtesy of the Arizona Historical Foundation

the Navajo called themselves, livestock reduction and World War II combined to begin to reshape the workings of the Navajo economy and society. Wage work gradually became more important, and although sheep remained central to the functioning of the Navajo social order, in the next generation it no longer could be assumed that every child would grow up amidst them. This is not to underestimate the symbolic significance of "tradition" nor the ability of the Navajos to incorporate new technology into their culture. But after 1950, new roads, new schools, and other developments broke down the old isolation and the relatively contained spheres of Navajo life. Because Goldwater took most of his photographs in Navajo country before 1950, they captured a sense of that transition.

He considered photography to be a hobby, "the most satisfying" among many. Adams noted that Goldwater was not a professional photographer, in the sense that he did not make a living through his work. As, in Adams's words, "a fine and eager amateur," Goldwater knew how to communicate a particular "vision of the Southwest," and, Adams added, he deserved "high accolades for his desire to tell us what he feels and believes about his beloved land." Goldwater "always loved his native land of Arizona and the other lands of the Southwest," Adams noted, and saw the region "in terms of images" which he conveyed in "photographs of historical and interpretive significance."

Goldwater's photography thus not only offered a kind of entry into politics but also ultimately reflected a certain vision of Arizona that always informed his politics. Well before the advent of a political career, he had come to know something about particular peoples and landscapes. He attempted to capture their spirit in his photographs—something of their resilience and their character. It is not surprising that such images later would be seen in his office in Washington. They were more than decorative. They reminded him of roots and responsibilities as well as of an Arizona that he tried to represent—both in photographs and as a senator.

At the same time, Goldwater's "Welcome to Arizona" message in Glen Canyon, his association with *Arizona Highways,* his background as a businessman, and his understanding of the barriers Arizona had faced in its history all speak to his interest in promoting economic development in the state through tourism and relocation of individuals and companies. In the longer term, such immigration inevitably affected the lands and lives of peoples whom Goldwater knew. Nonetheless, representing Arizona ultimately meant not only seeing it, but also building it. Development might allow natives and Natives a better chance to remain in the state, thanks to an invigorated economy. Such growth might well pose problems for the environment Goldwater cherished, that Raymond Carlson brought to the world. That fragile land, that unique sky might be endangered. However, that dilemma seemed distant when the Navajo girls, their sheep, and the snow graced the cover of *Arizona Highways.*

CHAPTER 3

Aviation, the Military, and Electronics

THOMAS Edison probably liked the letter he received from the thirteen-year-old boy:

> I wish to congratulate you upon your great success in the past years and hope your future years may be as fruitful.
>
> I am very interested in electricity and Radio. I operate a Radio Station here of 10 watts power under the call GB Pi. I have studied electricity since I was a little kid and I am going to keep it up until I am an old one.
>
> Sincerely yours,
Barry Morris Goldwater

And he did. Three of the keys to Arizona's growth in the twentieth century may be found in the interrelated areas of aviation, the military, and electronics. Barry Goldwater became involved in each as soon as he could and retained his fascination with each throughout his life. As the letter to Edison suggests, it began for him at an early age.

At the state fair in Phoenix in 1915 or 1916, Goldwater saw an airplane for the first time. He later recalled being "enthralled by the sight" and captured by the very idea that a person could fly. The example of Frank Luke, Jr., also made an impression. The local man, the namesake of Luke Field, received the Congressional Medal of Honor for his flying exploits during World War I. In addition, Goldwater's father purchased for him a crystal radio receiver. Without a radio station to listen to in Phoenix, he still could pick up the more distant signals from stations in Los Angeles. A year or so before he wrote Edison, he gave Earl Neilson a hand in starting KFAD, Phoenix's first radio station.

It did not take long for him to imagine possibilities and to make connections between the promises of these fledgling additions to life in twentieth-century Arizona. What if, he wondered, people on the ground could communicate with people in the air? It could help pilots with their landings. What if he could use an airplane to shorten the time it took to get from one point to another in the rugged country of his native state? It now took twelve hours and, perhaps, twelve tires to drive from Phoenix to Prescott. There had to be a better way. What if he and others could send messages that could warn of danger or send help in the case of emergency? Think of the advantages airplanes would have in spotting fires or delivering food to rural families stranded by a winter blizzard. Clearly such new technologies offered some significant possibilities. Through their advancement life in Arizona could be made better, and through their employment new states such as Arizona could become more competitive with other, more developed states already boasting more developed systems of transportation and communication.

The appeal of flying, to be sure, encompassed more than practicality and service. It just looked like fun. In addition, as Goldwater later mused in *With No Apologies,* it yielded "splendid isolation," a unique perspective on Arizona's extraordinary landscape—another way besides photography of seeing his native state—and a particular kind of discovery. Flying an airplane provided "the ultimate extension of individual freedom." It provided a new form of pioneering to a man who took pride in his own pioneer heritage.

After Goldwater returned from the University of Arizona, his interest in flying moved from daydream to reality. Walking down Central Avenue one day, he glanced in R. D. Roper's automobile show room and spotted not a car but an airplane. Goldwater ambled into Roper's and asked the price of the Great Lakes Trainer. The salesman informed him the plane could be his for a mere $2,500. Of course, there was a slight catch. It might make more sense to buy a plane if he knew how to fly one.

But, the salesman added promptly, that did not represent a problem. Go out to what passed for the airport, he advised Goldwater. Jack Thornburgh can teach you. Goldwater made his way over to the dirt strip at 24th Street and the railroad tracks, located Thornburgh, and soon began to take flying lessons, at ten dollars an hour, with Thornburgh and with Irving Kravitz, later a TWA pilot. Goldwater soloed after ten hours of instruction, taking to the bright Phoenix skies one lovely morning. In fact, he did all his early flying in the morning, before work, puzzling his mother, who wondered what in the world now inspired her son to rise and leave so early in the day. Goldwater knew he had not fooled her entirely but assumed she suspected a woman rather than a plane for his inspiration. She learned of his new love by way of a notice in the local paper after he had obtained his license. Josephine Goldwater would not have been reassured to learn that he had received no ground school training. "About all I knew," he recalled, "is one wing had a red light on it and the other one had a green light." Given the generally cooperative climate, he had also learned nothing about weather.

For that matter, the one-hundred-dollar investment had not covered spins, other than the cheerful counsel that if he got in one to let go of everything and to launch into the Lord's Prayer. Goldwater remembered vividly that first experience: "The first goddamn time I went up with a passenger I said, 'Well, I'll give her a tight circle over her house.' I did, it flipped over, and started to spin, and I said, 'Je-esus Christ!' So I let go of everything, by God, and it just came right out. I put both hands on the stick, shaking like a dog, flew it back to the airport, went home and got drunk." Undeterred, he kept flying and quickly became a booster of air transportation. The field on which he had learned to fly had been closed and the land temporarily transformed into a lettuce patch. When the American Legion post in Phoenix sought to present a gunnery trophy to the 27th Aero Pursuit Squadron in San Diego, the

squadron wanted to fly over to Phoenix but lacked an adequate place to land. Goldwater enlisted a friend, Lee Moore,
borrowed a tractor and drag from a Japanese American farmer,
and carved out a landing strip for the visitors in the middle of
the now abandoned lettuce patch. The T-12s had a place to
land, even if the runway had to be dragged every two weeks
and after every rain. The job took a day and a half, with go-
pher holes lengthening the time needed for the task.

The location became known as "the farm." Pilots buzzed
the field before they landed, thus helping to clear cattle off the
landing strip and alerting the only taxi in town that perhaps a
fare or two was about to land. Night landings furnished the
possibilities of additional excitement. Even after a beacon and
boundary lights had been added at the strip, they did not go
on automatically when a plane approached. The person in
charge of turning on the lights could forget when a plane was
scheduled to come in, could fall asleep, or could just be un-
prepared for an unanticipated landing. On such occasions the
pilot flew over the field and yelled, "Lights!" In 1935 the city of
Phoenix bought the field from Acme Investment Company for
one hundred thousand dollars. Phoenix decided to keep the
name "Sky Harbor," which had been applied to the site by the
board of directors for Scenic Airways, an airline which briefly
served Arizona.

As he continued to gain more experience as a pilot, Goldwater attempted to link this activity with military service. He
had joined the Army Reserve as a second lieutenant and hoped
to enter the Army Air Corps. However, his effort in 1932 did
not succeed; poor vision denied him the opportunity. The
middle and late 1930s were so busy that Goldwater found it
harder to record hours, even though he did keep adding to the
total. He had met and married Peggy during this interval, and
she had not been entirely impressed by his passion for planes.
I'll marry you, she said, but you'll have to give up flying and
learn to play bridge. The smitten Goldwater made a relatively
solemn vow to that effect. After the wedding he somehow
managed to keep flying and never to play bridge.

By the time World War II erupted, Goldwater had flown for more than four hundred hours and had graduated to larger planes. The war gave him a second chance, even though his eyes combined with his age to prevent entry into the Army Air Corps. As chairman of the Chamber of Commerce committee responsible for checking on the welfare of the troops and airmen who would be at Luke Field, Goldwater went over to Luke in the summer of 1941. He asked the commanding officer, Colonel Ennis Whitehead, if he might be of assistance. The exasperated Whitehead, known to his associates as "Ennis the Menace," happened not to be having a very good day. When Goldwater asked more particularly if Whitehead could use a second lieutenant, the colonel replied, "My God, are you a reserve officer?" When Goldwater affirmed his status, Whitehead instructed him to sit down and type out his own application for assignment. Three weeks later, magically, he had been assigned to Luke, and a cherished association with the Air Corps had been established at last.

There seemed to be no way for him to fly in combat, but he maneuvered to find ways to fly. Goldwater had the only camera on the base and had taken on public relations work along with other duties. When the word got out about his skills as a photographer, the officers besieged him to take their pictures to send back to their mothers and girlfriends. Goldwater would go along in the back seat of an airplane, an AT-6, and ten or twelve of the planes would fly off to some scenic backdrop such as Grand Canyon, Oak Creek Canyon, or the Verde Valley, where they flew by the right wing of Goldwater's plane. He related: "Now the deal I made with them was that I would take the pictures and give them the pictures, but I had to have an hour's stick time for each flight, so before anyone knew it I piled up about 300 hours in the AT-6."

During the war the Air Corps confronted a quandary. It did not have enough pilots to ferry planes, haul targets, fly the mail, and perform other chores. So it created a new category of pilot. Service pilots could not fly in combat, but they could fly for other purposes if they had four hundred hours or more in aircraft over four hundred horsepower and if they could pass a flight test in an AT-6. Goldwater just happened to qualify, and by October 1941 he had received his first set of Army Air Corps wings. The man who had started to fly without ground training soon received the assignment of ground school instructor.

Assigned to Yuma Air Base in the spring of 1942, Goldwater gained access to all sorts of interesting airplanes as he took messages to Luke Field and ferried different aircraft to and from Luke. He flew "the old bamboo bomber, the twin Cessna, that we later used, the AT-9 which was a monstrosity of a twin engine airplane," a P-40 that he loved, the A-20, and then the B-26. In the fall he moved on to the Second Ferrying Command in Wilmington, Delaware; earned promotion to captain; and became an operations officer for the 27th Ferrying Squadron. There were more planes to fly: P-47s all over the United States, B-17s to England, A-36s and B-26s to the British in the Bahamas, P-39s to the Russians in Alaska. The orders came. Goldwater participated in the first, and it turned out, only attempt to ferry fighter planes across the Atlantic. With nine others he piloted his P-47 Thunderbolt from New York to Maine, to New Brunswick, to Newfoundland, to Greenland, to Iceland, and finally to Scotland.

Goldwater's diary of this journey still makes compelling reading. He named his plane *Peggy G* after "you-know-who"; "She (Peggy) led me through the best part of my life, so I figured I might as well follow her across the Atlantic." Each leg of the flight had to be made by contact flight rules, allowing for at least a fifteen-hundred-foot ceiling. Those who knew the weather in Newfoundland assured the pilots they could count on such conditions perhaps once a year. Goldwater and his colleagues chafed at the delay. "Today is a stinker," he wrote. "Wind, rain and cold. The sun hasn't been out all day." Four days later, August 1, 1943, he noted: "Ye Gods! . . . still no weather for us to clear." Fortunately, his superiors changed their minds about the rules, and by August 6 the fliers had resumed their travels.

The *Peggy G* in Greenland, 1943. Barry Goldwater Photograph Collection, courtesy of the Arizona Historical Foundation

The trip to Greenland represented Goldwater's first solo flight over an ocean. He admitted to being "a mite squeamish" as he approached Cape Hanison before heading out over open water. After saying the Lord's Prayer, "I touched my Flying Saint Christopher, which Peggy had given me, looked over my instruments, felt of my already tired rear end, and settled down to my job." After three hours he could see "way, way ahead" land which looked "darn good," even if it remained 150 miles out. As he passed over the Greenland coast, below him loomed a vision that, Goldwater said, if he lived to be one hundred years old he would never forget: "a rich blue quiet sea, flanked by a very rocky coastline, and miles of deep cut fjords along this coastline." He landed, having flown 776 miles in four hours and fifteen minutes.

On August 8, after four hours and twenty minutes in the air, Goldwater reached Iceland. Following a two-day interlude occasioned by the weather, including one of rest and relaxation in Reykjavik, he and *Peggy G* completed the final installment of their mission on August 11. Miles flown, 3,750. Time: nineteen hours, forty minutes. Average speed: 190 miles per hour. Returning back across the pond, Goldwater wrote to Peggy an hour before landing at Goose Bay, Labrador: "Well, darling. . . . There should be a lot of letters and two bottles of whiskey waiting at Goose for me. . . . It has been a glorious trip and I am happy it is over and happy that I made it. It was the first time in history that a single engine fighter plane had been flown across the ocean." He concluded: "While my pride in being part of the flight is great, I think my pride in a country that can make engines and planes that will stand such a trip is greater."

Even though Goldwater suggested that not getting into combat remained one of the greatest disappointments in his life, he clearly took satisfaction in this achievement. And there were other compensations. During the remainder of the war he also had a tour in India, where he met again some of the Chinese pilots he had helped train at Luke and at Yuma. He received the "yearbook" published by the aviation cadets of class 43-E of the Army Air Force Advanced Flying School at the Yuma Army Air Field. The cadets dedicated the volume to him and observed that he was "the type of Officer and Gentleman after which we would like to pattern ourselves."

If the war brought new horizons to Goldwater, it certainly offered them as well to his home town and soon to be adjacent communities. The 1940s ushered in an era of unparalleled growth for what now could be called the Phoenix metropolitan area. The census figures reported that from a population of 65,414 in 1940, Phoenix had grown to 106,818 in 1950 and 439,270 in 1960. During the same two decades Mesa expanded from 7,224 to 16,670 to 33,772; Tempe's population increased nearly tenfold, from 2,906 to 7,684 to 24,897. Other Salt River valley towns recorded comparable gains. Maricopa County's figures were especially revealing, with the county population more than tripling in a generation, from 186,193 in 1940 to

Barry Goldwater, pilot. Goldwater flew 165 different airplanes, including the F-16 and SR-71. Barry Goldwater Photograph Collection, courtesy of the Arizona Historical Foundation

331,770 in 1950 and 663,510 in 1960. Although many reasons could be cited for this demographic explosion, aviation, the military, and electronics had been crucial in propelling the expansion.

In this expansion came opportunity for individuals to create new lives and realize old dreams. Goldwater applauded growth for making it possible for people to achieve their social and economic goals. However, he did not want to emphasize individualism at the expense of the larger needs and concerns of the community. As a native of Phoenix, he possessed the kind of pride, if not chauvinism, that a member of an old—by Arizona standards—family had in his home town. He saw individual opportunity and community growth as inextricable; one encouraged and assisted the other. But he hardly wished to promote a kind of environment in which individuals denied common responsibility for their fellow residents. That ran against the grain of what the Goldwater family had understood about citizenship. Nonetheless, as a businessman and as an unabashed advocate of private enterprise, as well as a steady foe of federal intervention against the wishes of local people, Goldwater almost inevitably became part of the vanguard of a new political order which surfaced in Arizona life in the decade following World War II.

Goldwater continued to promote commercial aviation and the presence of the air force in the Salt River valley. Commercial travel was still in its infancy, but the feeling of complete isolation had begun to dissipate; one began to believe that it was possible to get there from here. Goldwater understood that Sky Harbor could provide the necessary links with the rest of the United States that encouraged people to travel to Arizona on business or on vacation. He appreciated the possibilities for air transportation to allow individuals to visit more quickly their families in other parts of America. He had participated in the discovery made by the armed services during the war that Arizona presented extraordinary conditions for the training of pilots. In addition to the exceptional weather— marked by very few rainy days and the relative absence of wind—Arizona boasted open space. There would be few problems in expanding air bases or in reserving desert lands for aerial exercises. Luke Air Force Base in the northwest valley and Williams in the southeast remained viable after the war had ended, together with Davis-Monthan Field in Tucson. Moreover, many of the servicemen who had passed through Arizona during the war years had not felt deprived by the absence of snow and ice in winter. Now that air conditioning seemed to be more efficient, one could imagine living in the desert. The climate allowed for extended seasons and almost anything seemed to grow here, including the plants and trees from around the country that newcomers transplanted from back home.

During Goldwater's absence during the war, Arizona's economy began to be redefined. The traditional sector, based on the use of natural resources, rebounded. The moribund copper industry revived because of the overwhelming need for copper; the Metals Reserve Corporation of the federal government provided a reliable and generous purchaser for the mineral. Cattle ranchers and cotton growers also improved their situation. However, industrial enterprises became much more important. A series of new developments emerged in the state, prompted by climate and convenient access to the industrial economy of southern California. For example, Consolidated Vultee came to Tucson. Goodyear Aircraft built in Litchfield Park. The Aluminum Corporation of America, or Alcoa, constructed a plant at 35th Avenue and Van Buren in Phoenix in 1942. Later in the same year, AiResearch, which manufactured airplane parts, occupied a building near Sky Harbor Airport. The federal government assisted Alcoa in its startup and AiResearch in acquiring its building. Given the inevitable housing shortage for workers, the government also hastily threw together housing for workers at such facilities.

Members of old Arizona families, including the Goldwaters, understood that such industries represented part of the means through which their ambition of an expanding state economy could be achieved. The new migrants lured by such industries not only might shop at Goldwater's, but also in time might contribute to the growth of interrelated concerns, such as housing and automobiles. Rural people could count on hourly wages instead of the uncertainties of working on a farm or ranch. In *Heart Earth*, Ivan Doig remembered his father's being enticed to work at Alcoa. The Doigs moved to

Arizona from Montana. "Surely this," Doig wrote, "the state of Arizona humming and buzzing with defense plants and military bases installed for the war, this must be the craved new world, the shores of Social Security and the sugar trees of overtime." He and his father were equally mesmerized by the sight of an illuminated sign at night on top of the towering Westward Ho Hotel; perhaps just then, he mused, Arizona "must have seemed just what my parents were looking for after their recent Montana struggles."

Arizona could not hold the Doig family. The Doigs returned to Montana after the war, and Ivan Doig went on to become a bard of the north country. For many others like the Doigs, the end of the war did not mean a return to a former residence. Rather, they stayed on, applauding the winters, cherishing new chances, even if they felt initially like strangers in a strange land. For their children, snow became abnormal and the desert surroundings had a far better chance of appearing beautiful. The parents were more likely not only to plant familiar shrubs but as well uproot their political views and bring those, too, along with them to their new residences. Because they had acted more independently, because they believed that through their own initiatives they had improved their lives, they were ready to support politicians, such as Barry Goldwater, who underscored their judgments. Such voters brought their political affiliations with them, too, and a great many of them were registered as Republicans.

Arizona benefited from both the war and the cold war that followed. Defense-related industries expanded in the years after 1945. Goldwater and other Arizona businessmen had encouraged an economic climate that seemed ideal for the new electronics companies that readily served the needs of the Defense Department. Such companies were exactly what the boosters of the Phoenix area had in mind. They quickly gained the label of "clean industries," far preferable to the smokestack industrialization characteristic of the urban East. Few individuals imagined at the time that electronics companies could have any negative impact upon the land or water. Such firms could count on a warm Arizona welcome from the business leaders of the state.

Frank Snell, Eugene Pulliam, and Walter Bimson numbered among those leaders. Snell, a Phoenix attorney, Pulliam, the publisher of the Phoenix newspapers, and Bimson, the head of the state's major bank, Valley National, all worked in concert to attract corporations to come to the Salt River valley. These same men were friends of Goldwater and played important roles in promoting his early political career. They sought to establish in Phoenix in particular and in Arizona in general the right kind of climate and the appropriate political leadership that would be responsive to the needs of the city and the state. They knew if they could bring in new major companies in the postwar years that other concerns would follow.

The decision of Motorola officials in early 1948—no doubt on a frigid winter day in Chicago—to construct a research and development center in Phoenix altered the future of Arizona. Despite some anxiety over the inferno their employees would face in the summer, Motorola executives had sufficient confidence in the technological advances achieved in air conditioning to approve the deal. The initial plant, devoted specifically to defense work, later was joined in 1960 by two additional plants constructed by the company. Motorola had emerged as the largest single private employer in the state of Arizona, a position it still holds today. As Brad Luckingham recorded in his history of Phoenix: "With Motorola setting the pace, manufacturing had become the city's number one source of income by 1955, with farming and tourism in second and third place. Between 1948 and 1960 nearly three hundred manufacturing enterprises opened their doors and manufacturing employment in the metropolitan area tripled. The annual income from manufacturing rose from under $5 million in 1940 to over $435 million in 1963."

Following Motorola's lead, General Electric, Sperry Rand, and Kaiser Aircraft and Electronics joined the parade into Phoenix in the 1950s. Goldwater would work directly with the financial community to encourage this commitment, meeting

company officials at various gatherings and encouraging helpful changes in state laws in order to promote corporate investment. He realized that if a few companies came, others might
follow, and he instinctively backed this kind of new frontier
for Maricopa County. Given his enthusiasm for technology, he
delighted in the innovations made possible through electronics. In later years he thus observed a procession of electronics
industry giants such as Honeywell and Intel arrive in the area.
This growth spurred the rapid expansion of metropolitan
Phoenix and, in turn, affected every sector of life in Maricopa
County. Arizona State University serves as but one example. A
tiny teachers' college at war's end, by the end of the 1950s Arizona State University had changed its name and its mission,
with its enrollment swelling from well under a thousand to
over eleven thousand in a fifteen-year span. The needs of the
manufacturing community contributed to its skyrocketing
numbers; returning veterans, buoyed by the G.I. Bill, also
added to the process through which the institution redefined
itself.

Such dramatic change could not have been guaranteed by
civic leaders during World War II. They agonized over contemporary realities that stood in the way of the growth they
desired. The war brought unprecedented challenges to the
prevailing social and political order of Phoenix. In November
1942, for example, a riot involving servicemen had startled the
community. Throughout that year military officials had complained about the prevalence of prostitution. The fear of vene-
real disease more than the fear of civic disorder inspired
Colonel Ross G. Hoyt, commander of Luke Field, to declare
Phoenix off-limits for his personnel. The *Arizona Republic*
blasted city officials for tolerating nine houses of prostitution,
a "massage parlor," and bars which provided meeting places
for prostitutes and their customers and which generally promoted disreputable behavior. Snell, Pulliam, Bimson, and
other local political heavyweights had had enough. They pres-
sured Phoenix city government, and in December the government fired its city manager, police chief, city clerk, and city

magistrate. A few days later, on December 21, Hoyt rescinded his off-limits order. Even with this victory, boosters remained uncertain about the future direction of Phoenix. Politics as usual was not going to be sufficient, they concluded, and members of the business community were going to have to become much more directly involved in the political process if Phoenix were to achieve a proper future. This conclusion inspired Snell, Pulliam, Bimson, and their allies to search for like-minded men to seek public office. It is not surprising they would soon turn to one of their own in Barry Goldwater.

Although Goldwater was one of the unique personalities who figured in this scenario, Phoenix was hardly alone in confronting the general question of postwar governance. It numbered among many municipalities that struggled with the growing pains brought by the first half of the 1940s. For example, a coalition of merchants, lawyers, and industrialists in San Jose established the Progress Committee in 1944 to try to create a more progressive political order in the city. In Denver, forces mustered to try to find an alternative to "Interminable Ben" Stapleton, who had served as mayor since the 1920s. Albuquerque witnessed a Citizens Committee, formed by middle-class residents who sought to achieve a more efficient and productive city government. Thus Phoenix may be seen as rather typical in the situation it faced and the links its leading citizens drew between efficiency and honesty and insuring a kind of climate that promoted growth. Phoenix may not have possessed the equivalent of an A. P. Hamann, the San Jose city manager who pledged earnestly in 1950 to make San Jose "the Los Angeles of the north." Nonetheless, it definitely wished to forge opportunities for what it deemed progress.

However, not all western cities exactly duplicated each other in how they defined progress and opportunity. Cities that had already experienced substantial growth before the war and yet had not become enormous, historian Carl Abbott has argued, stood a better chance of fashioning what he termed civil communities, where avenues for individual initiative could be balanced by a commitment to republican virtues and community values. By 1940 Seattle and Portland ranked only behind Los Angeles and San Francisco–Oakland—if one does not count Houston as a western city—as the largest metropolitan areas in the West. Barry Goldwater's Phoenix, small and more diverse in its population than Seattle and Portland, faced more of a challenge in building a civic culture. In addition, the postwar boom in Maricopa County fostered the growth of decidedly independent neighboring communities: Mesa, Tempe, Glendale, Scottsdale, and Chandler. The major electronics companies did not build only in Phoenix. This suburban development influenced the contours of Maricopa County and, thus, Arizona politics.

As a Phoenix native, Goldwater wanted to encourage a civic culture. At the same time, his commitment to individualism and private enterprise fit the kind of city Phoenix was becoming. More like Dallas in its ethic, which gave priority to the individual and to the needs and wants of business, Phoenix struggled to construct a more cohesive civic culture. All the while, its boundaries expanded and the corresponding sprawl worked against such an identity. Phoenix was too new to most of its residents, who often remained loyal to their old cultural homelands in everything from their continuing adherence to sports teams elsewhere to their persisting preference for lawns rather than desert landscaping. The average Phoenician railed against initiatives in the decades that followed the war—whether they were designed to provide minimal public transportation or even add more miles to the clogged freeways through slight tax increases—as governmental intrusion contrary to individual well-being. That kind of selfish individualism ultimately disappointed Goldwater, who did not see civic and personal advancement as being in competition with each other.

The political and economic climate at the end of the war did at least promise that Arizona could realize its destiny in the twentieth century. In the past, too many people had migrated to the state before the war and had not remained. The weather and the economy had discouraged extended residence. Now, along with the winter visitors, who had always flocked to Phoenix, would be those new suburban pioneers who anticipated correctly the promise of the postwar period. Especially the younger ones, their tastes and perspectives more fully shaped by the past decade, had some instinctive sense that this new economy would prompt a classic real estate boom of wonderful proportions. Land was both plentiful and inexpensive; the benign winters aided rapid construction of new homes. The new arrivals generally may have wanted familiar trees and plants, but they did not want to re-create the urban scenario they had experienced or observed in the Midwest and in the East. More slowly than in California, but following a very comparable pattern, they sought a different kind of urban life, characterized by single-story residences and what proponents called "low density" and outnumbered opponents labeled "sprawl."

The automobile coupled with the climate provided the ingredients for these desires, at least in the short run, to be realized. Historian John Findlay has written about the kind of mental maps constructed by the residents of such postwar areas as Phoenix. While people accustomed to the old mixed-use city center decried the new trend, westerners embraced the city, Findlay argued, "not as a single place but as a series of environments catering to different needs and tastes." In the Phoenix metropolitan sector, as elsewhere in the new urban West, middle-class and upper-income people "dwelled in housing subdivisions, worked in industrial or business parks, shopped at shopping malls and commercial strips, and found entertainment at recreational and cultural centers." To the uninitiated the resulting, evolving place seemed chaotic, without order. To the person more familiar with the place, it did not appear that way, for he or she had learned how to navigate easily by car through the wide, new streets. The resident followed certain corridors, knew certain orbits. With the federal government and private sources offering accessible loans to new home buyers, the commuter pattern quickly formed.

"Boosters in Houston and Phoenix," commented historian

Richard White, "liked to emphasize their cities' dependence on free enterprise, but these cities, too, had close links with local, state, and national governments." He added: "A free enterprise strategy did not necessarily equal a devotion to the free market. Houston and Phoenix sought federal aid; what they sought to avoid was federal regulation." In due course, Federal Housing Administration and Veterans Administration loans to both Phoenix and Tucson played a central, essential role in the real estate boom, just as federal investment in wartime industries had helped build a foundation for postwar economic growth.

If the federal government had a stake in postwar western economic expansion, civic boosters such as Barry Goldwater obviously had a particular stake in it, too. Not that he tried to manipulate the era to his own financial advantage. In fact, one could contend, as Goldwater often did in later years, that he made considerable financial sacrifices by choosing a career in politics instead of remaining in the business world. Goldwater never pretended that he was a candidate for the poor house, although in private correspondence and eventually in public interviews he intimated that he surely could have been far more prosperous had he remained fully in the private sector. His honesty did not permit him to use politics to gain financial wealth. Already a prosperous, successful businessman, he felt no need or temptation to do so.

What Goldwater did experience was the need to contribute directly to the process through which Arizona's potential could be realized in the years that followed the war. Without planning it, he had placed himself in a position where he was almost uniquely suited to represent Arizona as a politician in this new era. He understood how things worked. He knew that Arizona could realize the kind of prosperity he had always believed it could attain. He should not have been entirely surprised when his friends and colleagues urged him to take part in the political work that they believed needed to be done. A pilot, a veteran, a man with a lifelong fascination with technology, a businessman with a well-known and well-regarded family name, a native of Arizona, and, just for good measure, a man you could not help but like, regardless of how you might feel about all the details of his views, Barry Goldwater looked liked a natural for the postwar politics of his city and his state. One might have anticipated that he would be a leader. And one might have anticipated that aviation, the military, and electronics would continue to be important to him in the political career that lay ahead.

CHAPTER 4

Entering Politics

"I STARTED my career in politics in the city of Phoenix," Barry Goldwater once said, "in the firm belief that if a man told the truth, that if a man acted according to his honest convictions and the feelings of his heart, that a man, even though defeated, would be a man who could live with himself in the years to come."

Morris Goldwater's nephew learned at an early age that one should care and speak out about one's own community. He also believed that with social advantage came some degree of social responsibility. Before he reached the age of thirty, Goldwater began to air his views in the newspaper. Responding to a man in Phoenix who had criticized his opinions, Goldwater displayed the sense of obligation, a sort of noblesse oblige, that would carry him into the political scene. "I did not get my start selling old boots and bottles," he reminded his adversary. "I was one of the lucky few who was born with a silver spoon in my mouth and I am doing my best to keep it there." Goldwater was amused by a question "as to whether I have the guts to repeat my statement. . . . I will say what I damn please any time I feel like saying it to anybody I feel like saying it to." He concluded: "I just happen to be an American citizen who has a perfect right to feel like he wants to feel, to think what he wants to think and to say what he wants to say about it."

The voice was already emerging. In the following year, Goldwater gave radio talks over radio stations KTAR and KOY dealing with such varied subjects as cattle feeding, the Community Chest, and summer camps. In one such commentary, on January 12, 1939, he suggested to his listeners that Phoenix's economic growth had not been "a Jack and the bean stalk" overnight effort. "The city had been constructed on the foundation erected by men who came to this valley over seventy years ago and settled here with the determination growing only from unselfish motive to make Phoenix a city." Such individuals had envisioned "a city their children and their children's children would be proud to work in and call home . . . a city that would be respected by the world and loved by its citizens."

However, during the 1940s the city of Phoenix experienced what can be politely termed "growing pains." Almost overnight the war years sparked an unprecedented influx of new people. In 1940 Phoenix counted 65,414 inhabitants; by 1950 the population reached 105,818, not counting individuals already residing in land about to be annexed by the city. And the next decade promised extraordinary expansion of this total. Businessmen such as Harry Rosenzweig and Barry Goldwater had a natural interest in urban growth but also in urban management. Along with others in the Salt River valley, they sought ways to bring new industry to the area, as well as to find the means to govern it.

Returning home from the service, Goldwater quickly plunged into a number of civic activities. In 1948 he was chosen as the first vice president of the Boys Club of Phoenix and reelected to the Community Chest board. In the same year Sidney Osborn, Arizona governor, appointed him to the Arizona Interstate Stream Commission (AISC). Along with fellow members Alfred Atkinson of Tucson (a former president of the University of Arizona), merchant Jay M. Gates of Kingman, Judge Jesse A. Udall of Thatcher, and three men with farming and business interests—Wayne M. Akin of Phoenix, John A. Roberts of Casa Grande, and R. H. McElhaney of Wellton— Goldwater fought for more Colorado River water for Arizona. In the small world of Arizona politics of that era, they worked with AISC Executive Secretary Ray Killian, a Mesa farmer.

Such roles brought the Goldwater name into the papers from time to time, but the activity that surely provided the

most publicity also likely was the most fun. Goldwater never
tired of showing his film about his journey down the Colorado
River to appreciative Arizona audiences. In later years he gave
the credit for his success in Arizona state politics to the exposure the film provided. Goldwater did more than turn on the
projector when he spoke in Kingman or Coolidge. He linked
the joy of his trip with, in the words of the *Mohave County
Miner,* the "potentialities" of the river. The *Miner* informed
its readers about "the unsurpassed beauty that radiates from
the tall sandstone canyon walls." It also reported Goldwater
had argued that "God put that river here for the service of
man" and that Arizona was "being cheated of its rightful share
of the river water" by California, which contributed "absolutely nothing to the river and wastes a great percentage of
the water it takes from the channel."

This utilitarian philosophy influenced Goldwater's perspective on the natural resource issues throughout his political career. That notion of service, be it by a river or an individual,
never drifted far from his consciousness. He maintained a
turn-of-the-century perspective about this responsibility. He
had an obligation, with that silver spoon in his mouth. His
mother had instilled the proper values; as a child he had heard
the Episcopal Church reinforce the message about being saved
for service and saved through service. And Goldwater already
realized that in his home town there were problems requiring
prompt attention.

Phoenix politics had been characterized by instability and
lack of accountability. City managers had little job security;
no fewer than thirty of them had been fired in the previous
thirty-five years. At the same time, the current city manager,
James Deppe, was rumored to be susceptible to bribes. Such
conditions would not do in an up-and-coming community. In
an alliance that had a powerful effect on Goldwater's political
career, the *Arizona Republic,* along with business and commercial interests, worked to promote a change in city government. New people had to be drafted to run and to be elected
to the city council. With the right candidates, the council

could be transformed and Phoenix governed in the kind of effective and responsible manner the times demanded.

Who could be tapped to seek spots on the council? The reformers, who had founded the Charter Government Committee and nominated candidates in the last election, called upon two incumbents whom they had endorsed previously: Mayor Nicholas Udall and Council Representative Charles N. Walters. An attorney, a native of Saint Johns, Arizona, and a member of the Church of Jesus Christ of Latter-day Saints, Udall, thirty-six, was part of the family that also would contribute Morris and Stewart Udall to Arizona politics. Born in Phoenix, Walters was also a lawyer; he had been appointed to the council in May 1948. Hohen Foster (coowner of Barq's Bottling Company), Margaret Kober (active in the community and married to well-known physician Leslie R. Kober), Frank G. Murphy (an underwriter for Mutual Life Insurance Company), and Harry Rosenzweig (a partner with his brother, Newton, in I. Rosenzweig and Sons jewelry store, founded by their father in 1897) also emerged as Charter Government candidates. During an era when voters perhaps cared more about religious affiliation, Foster (a Methodist), Kober (a Presbyterian), Murphy (a Catholic), and Rosenzweig (a Jew) professed different faiths but shared common concerns. They had all been active in civic organizations. Foster and Murphy had been president, for example, of the Phoenix Junior Chamber of Commerce; Kober had been president of the Phoenix Junior League. They were all married, with children; they had all lived in Phoenix for at least a decade.

One place on the ballot remained, and as the days dwindled before the deadline to complete the slate, Rosenzweig decided to persuade Goldwater, his friend from childhood, to join him in the race. Despite his admiration for his uncle Morris and his own engagement in civic matters, Goldwater paused before he pounced upon the opportunity. Rosenzweig later recalled taking him to dinner, armed with Old Crow, Goldwater's favorite bourbon. Talked by his pal into taking on the assignment, Goldwater told his brother, Bob, and a Goldwater's store manager: "You both will probably call me seven kinds of a dirty bastard when you hear that I have decided to run for councilman with Harry."

"Don't cuss me too much," Barry Goldwater added. "It ain't for life, and it may be fun." The forty-year-old capitalized on his name, his charm, and his involvement in everything from the Masons—he and Rosenzweig were 32d-degree Masons—to the Elks Lodge to lead the Charter Government ticket to an impressive victory that fall. With each voter able to vote for eight candidates, Goldwater received 16,405 of 22,353 votes cast by 22,353 voters in the at-large election. Rosenzweig and Kober came in second and third, with 14,887 and 14,498 votes, respectively. All the Charter Government candidates won. Goldwater carried every precinct in the city and emerged as a natural choice for vice-chairman of the new council under Mayor Udall.

Goldwater quickly figured as a possibility for other elective offices. No sooner had he been sworn in as a councilman than reports surfaced in the local press about what he might do next. The *Phoenix Gazette,* the afternoon paper of the Pulliams, declared on February 14, 1950, that Goldwater had been approached to run for governor in the autumn of 1950. "He is capable, knows governmental problems and needs, and has a vote getting personality," the *Gazette* noted. However, Goldwater had "demurred," observing that he had just begun his council term. Not to be deterred, the newspaper observed that in 1952 "some of his close personal friends would like him to be a Republican candidate for U.S. Senate at that time." As for the governor's race, Phoenix radio announcer Howard Pyle had come "within a gnat's eyebrow" of running in 1948. Perhaps he might be cajoled into seeking the post this time around.

In the meantime, Goldwater became a high-profile member of the Phoenix City Council, scoring points in the public eye for blunt talking and an already well developed sense of humor. Attending his first meeting of the council on January 3, 1950, he joined in the chorus for Deppe's resignation. When Deppe

Phoenix City Council, November 1951. Seated (*left to right*): Margaret Kober, Nicholas Udall (mayor), Charles Walters, Harry Rosenzweig. Standing (*left to right*): Frank Murphy, Barry Goldwater, Hohen Foster. Barry Goldwater Photograph Collection, courtesy of the Arizona Historical Foundation

protested, Goldwater replied, "Now, let's not gum up the works here anymore." Deppe departed, to be replaced by Ray Wilson, who had worked in city government in Kansas City, Missouri. Goldwater earned high marks from his peers for taking his duties seriously, but he was not above taking them down a notch if he thought they were getting out of line. Exasperated by a particularly long-winded colleague, Goldwater put a set of wind-up teeth on the council dais and let them chatter away to accompany the endless talk. The chagrined offender, Nicholas Udall later recalled, "grabbed for them and tried to stop them." But the point had been made, with characteristic Goldwater subtlety.

As the new decade began, Goldwater had already become

much in demand as a public speaker around the state of Arizona. In one of innumerable Lincoln Day dinner talks he presented for Republican fund-raisers, he spoke to Yuma County Republicans assembled for the occasion. The five things he asserted Republicans must do reflected the Goldwater agenda and political platform under construction. Stop being ashamed of being an American and a Republican, Goldwater advised. Put human freedom as the first and primary demand of the Republican party. "Stop apologizing for our capitalistic society, which has given Americans the highest standard of living with the greatest amount of personal freedoms." Get rid of compromising Republican leaders, he urged, and "stop planning for socialism and start planning for the continuation and the improvement of our free enterprise system."

Howard Pyle did accept his party's call to run again for governor. To manage his second campaign he named Goldwater. The *Arizona Republic* called the selection "a particularly fortunate one." The newspaper added, "He is a young man, full of enthusiasm as well as sound ideas and should add a great deal of strength to the already formidable movement to give new life to the party in Arizona." Publisher Eugene Pulliam liked what he saw. Neither Pyle nor Goldwater, the *Republic* concluded, "is a saddle-galled politician who has spent his life at the public trough. Both are young businessmen with a fresh viewpoint and progressive ideas."

It may be difficult now to recall or even imagine Arizona as a rock-ribbed Democratic state. Nonetheless, before World War II the Democrats vastly outnumbered their Republican counterparts in voter registration. Not surprisingly, the Democrats dominated state offices. But with the arrival of new Arizonans during and after the war, the political winds began to shift. Technological change, including the addition of air conditioning, combined with the movement of electronics firms, military bases, and other enterprises particularly to the Salt River valley, promised altered political circumstances. Many of the newcomers brought with them as part of their cultural baggage Republican party affiliation. There is an old folk saying in Arizona that "with refrigeration came Republicans." It may well be true.

Barry Goldwater numbered among those who sensed a changing political tide, and he labored tirelessly in the early 1950s to hasten that transition. The Pyle campaign offered a particular opportunity to spread the Republican gospel. Goldwater knew how to have his candidate meet more people more quickly throughout the state. Even though a significant portion of voters resided in Phoenix and Tucson, Pyle had to reach beyond the two cities of Arizona, and Goldwater knew how to give him that reach. He flew Pyle from one campaign stop to the next, thus making it possible for the candidate to meet with political leaders in Yuma at noon and in Kingman that evening, make it to Safford for breakfast, and have lunch in Casa Grande. For 1950, this represented a real breakthrough in how campaigns could be conducted. Pyle won, defeating the first woman in Arizona to run for governor, Ana Frohmiller.

Goldwater and Pyle remained close after the election, with the councilman often providing advice to the governor. In later years Goldwater gave Pyle the credit for initiating his race for the U.S. Senate in 1952: "I will never forget the day I was talking to a service club in Glendale, Arizona, and Howard was there. He drove me back in his governor's car to Phoenix and on the way he said, 'Barry, why don't you run for the U.S. Senate?' I said, 'Howard, if that is your wish, I will do it.'"

Although the thought obviously had occurred to Goldwater and to others before that conversation in February 1951, he had always professed to some reluctance to enter the race. The encouragement of his friends and his belief that "more businessmen should enter the arena of politics" influenced that decision. Goldwater knew he had an uphill battle, even with a well-known name and the backing of the Pulliam newspapers. The Democrats held a substantial edge in voter registration, and he confronted a popular incumbent, Ernest McFarland. In an era when one did not announce one's candidacy a long time before the election, Goldwater waited until April 24, 1952, to declare officially his intentions. He actually began the cam-

Republican nominee for governor Howard Pyle and his campaign manager, Barry Goldwater, 1950. Pyle's successful campaign marked an important turning point in Republican fortunes. Photograph by Herb McLoughlin. Barry Goldwater Photograph Collection, courtesy of the Arizona Historical Foundation

paign in February 1951, and despite his protestations to the contrary, he probably did not need all that much prompting.

Politics presented Goldwater with an ideal outlet for a man with energy to burn and an unwavering conviction that his values and priorities were needed in government. At the same time, there was a price to be paid. Running for the Senate involved a different level of commitment from seeking a seat on the city council. He later recalled: "That campaign went on and on. . . . I dropped my business, I dropped my family life, I dropped the life of my friends. In thirteen months of the last phase of my campaign, I made nearly 700 speeches and appearances in the state of Arizona, traveling by airplane over 50,000 miles and by car another 10,000 miles."

Upon occasion, Goldwater could be guilty of slight exaggeration, but on this score he did not embellish. Fueled by the kind of zeal that empowers a man starting a new career in what seemed to him to be middle age, he devoted himself to the task at hand with a single-mindedness that did not leave much room for other dimensions of his life. In keeping with the mores of the time, Peggy Goldwater devoted herself to their four children. She was not one publicly or privately to express anything other than loyalty to her husband and what he wished to achieve. His life was hers, and she wanted him to be happy. Although fiercely loyal to the Goldwater name and the legacy of the store, he was not a person who would have been fulfilled by a life spent in making decisions about the direction of the store. Politics supplied another avenue, and once he made that turn in the road, he did not ever reverse his direction. As any person, he had his second thoughts about what might have been; he mused more than once about what a life in the military might have been like, and the longer he stayed in Washington the more he missed his family and the familiar environment of his native state. Once he had made up his mind, however, it was full speed ahead. Mindful of the adage that it doesn't matter whether you win or lose until you lose, he intended to win.

Republican candidates for state office in Arizona in 1952 had a mountain to climb. No Republican served in the state senate, and only eleven held seats in the eighty-two-person house of representatives. No Republican had ever been elected to the U.S. House of Representatives. Democrat Carl Hayden held the other U.S. Senate post. The Strom Thurmond of his day, Hayden had served Arizona in the U.S. House and Senate since 1912, and it appeared as though he could go on forever. Yet the election of Howard Pyle in 1950 indicated that Republicans could win under the right circumstances, and the year 1952 happened to be tailor-made for alterations in the Arizona political landscape.

Individual Republican candidates had several things going for them this time around. As already noted, newcomers to the state were more likely to be Republican than Democrat. McFarland, for one, would place the blame for his electoral defeat in 1952 squarely on that demographic factor; the new people did not know him and did not appreciate his prior service in Washington. There is a certain degree of validity to this assertion. Goldwater benefited from the arrival of Republican voters, and new voters, regardless of party affiliation, had to become acquainted with incumbents. Yet even with the upswing in party affiliation, Arizona remained Democratic. Goldwater and others, such as John Rhodes, who sought the U.S. congressional seat held by Democrat John Murdock, gained from the increasing tendency of American voters to vote, as they said in the 1950s, for the man, not the party, and from Democratic apathy. If Goldwater could convince some Democrats and some independents to vote for him, and if he could hang on to most Republican voters, he could win.

No one more personified that growing proclivity of American voters to look to the individual rather than to the party than Dwight Eisenhower. Eisenhower had been sought by both the Democrats and the Republicans. His personal appeal transcended party lines, and Republicans in 1952 knew they had a winner who might even pull those who did not usually vote for a Republican into the Republican column for more than the presidential balloting. Goldwater had opted for Eisenhower over Ohio senator Robert Taft to be the GOP standard bearer, despite Taft's impeccable conservative credentials. Goldwater sensed correctly that Americans liked Ike, noting as well the former general's effect upon young Republicans in Arizona, and was willing to endure some criticism for throwing his support behind the candidate most likely to give Republicans their first man in the White House since Herbert Hoover. And, to be sure, Goldwater applauded Eisenhower's military credentials and perceived him to be a leader who as president would encourage investment in national defense.

Goldwater easily won reelection to the Phoenix City Council in 1951, again topping the slate of candidates with 18,016 votes. He continued to give necessary attention to council matters, but by then his primary focus lay elsewhere. His announcement for the U.S. Senate in April 1952 made official what everyone had known for months. Three months before, for example, the *Holbrook Tribune News* declared it "no secret that U.S. Senator Ernest W. McFarland is deeply concerned over the possibility that Barry Goldwater will be nominated for the U.S. Senate by the Republicans." When the announcement came, it contained unmistakable signals of Goldwater's emphases in this campaign and, for that matter, others to follow.

In what has become familiar fare for Republican candidates from the American West, he began by pledging he would make "every effort to re-establish local self-government and responsibility and to combat the efforts" of what he termed the "New Deal" party "to nullify the rights of the states." Goldwater noted the degree of federal control over state land resources and called for "decentralization of the bureaucratic power" of Washington. Echoing Richard Nixon and other Republicans of the era, he also warned of "the aping of socialism and the appeasing of the Communists of Russia." Thus "the great issue" facing Americans, in his judgment, was "the restoration, the preservation, and the perpetuation of human liberty."

If Goldwater ran against Washington and Moscow, he, as does any candidate for local office, reminded voters of his attachment and dedication to his locale. From April until election eve he stressed his "life-long familiarity with Arizona." He also put stock in his business background. Such themes were quickly picked up by the Pulliam newspapers. On April 26 the *Arizona Republic* labeled him "an outstanding candidate." Leaving little doubt whom it favored in the fall election, the newspaper concluded that "no one could be better fitted to represent Arizona. He knows the state like the back of his hand." Citing his achievements in business and on the city council as well as his involvement in civic enterprises, the *Republic* asserted that Goldwater was "known, admired, and respected the length and breadth of the state." It argued that his race strengthened the two-party system in Arizona and even dared speculate that he had "a very good chance" of beating McFarland.

Stephen Shadegg (the father of John Shadegg, elected to Congress from Arizona in 1994) stepped in to run the Goldwater campaign. A valuable associate of Goldwater throughout most of the senator's long career, he demonstrated his talents early in the 1952 race. Goldwater ran not only against Washington and against McFarland as Senate majority leader, but also against Harry Truman. In 1952, Truman had not yet begun to be rehabilitated by historians and featured in Home Box Office films; the polls mirrored his dramatic lack of popularity. He made a convenient symbol, a target for Republican brickbats and campaign signs. Shadegg had an idea. Why not put up signs along the road linking "Mac" (McFarland) with Truman and Barry with the people? Carrying on the Burma Shave sign tradition, the effort allowed drivers in Arizona to begin to notice a quintet of properly spaced signs:

> Mac is for Harry
> Harry's all through
> You be for Barry
> Cause Barry's for you
> Goldwater for Senate

The Korean War, coupled with Truman's decision to remove General Douglas MacArthur from command, made such a strategy especially effective. When McFarland allegedly called the war "cheap . . . because we are killing nine Chinese for every American boy," Goldwater jumped on this remarkable statement. Again and again radio listeners heard an advertisement with the sound of airplanes and machine guns and men yelling and a voice in the background commenting, "This is what McFarland calls a cheap war." Shadegg and others believed the ad and Goldwater's relentless attack on McFarland related to the war made the difference in the campaign.

Inaugurating a tradition, Goldwater opened his drive for the Senate not from his home in Phoenix but from Prescott. Uncle Morris had been Prescott's mayor, and the Goldwater store had been opened in that community in 1874. So starting in Prescott made cultural sense. It also made political sense, for it reminded voters of how well established the Goldwater name had become in Arizona, and it identified Goldwater as not only a candidate from Phoenix. Even in 1952, although not to the degree it does today, Phoenix, for those who hailed from outside the state capitol, exemplified the ills of urbanism and the problems of tomorrow. Prescott, by contrast, with its Victorian homes, more benign climate, and forested surroundings, enjoyed the image of being "everyone's home town."

Goldwater seized other means to imprint his stature as an Arizona native and his love for the state. His campaign cards featured photographs of scenes from throughout Arizona. According to the *Apache County Independent News,* published in Saint Johns, Goldwater said that "people get awfully tired of looking at a candidate's face, but they never get tired of looking at the beauties and wonders of Arizona. And he says he couldn't pass up the opportunity to advertise Arizona among Arizonans." Score one for Goldwater. In the eyes of the editorial writer for the *Independent News,* and no doubt others, it reinforced his standing as a native son.

Newspaper and other endorsements echoed the refrain. As one might anticipate, the *Yavapai County Messenger* of Prescott stated that Goldwater's "roots are deep in this county" and suggested he represented "the best of its pioneer traditions." The *Phoenix Gazette* highlighted Goldwater's being born in Arizona and being "the son of a pioneer merchant." The Arizona Sales Executive Club described him as "a native Arizonan whose enthusiasm for the Southwest is well known throughout the United States," emphasizing that such enthusiasm was "much more than mere flag-waving loyalty to his birthplace" but was "based on a thorough knowledge of the area—its people, its geography, its way of doing business, as well as an understanding of the problems of its almost fantastic development in the past few years." Goldwater underscored the point at every juncture, maintaining that his first-hand knowledge of Arizona's geography, economy, and people "eminently qualified" him to represent the state in the Senate.

In an attempt to counteract the Goldwater barrage, the low-key McFarland reminded voters of his seniority and service. Tied down by his duties in Washington, he underestimated his opponent until too late in the campaign, by which time the Goldwater bandwagon had picked up considerable momentum. For his part, McFarland used the familiar style of joining with other Democratic candidates in joint appearances, trooping loyally from one county to the next to stage enthusiastic rallies. Such a strategy counted on party loyalty and proved much more suited for an earlier political era than for the new one which emerged in 1952. McFarland might have been better served to campaign on his own, stressing his qualifications. That, of course, is just what Goldwater did, again using the airplane for solo appearances throughout Arizona.

By October the upstart Goldwater had begun to gain some national notice for his efforts, even if observers continued to discredit his chances. *Fortune* magazine, for one, in its October issue, reported that "a would be David is stalking a mild, pink cheeked Goliath." It continued: "Goldwater has been campaigning since January, covering the state in his own plane, making house-to-house calls. But for much longer than that he has been informally dashing around the state snapping pictures, giving lectures, and taking part in cultural programs, until he may be even better known than McFarland. . . . In fact, he is sometimes called 'Mr. Arizona.'"

Nonetheless, even *Fortune* rated his chances as "poor." Those closer to the scene realized he had a real possibility of winning. It did not hurt Goldwater's chances to have Eisenhower appear in October, speaking before an overflow crowd of at least twelve thousand at the old Montgomery Stadium in Phoenix. Goldwater recalled a blackboard in the Rosetree Bar on Adams Street in downtown Phoenix where they listed odds on bets one might care to make. With two weeks to go, it had become a horse race; Goldwater was now even money to win. "I thought," Goldwater said cheerfully, "by God, I might have

a chance." If McFarland had come home earlier and cam-
paigned more vigorously, "Mac would have beat my ass off."

Arizona voters turned out in extraordinary numbers in November 1952. Eighty-one percent of those registered cast their
ballots. Eisenhower trounced Stevenson 152,042 to 108,528.
John Rhodes unseated John Murdock by a comfortable margin of 66,512 to 56,622. And Goldwater had won as well. The
final tally of 132,063 to 125,338 represented a bit of a turn-
around from the primary just two months before. Then Goldwater had defeated his token opponent, Lester Kahl, 33,460 to
3,297, while the unopposed McFarland had received an impressive 108,992. But primary results, particularly in 1952, did
not predict what might happen in a general election. At the
age of forty-three, Barry Goldwater had been elected to the
U.S. Senate.

The victory did not go unnoticed. The veteran political editor of the *San Francisco Chronicle*, Earl Behrens, wrote
effusively about the person he termed "a true son of the
West." After tracing Goldwater's family background, Behrens
credited him with understanding how immigration after the
war had altered Arizona's political picture. While Goldwater
might have acknowledged the utility of the Eisenhower and
Pyle coattails in pulling him through, he did not concede
sufficiently his own role in careful planning, attracting
younger voters, and capitalizing on the "time for a change"
attitude of Arizona and the nation. Behrens also perceived the
personal appeal of the man. In the 1960s it would be called
"charisma," but in the language of the previous decade Goldwater was portrayed as "tall, hard-muscled, good looking."
The senator always professed not to understand it, but this
magnetism provided an integral element for Goldwater's political success, just as it did for John F. Kennedy, elected to the
presidency eight years later at the same age of forty-three.

Behrens chose to highlight two other dimensions of Goldwater's background. He spoke of the senator's knowing Arizona "from stem to stern." Goldwater, Behrens wrote, had
"traveled the back country, fished in its streams, is one of the

few men who have traveled the entire length of the hazardous Colorado River in a boat and has been a part of every business, political, and civic movement for the betterment of his state in recent years." That kind of engagement and experience, which already had catapulted Goldwater to the status of "authority" in regard to Indian affairs in particular and Arizona history and culture in general, remained a political calling card throughout his career.

Behrens also predicted that Goldwater would be "a liberal in the best Western tradition." He based this assertion on the kind of benefits Goldwater's store employees had enjoyed "many years before such things became commonplace," such as " profit sharing, health and accident insurance, retirements and pensions, summer vacation cottages, a shortened work week and excellent wages." Here Behrens missed the mark, but not entirely. Behrens understood that because of his association with the family business, Goldwater cared about such matters. He believed that good workers, especially those who had demonstrated competence and loyalty over a period of time, deserved to be compensated in an appropriate manner. Goldwater's store provided the lens through which he viewed the workings of the private sector and, correspondingly, the place of government. This paternal perspective assumed the benevolence of a conscientious company, one which knew and rewarded its faithful employees. The store assuredly lived up to its obligations. And if it did so, then the government, and for that matter, organized labor, did not need to get involved. The problem came when American business did not resemble Goldwater's—when the owners, either of large corporations or of small businesses, could not or would not uphold their part of the bargain.

As does any newly elected representative, Goldwater brought to Washington his own particular agenda. With jubilation over his electoral triumph tempered considerably by fear—"I was scared to death, I really was," he later told *Phoenix Gazette* reporter John Kolbe—he headed east with a message and a mission. In these strange new surroundings he began to share the gospel learned on the Sonoran Desert and the Colorado Plateau.

That gospel included its share of consistency and contradiction. Goldwater preached pioneer virtues: opportunity, hard work, building for the next generation. He saw in his family's and his state's history the reaffirmation of such values. At the same time, he mixed in the brew of rugged individualism and distaste for federal regulation of natural resources an additional ingredient needed for that concoction to reach its full potency: a dollop of federal dollars. The federal government represented both a distant foe and a ubiquitous neighbor in Arizona. It held Indian lands in trust, maintained military bases, managed national parks, monuments, and forests, and built dams. Rugged individualism would not do the trick all by itself. For Arizona to grow, the feds had to help. For Arizona to prosper, the feds had to contribute. Goldwater hardly invented this plea; in Arizona it dated back not only to the turn of the century and the passage of the Reclamation Act but also into the nineteenth century and federal investment in military campaigns against the Apaches as well as federal support for railroads, to cite but two examples. In this part of America, the federal government controlled the most land and gave the most back to its citizens in terms of per-capita expenditures. Each October before the election one reviled its role in regulation; each January after the election one asked for, indeed demanded, its assistance. That is how the world worked, at least from the vantage point of the Salt River valley.

When Goldwater reached Washington, he gained a broader view of what the federal government gave back as well as what it appeared to take. For example, in October 1953 he admitted he had been wrong in the past in stating that the federal government collected more from gasoline taxes in Arizona than it returned to the state. But he continued to emphasize what the individual had to do. Speaking to a Lincoln Day dinner crowd of two hundred in 1953 in Alhambra, California, Goldwater called for a "return to faith in the flag, Bible, family and self." Using a metaphor his audience understood, he emphasized:

"We still have many Donner Passes and deserts to cross. No government can smooth out the hills and valleys of the world." Or, as he delighted in reminding his Arizona audiences about his own family, who made their way to Arizona: "How they crossed the desert without federal aid, I'll never know."

Goldwater's first term witnessed his gradual emergence into a national figure. He ultimately became better known for the speeches he gave than the bills he wrote. As a junior senator from a small western state, he had little clout. He learned that more senior senators tolerated his speaking out more easily in Walla Walla than in Washington, D.C. That suited Goldwater just fine. He loved giving speeches, and he did not mind at all flying in airplanes. Committed to the Republican party and hoping to do his part to make it a truly national party—less controlled by the East and more viable in the South—he readily accepted the offer in January 1955 to become chairman of the GOP Senate campaign committee. That meant celebrating Lincoln Day for all of February rather than just on one day of the month. It meant cruelty to his digestive system as he munched his way through countless rubber chicken dinners. And it meant that more and more people across America began to become acquainted with Barry Goldwater.

February 1955 provides a case in point. On February 5 Goldwater spoke at the North Carolina Lincoln Day dinner in Winston-Salem, North Carolina. The local headline began: "Rapidly Rising Political Figure to Address." By the middle of the month he had given Lincoln Day dinner addresses in Evanston, Illinois, and Boise, Idaho. February 22 found him in Muncie, Indiana, to talk at the Ball State University Student Center. At the end of the month he greeted the inimitable Lawrence Spivak on NBC television's "Meet the Press."

Even after Lincoln Day could no longer be observed, the long march continued. On one night he appeared before the Republican Victory Fund Dinner in Brockton, Massachusetts; by the next evening he had flown to Richmond, Virginia. Another week included the Southern Nevada Knife and Fork Club at the New Frontier Hotel in Las Vegas and the folks at the Nogales, Arizona, Rotary Club. It almost did not seem to matter who issued the invitation. If the Michigan Christian Endeavor Convention in Grand Rapids had room for him on June 18, he found a way to be on hand.

Before Goldwater knew it, 1955 had come and gone, and with the advent of 1956 another smorgasbord of Lincoln Day feasts loomed. Off he went to the Saint Petersburg Republican Club Lincoln Day Celebration; to Oakland County, Michigan; to San Diego. GOP fund-raisers discovered that in Goldwater they had a person who could generate enthusiasm and, as importantly, draw a crowd. The *Dallas Times Herald* described Goldwater as "tall, lean, and granite-jawed" and as one with "unbounded optimism" about his party's chances in November. He aimed his remarks at both Republicans and conservative Democrats as he helped lay the groundwork for a GOP breakthrough in Texas. The San Angelo, Texas, *Evening Standard* quoted him as telling reporters that "Southerners must ultimately realize—and the sooner the better—that their Democratic party is controlled by northern liberals with no sympathy for either the South or the principle of state's rights." Lyndon Baines Johnson, he assured his listeners, would never gain the Democratic nomination for president as long as Harry Truman, the Americans for Democratic Action, and Walter Reuther controlled the party.

The Americans for Democratic Action saw eye-to-eye with Goldwater only by accident. Their rating of what they termed the "liberal quotient" of the voting records of congressional representatives generally featured Goldwater at either the bottom or the top of the heap, depending on how one saw such things. For example, in September 1957, on a scale from 0 to 100, Goldwater earned precisely 0; by contrast, fellow Republican John Rhodes obtained a 33, Carl Hayden a 57, and Democratic congressman Stewart Udall a 100. "Nothing could have made me happier," Goldwater gloated, "than this recognition from this socialist group."

Walter Reuther had furnished Goldwater with a useful symbol of the ills brought on by big labor. Membership on the

Committee on Labor and Public Welfare endowed Goldwater with a conspicuous platform from which to assail the United Auto Workers leader. The UAW and other major labor unions did have a decided tendency to support Democrats; Goldwater accused them of using union funds for this very purpose. He depicted Reuther as an enemy rather than a friend of the working man and woman; right-to-work states, he argued, provided a better climate for business and ultimately for employment than states where, in his opinion, the unions had too much power. Goldwater's antiunion stance represented a crucial dimension of contemporary conservatism. He still wore his Goldwater's store hat; as an employer he wanted to be free to hire or not hire any person. Goldwater was in the vanguard of those who anticipated and promoted a new day when the influence of unions would decline and employers would be less constrained, as they saw it, by union demands. His career clearly benefited from the growing antiunion backlash.

Reuther did not hesitate in responding to Goldwater's charges, labeling the Arizonan "mentally unbalanced" and "a political hypocrite and a moral coward." This kind of attention, in turn, yielded still more dinner speaking engagements as well as articles in the major news magazines, such as *Time* and *Newsweek*. The Merchants and Manufacturing Association of Los Angeles, for example, invited Goldwater to speak on "The Right to Work" at its sixtieth annual banquet on April 4, 1956. This organization depicted him as "an ardent champion of many of the sound objectives enunciated in your Association's Declaration of Principles." The Executives' Club of Chicago on December 13, 1957, called its speaker "A Two-Fisted Foe of Walter Reuther." The club commented, "You expect a powerful address from this man, and you'll get it."

It played well in Peoria, Illinois, and Peoria, Arizona. Illinois senator Everett Dirksen praised Goldwater for his "plain, unadulterated courage" and termed his reelection in 1958 "a great moral issue." Paul F. Healy of the *New York Daily News* wrote, "Barry's got all the guts in the world." In its June–July 1958 issue, the *Saturday Evening Post* claimed Goldwater possessed "more leadership potential than any other Republican in the U.S. Senate during the last ten years." Back home, readers of Arizona newspapers read continuing coverage of Goldwater, for his office staff tirelessly dispatched copies of his speeches as well as other press releases. As the *White Mountain Eagle* of Show Low, Arizona, noted: "Every editor in the state knows pretty well what Senator Goldwater is doing." The Show Low paper in May 1956 sang his praises as "one of the most capable, hardest working men the state of Arizona has ever produced." The *Eagle* admonished, "Let us not ever turn our heads (and votes) against Barry Goldwater. We need more like him in public life, fighting for what is right."

Goldwater's first term in the Senate included one fight that permanently scarred him. In 1946, Wisconsin voters had elected Joseph R. McCarthy to the Senate. McCarthy aided and abetted the anti-Communist crusade that gripped America by the end of the 1940s. Following in the footsteps of Richard Nixon, who had established his national political career through well-publicized forays against alleged Communist influences in the United States, McCarthy became a household name in his manipulation of contemporary anti-Communist paranoia. He accused Secretary of State Dean Acheson of hiring 205 Communist party members in the State Department; he contended that through its negligence the United States had prompted Communist aggression in Korea. McCarthy obtained an ovation at the 1952 Republican convention, but by early 1954 his erratic behavior and wild accusations, including the charge of Communist infiltration of the U.S. Army, had initiated what became a rapid political decline. At year's end, safely after the November election, the U.S. Senate formally censured him by a vote of sixty-seven to twenty-two. Barry Goldwater joined twenty-one other Republicans in voting against the motion. McCarthy remained a senator, but his influence had ended, and he died in 1957, an alcoholic demagogue who once had exerted a disturbing power over a sizable portion of the American public.

Goldwater's willingness to defend his colleague from Wis-

consin earned undying enmity from those who pronounced
McCarthy a demon. McCarthy's vigorous polemics against
the evils of Communism, however, were sufficient to win
Goldwater's support for "the most contentious, controversial,
and stubbornly cussed character that I ever met in my life." As
political scientist Michael Rogin remarked, many Republicans
did not wish to criticize McCarthy for fear of splitting a resur-
gent party; many liberal Democrats shied away from attacking
a politician with significant grass-roots support. In his autobiography, Goldwater admitted, "I was probably wrong in de-
fending him," but suggested, "A man can be put out of action
without a public lynching." Goldwater's loyalty to a friend,
nonetheless, had caused him to be branded as a reckless man
with poor judgment. When Goldwater ran for president, the
memory of his publicly uncritical support of "low blow Joe"
had not been erased.

Back in Arizona, Goldwater had to confront the continuing
presence of a political foe. Ernest McFarland did not go qui-
etly into the night after his defeat in 1952. Instead, he took on
Howard Pyle and defeated him in the governor's race in 1954.
Very much back in the public eye, McFarland challenged
Goldwater for reelection in 1958. Democrats still outnumbered Republicans in Arizona by more than two to one; in the
fall of 1958, Democrats had 226,000 registered to only 106,000
for the Republicans. The primary results in early September
looked familiar. McFarland had defeated his opponent by
nearly a three-to-one margin and had racked up 104,333 votes,
while Goldwater tallied 36,099. The former senator no longer
took his opponent too lightly, and the *Wall Street Journal* on
October 24 called it a very close race. On election eve, the
New York Times concluded Goldwater had gained ground and
the race was now nip and tuck.

Yet on election night, Goldwater won in convincing fashion. The final count showed McFarland with 125,473 votes and
Goldwater with 161,881. The *Wall Street Journal* and the *New
York Times* had done their homework, if one could ignore
only one county out of Arizona's fourteen. In the state's

largest county, Maricopa, Goldwater drubbed McFarland 88,043 to 59,431, or nearly 80 percent of his margin of victory. McFarland had defeated Goldwater in five counties. He did best in counties such as Gila and Greenlee, where mining interests predominated, and also carried Cochise, Pinal and, barely, Yuma. But Goldwater had beaten McFarland solidly in northern Arizona, winning the northern tier of Coconino, Apache, and Navajo counties by 2,381 votes and Yavapai County, the site of Prescott, by another 2,114. And he carried the rural counties of Graham, Mohave, and Santa Cruz, along with Pima County, usually a Democratic bastion; Goldwater won in Pima by an impressive 4,133 votes. Nonetheless, Maricopa had been the key to victory. In a precursor of elections to come, Phoenix and its suburbs decided the contest, with more than half the ballots cast in that metropolitan area.

Goldwater lived in Phoenix, and one anticipated his success in the Salt River valley. However, the steady drumbeat of positive coverage through the *Arizona Republic* and the *Phoenix Gazette* helped him, and favorable editorial stances elsewhere in the state bolstered his chances. At a time when newspapers played a more major role in presenting and interpreting the news, Goldwater had enjoyed the support of almost all of those published in Arizona. Only one daily, the *Arizona Daily Star* of Tucson, had backed McFarland, whereas in addition to the Phoenix papers, the *Mesa Tribune, Tucson Daily Citizen, Yuma Daily Sun, Arizona Daily Sun* (of Flagstaff), *Douglas Dispatch,* and *Prescott Courier* had endorsed Goldwater. The rural papers that published less frequently also opted for the incumbent.

Anticipating some of the criticism about to greet Goldwater as a national figure, the *Arizona Daily Star* determined that "Senator Goldwater has been comparatively useless in Washington" and "has shown himself to be one of those absolutist thinkers who would burn the barn down to kill the rats." Citing foreign aid as but one example of this thinking, the *Star* contended Goldwater had "no answer to the troubles that beset us throughout the world, other than a military answer." By contrast, the *Arizona Daily Sun* sounded a more familiar theme: "We will choose between a man of proven integrity, independence, and courage and a typical machine politician whose concern is to be elected and re-elected by whatever means." The Flagstaff paper anointed Goldwater as "the legitimate heir of those hard-hitting, non-compromising pioneers who conquered the last frontier." Although the *Douglas Dispatch* had not endorsed Goldwater in 1952, it now believed he should continue to represent Arizona. It praised him for being "aggressive, firm, and outspoken in his convictions" and for providing "the outstanding leadership Arizonans asked for."

During the campaign, Goldwater portrayed himself in the words of his announcement of candidacy in May: "As a native son, a citizen who loves Arizona, its people, and its opportunities." He had been for five and a half years what he termed a "nominal resident" of Washington, but "my heart," he said, "and my interest, and my concern have never left the state of Arizona." Goldwater again used photographic images of Arizona in his literature; one brochure, entitled "The Measure of a Man," featured a map of Arizona with lines drawn to demonstrate his connections to different communities in the state, from Flagstaff to Yuma, from Navajo country to Bisbee.

McFarland, of course, could have drawn a similar map, even if the connections would not have been the same. The resident of Florence had also served the state over many years and could also recite examples of his accomplishments for the people. He believed his chances had been thwarted by the biased coverage of the Phoenix newspapers and a bizarre incident in the final days of the campaign. A flier mysteriously appeared with a caricature of Joseph Stalin, smoking a pipe with a hammer and sickle emblazoned on it, emitting smoke and the message, "Why Not Vote For Goldwater?" Those responsible for the fliers, voters learned well after the election, were affiliated with the labor movement and thought the confusion surrounding their handiwork might work to McFarland's advantage. Instead, Goldwater denounced the fliers without suggesting McFarland had had anything to do with the strange cartoon, and McFarland, who knew no more about its origins, was left to wonder what had happened.

In retrospect, it seems clear that Goldwater would have won without this last-minute episode, although it likely padded his margin of victory. The decisive win strengthened his position not only in Arizona, but in the entire country as well. The Democrats had gained major victories nationally; they added seventeen Senate seats and fifty-nine seats in the House of Representatives. Democratic candidates defeated ten Republican incumbent senators. The inability of the Democrats to vanquish Goldwater heightened his profile among Republican activists; the Democrats' success transformed him into a much more senior Republican senator. A number of important Republican conservatives had lost, including John Bricker of Ohio and William Knowland of California. Those who had won included moderates or liberals in the East such as Kenneth Keating of New York and Hugh Scott of Pennsylvania. Thus, Goldwater also achieved greater prominence within the Republican party as a conservative. Not all party regulars waxed as melodramatically as the editor of the *Glendale News,* who proclaimed Goldwater "was as tough as the native copper ore that lies buried in the rocks of his own beloved Arizona." They did notice a variety of regional and national journalists who noted in the usual post-mortems of the election that in six years' time Barry Goldwater had become a political voice heard well beyond the borders of Arizona. Regardless of the senator's heightened profile, even the Glendale editor could not have anticipated that in six more years Goldwater would be the Republican nominee for president of the United States.

CHAPTER 5

Gaining the Nomination,
Losing the Race

THE year 1960 marked a kind of watershed for Republicans. With Dwight Eisenhower leaving the presidency and Richard Nixon's political future very much in doubt, party members continued their internal debate about the appropriate direction for the new decade. The growing conservative presence in the party could hardly deny the more moderate Nixon the nomination for president. As Eisenhower's vice president for eight years, he clearly was the heir apparent. But this fact did not prevent Republicans on the right from banging the drum for a more congenial alternative. The 1958 elections, after all, had been a disaster. The loss of so many Republican seats did not bode well. Brent Bozell and others at the *National Review,* a widely read conservative publication, argued for a new direction. Nixon continued to win applause for his stance as a staunch opponent of Communism, but he did not echo the Republican right on the role of the federal government in internal affairs. Although he was from the West, Nixon appeared to be too closely allied with the more moderate wing of the party, whose base of influence clearly lay east of the Mississippi River.

Publication in January 1960 of *The Conscience of a Conservative* had vaulted Barry Goldwater to national prominence, and as the year had progressed it had become more and more evident that he had emerged as the symbol and the hope for conservative Republicans who wanted to change the course of their party and, in turn, the direction of America. The book confirmed what conservatives had already suspected: Goldwater had the kind of backbone and the kind of vision needed. They saw him as a man who, unlike Eisenhower and Nixon, had stood up to the demands presented by such establishment figures as New York governor Nelson Rockefeller. They observed that Goldwater, for example, had been virtually alone in decrying the Eisenhower budget in 1957.

Although *The Conscience of a Conservative* had been published in Shepardsville, Kentucky, instead of New York, its sales proved to be nothing less than astonishing. The book eventually sold well over three million copies. It did not matter that Victor Publishing Company instead of Random House had been responsible. If anything, the obscurity of the publisher added to the appeal of the 123-page book. What mattered was the message—a kind of conservative call to arms that appealed to people throughout the nation. It did not even matter that Goldwater had not been the sole author. His name was on the cover, and the public did not care about the process through which the words had come into print. Within six months the book had reached the national best-seller list of the *New York Times*.

Who wrote *The Conscience of a Conservative*? In *Goldwater*, written with reporter Jack Casserly, Goldwater says: "The work was adapted by Brent Bozell, an editor at *National Review* and longtime Republican activist, based on speeches I'd given and his own research." Those speeches, in turn, usually had been crafted by Stephen Shadegg, who had managed Goldwater's campaigns in 1952 and 1958. An experienced political hand, Shadegg was a registered Democrat who had directed Carl Hayden's campaign for reelection to the Senate in 1950. He had moved to Arizona from California, where he had been a writer for radio and film, and quickly had become active in the Phoenix community. His wife had known Peggy Goldwater in the Junior League and had worked with her in starting the Planned Parenthood clinic. So the partnership between Shadegg and Goldwater had a personal and professional foundation. While Goldwater was more than a mere mouthpiece for the sentiments of others, he did not pretend to be a wordsmith. He had a hand in the process, and he would not put his name to sentiments he did not embrace. In that sense, of course, he resembled countless other elected officials at the state and national level who utter words not entirely their own. Unlike most of these compatriots, Goldwater found a means to keep saying the words, through his books and through a column syndicated by the *Los Angeles Times*. By the middle of 1961 the book had sold over seven hundred thousand copies, and the paperback version had gone into its twelfth printing; the column—again a collaboration between Goldwater and Shadegg—was being published in 104 newspapers.

The announcement of the column coincided with the publication of the book. In its initial publicity, the Los Angeles paper labeled Goldwater "the leading conservative thinker in American political life" and declared itself "proud to publish the opinions of the senator from Arizona." It added, "In the struggle for men's minds he has won victories where the odds seemed insurmountable." Goldwater, in turn, paid tribute to his roots:

> I was born in Arizona in territorial days. My grandfather and his family were immigrants who had found a new life and maximum opportunity in the United States. There was great personal freedom and opportunity in the Arizona of my childhood. . . . I came to realize that freedom was a gift to man from God. When I was a boy, there were no sophisticated critics to sneer at a patriotic love of country. My mother used to take us—my brother, my sister and myself— out to the Indian school (quite a journey in those days) to be present when the flag was raised or lowered.

The column required a straightforward division of labor between Shadegg and Goldwater. Shadegg would grind out the weekly quota of columns, dictate the initial draft to Goldwater, and then edit the final product after receiving the senator's comments. "I'm no writer," Goldwater acknowledged at the time, "but I'll learn bit by bit and at least the ideas will be my own." Neither Goldwater nor Shadegg profited directly from the column. The Prescott Community Hospital received the proceeds.

Indirectly, to be sure, Goldwater profited politically from this bully pulpit. It offered a valuable forum for his views; it kept his name before the nation. Combined with his continuing whirlwind of speeches and party appearances, Goldwater could not be ignored. In the first few months of 1960 he spoke to the National Cattleman's Association, and he traveled to talk in Kalamazoo, Omaha, Muncie, and Orange County. Even as he gained more adherents, he also began to attract his share of brickbats, well before 1964.

The *Baltimore Sun,* for example, called his "hard counsel" in *The Conscience of a Conservative* "nonsense." It shuddered: "The idea that this nation abandon the defensive policy which is traditional with free countries, particularly those of Anglo-Saxon origin and go in for an offensive system of alliances is in effect a policy which could lead to the fighting of a preventive war, and a preventive war in which, if the Arizona senator had his way, nuclear weapons would be used." Joseph Alsop referred to Goldwater in his column as "the Republican party's most extreme right-winger above the crank class."

Others questioned the degree of appeal Goldwater's perspectives had for more than a narrow portion of the American electorate. Writing in his widely distributed "Today and Tomorrow" column, syndicated through the *New York Herald Tribune,* Walter Lippmann scorned the notion of "a great hidden majority in the country . . . of a large number of people who do not vote" and can only be lured to the polls by a candidate of the "extreme right." Lippman concluded, "Men like Senator Bridges and Senator Goldwater really believe that the more the Republican party follows their leadership, the more stay-at-home Republican voters will come to the polls." Lippmann dismissed this notion as "an extraordinary fantasy, rather like that of thirsty men in a desert who see mirages of green oases with plenty of water."

Reading the yellowing pages of newspapers published in 1960, one recognizes a kind of rehearsal for 1964. The battle lines are already being formed. The initial skirmishes do not take place in the wake of the Republican convention at the

Cow Palace in San Francisco in the summer of 1964, but occur four years earlier. The New Plymouth, Idaho, *Payette Valley Standard* on May 5, 1960, for example, backed Goldwater for president. "There isn't a man running for President today," it argued, "that has the courage to match or even come close to him. . . . We think this is the kind of man we need to run the nation." By distinct contrast, the *Washington Post* three days later published an editorial entitled "Frothing at the Mouth." The *Post* termed Goldwater the "darling of the Chester Alan Arthur wing of the Republican party." The *New Republic* in April contended Goldwater was "as far to the right as man can get without being a crackpot."

Many publications found it easy to ridicule Goldwater and his followers. However, in a time in our country's history when to many Communism seemed on the march, when the success of Sputnik and other Soviet undertakings threatened American supremacy, when in an urbanizing, mobile society the individual might not feel as though he or she mattered, Goldwater's message came through loud and clear. Goldwater later summarized: "In the book I said that the liberal agenda for the country was not working. I criticized increasing state paternalism at the expense of individual self-reliance. With new decentralized government, individual liberty and economic initiative could flourish." He warned: "Collectivism and the welfare state were our greatest enemies at home, while communism had become our foremost enemy around the world. Either could destroy us."

In the heady days of spring in 1960, in the wake of publicity surrounding the book, Goldwater's name became mentioned with increasing frequency for a possible spot on the Republican ticket. Nixon seemed to have the nomination wrapped up, but what about Goldwater for vice president? When asked, Goldwater responded that he would accept the honor, but he thought the combination of a Californian and an Arizonan extremely unlikely. Or as he phrased it, "I have about as much chance as a snow ball in hell." Conservative writer Russell Kirk, for one, said Goldwater was "too good and too important" for "that powerless post." Goldwater acknowledged in June that he really was not seeking the vice presidency, noting that "perhaps by 1964 we will be strong enough to make our weight felt on the party."

Realistic about his status in 1960, Goldwater nonetheless used what influence he possessed to try to keep the party from turning more to the left. In Nelson Rockefeller he perceived the kind of person he certainly did not want in a position of Republican national leadership. Rockefeller did not lack ambition to become president, Goldwater observed, but if he wanted to gain a nomination, he might be better off traveling to Los Angeles, where the Democrats were holding their convention, "and have a pretty good chance of getting it." The two men made a joint appearance on "Meet the Press" in July. They did not sing a duet.

That month the Republicans gathered in Chicago and, as expected, made Nixon their nominee. Nixon turned eastward for his running mate, selecting Henry Cabot Lodge. Some of the party faithful wanted to place Goldwater's name in nomination, but the senator withdrew it. "We've had our chance," he told the assembled, "and I think the conservatives have made a splendid showing at the convention. Let's, if we want to take this party back—and I think we can some day—let's get to work." And work he did. He gave over 125 speeches in twenty-six states during the campaign, despite his dissatisfaction with the party's platform. In the morning, he spoke to 150 Columbus, Ohio, businessmen at a thousand dollars a plate. He then flew to South Carolina to address 300 at the Dillon ball park. On to the Orangeburg ball park to talk to 350 more people. Then he pressed on to Augusta, Georgia, before supper to a rally at a shopping center, before facing 700 who had paid $12.50 for a meal and the chance to hear him at the Bell Auditorium. A press conference inevitably followed and then a reception for key party workers. And then the next day dawned.

Moreover, Goldwater gained the kind of attention that most politicians could only dream about. Reporting for the

New York Times, Russell Baker spoke of Goldwater as "an urbane charmer and sometime jet pilot from Arizona, who is
rapidly emerging here as the exciting new idol of the party's
dispossessed." It would be easy to ignore Goldwater, Baker
admitted, given his "forthright call for a return to the Valhalla
of nineteenth century conservatism" and the "disordered as-
sortment" of people rallying in his name. One could be
tempted to write the whole phenomenon off "as a product of
the Chicago heat." Baker determined, "The evidence, however, suggests that it cuts much deeper and that Goldwater
may indeed prove to be a man of destiny in his own party."

The Phoenix newspapers had no doubt about that destiny.
"Goldwater has become a giant at Chicago," trumpeted the
editorial in the *Gazette.* U.S. conservatives had "had a good
look at Arizona's man" and had liked what they had seen. If
Nixon lost this year, Goldwater would then be "an ideal GOP
candidate for president in 1964—and probably a winning candidate." The *Arizona Republic*'s editorial cartoonist Reg
Manning on July 30 depicted Goldwater coming off a plane,
to be greeted by a sign saying, "Welcome Home, Barry! Well
done!" A figure blessed with a face in the shape of the state of
Arizona is so proud his buttons are popping off his shirt.

One can disregard such spoutings as local chauvinism, but
Baker's column mirrored sentiments heard around the nation.
Walter Trobham, chief of the *Chicago Tribune*'s Washington
bureau, proclaimed the "articulate and dashing" Goldwater a
winner, admired by the right and respected by the left. Other
conservative papers joined in the chorus: the *Mobile Press,* the
Los Angeles Times, and the *Charleston News and Courier* added
their plaudits. Columnists singled out his "guts," his "ele-
mental honesty," his willingness to speak his mind without
muffling his opinions in the usual cautious guise adopted by
most politicians. If Goldwater characterized Rockefeller as
"the rich man's Harold Stassen," then it also assuredly made
for good copy. In other words, well before 1964 the nature of
Goldwater's appeal and the qualities that gained him admirers
and attracted virulent critiques already could be detected.

Nixon lost the election by the narrowest of margins. Conservatives within the Republican party, disappointed and irritated by the defeat, began to plan for the future. They did not trust Nixon because they saw him as a person too intent on placating the Rockefeller wing of the GOP. They began to consider their options. The junior senator from Arizona had already emerged in their eyes as a possible candidate for the White House. Goldwater was perfectly aware of this attention but pondered what to do about it.

A month after the election, he dictated a letter to his legislative assistant, Dean Burch. In the letter he took stock of the current state of the Arizona congressional delegation and his own political future. "We have a fine Congressional team now," he noted. Although Morris Udall was a Democrat, Goldwater considered him "a very congenial and easy to get along with fellow." "Johnny" Rhodes would be a good leader. The aging Carl Hayden still had considerable influence. This group could "produce for Arizona more than has been produced over the past many years."

At the same time, Goldwater wondered about his own priorities. He had worked hard on issues relating to the state's Indian peoples, but he had not been as deeply involved in formulating congressional legislation relating to other matters. "Where do I fit into the picture relative to Arizona?" Goldwater mused: "Should it be confined to Indians, or should it be broadened to include everything that pertains to our state? . . . Do I make out of myself a senator with the narrow views of one state, or do I expand them, as I have in the past, to encompass the problems of the nation and the world?"

Goldwater had come too far on the national scene to be content with only being the junior senator from a small state, and he already knew his greatest strength did not lie in the day-to-day battles over the details of particular bills. He could also hear the clock ticking. About to observe his fifty-second birthday, he spoke in the letter to Burch of "approaching sixty." Regardless of his age, he believed he had "another chance to do something for people, my state, and my country." So, he reminded Burch, to achieve that goal he needed help from his friends. In a wonderfully mixed metaphor, he advised his associate that "if I put the elbow on you once in a while, it's not the elbow of an old man, it's the elbow of years still filled with a lot of pee and vinegar wanting to add the brilliance of youth to those years."

And so, four years before the next presidential election, he did not set his sights on the White House. Yet he wanted to do what he could to increase the power of western interests in the Republican party, and he wished to continue to speak out on matters about which he cared deeply. In the process, as 1961 began, he continued to fuel the energies of conservatives around the country who desired to place one of their own at 1600 Pennsylvania Avenue. Thus he spoke out on issues and concerns, both large and small.

He had the innate talent at times of making himself an easy target. Speaking to a meeting of the National Interfraternity Conference, the man who had pledged Sigma Chi at the University of Arizona termed fraternities "a bastion of American strength" and went on to chastise Harvard for its willingness to ban fraternities but permit faculty members to espouse Communist and socialist philosophies and thus breed a faithless generation. Communism and socialism, he alleged, flourished where fraternities were outlawed. Some Harvard students found this far too good an opportunity to ignore. They founded Iota Beta Phi, which they said stood for "inexperienced but faithful"; named Goldwater the honorable grand wizard of this fledgling outfit; and sent him an eighteen-inch crimson paddle.

Even given these tendencies—he worried aloud about the possibility that the newly established Peace Corps might become a "midsummer cruise for beatniks"—by early spring of 1961 the "Goldwater for president" boom could not be denied. One could see he was being taken seriously in part by the kind of commentary he received. Already the bumper stickers appeared: "Goldwater in 1964" and "Goldwater in 1864." In March 1961 the influential columnist Marquis Childs affirmed

that "the hottest stock on the political course today is Barry
Morris Goldwater, right-wing preferred."

In his column, "Washington Calling," Childs called Goldwater a "national figure" and noted two advantages Goldwater
possessed that had catapulted him to that status: "The first is
his personality. He is vigorous, vital, attractive, with seemingly
tireless energy . . . [and] a second conspicuous advantage is the
simple black and white with which the Senator views every
issue and particularly the issues of foreign policy." Childs
commented: "This has an appeal for a great many Americans
who are increasingly frustrated by the complexities of the cold
war."

The columnist made another very significant point about
Goldwater. It related not to the man but to his followers. Even
now Childs could see all those "to the far right of Goldwater . . . to whom President Eisenhower is a dangerous Communist." These people, Childs judged, "are troublesome even
though they are good people and in many instances the backbone of the Republican party." They helped lead the cheers in
Goldwater's audiences. "The senator from Arizona," Childs
said, "speaks of them more in sorrow than in anger." This
fringe contributed, financially and emotionally, to the gathering Goldwater boom. On the other hand, he would pay dearly
for their support in 1964, for they, too, provided easy targets
for reporters and others who leapt to facile conclusions about
the degree to which their views of the universe paralleled those
of Goldwater.

Another "Washington Calling" column highlighted two
other valuable perceptions. Republican senators such as Jacob
Javits of New York and Clifford Case of New Jersey had expressed their concerns about the direction a person such as
Goldwater might take their party. These fears did not dissipate,
for as Childs put it, GOP liberals feared Goldwater would
identify the party "with the radical right that would like to re-
peal the twentieth century." Goldwater could anticipate such
opposition continuing, especially in the face of his ongoing
diatribe against Rockefeller. Second, Childs understood why

Goldwater to date had succeeded in his political career. "Arizona," he wrote, "is in many respects perfectly tailored to the Goldwater approach. The salubrious climate has attracted many retired persons whose outlook is essentially conservative. The press in the capital, Phoenix, is unvaryingly ultraconservative." The unspoken implication was that Goldwater should also anticipate that as a national figure he could not expect such coddling by the national media.

Most of the harpoons had not been taken out in the spring of 1961. Columnists such as Childs or James Reston of the *New York Times* three years before the next presidential election mostly struggled to try to explain the Goldwater phenomenon. They tried to put their finger on the pulse of the public. Even if they frequently came away shaking their heads at what they had seen, they could not deny the ever-increasing tide. Reston traveled to the Midwest to review current sentiments. Goldwater, he stated, had "great" emotional appeal to Republicans in the region. Using language that he and others would later employ to delineate the rise of Ronald Reagan, Reston decided that Goldwater appealed to people's "wistful longing for the past." He offered "simple solutions to complex problems at a time when the diversity of events increases the general desire for snappy and tidy answers." Goldwater opposed the very symbols of frustration shared by midwesterners: big government, big labor, high taxation, and foreign aid.

When *Time* ran a five-page story on him on June 23, 1961, it sounded like Goldwater already had launched his campaign to capture the 1964 presidential nomination. The senator professed considerable irritation over the piece, but like it or not, the parade had begun. The next three years represented a kind of price Goldwater had to pay for his convictions and his zeal. He became part of something larger than himself. And he soon found that he could not control the process. It mattered too much to too many people. The stakes were too high.

The first stage of the Kennedy presidency also offered a cautionary tale. Shrouded today in the mists of the Camelot myth, it appeared a more troubled entity in 1961. The thousand days included many that did not go all that well. The ill-fated Bay of Pigs invasion of Cuba in April 1961 offered the most publicized catastrophe. Kennedy suffered through the whole misadventure. According to Goldwater, after he had answered a presidential summons to come to the White House to discuss the impending action in Cuba, Kennedy turned to him and asked, "So, you want this fucking job, eh?" Goldwater responded that Kennedy had been reading too many conservative newspapers.

Goldwater did not shy away from public acclaim, and any man who canvassed the country as he had could not be accused of lacking ambition. But many observers of the time noticed a contrast in his interest in the White House and that, for example, of Richard Nixon. Nixon continued to be consumed with the idea of becoming president; Goldwater did not have the same degree of ardor. Secure in himself, comfortable in his own company, he did not need to become president to prove anything to himself or anyone else. Columnist Robert Novak in 1961, for example, claimed that Goldwater's greatest handicap in the eyes of some political operators was his "lack of a single-minded ruthlessness that usually marks the successful national politician." The Cuban crisis caused him to reassess his prospects. The incident, Goldwater later said, stunned and saddened him. From his vantage point, Goldwater perceived Kennedy as something other than a profile in courage. He did not have the will to see himself and see the United States through to what had to be done in this situation.

However, Goldwater suddenly realized that he thought he did. Watching Kennedy waver, Goldwater concluded: "For the first time, I saw clearly that I had the toughness of mind and the will to lead the country. Others might be more educated or possess greater speaking and social skills, but I had something that individuals of greater talent did not have. I had an unshakable belief in, and willingness to defend, the fundamental interests of my country."

This is a particularly revealing quotation, even if uttered in retrospect. To this day Goldwater remains modest about his intellectual abilities and regretful about his lack of formal education. The contrast between his one year at the University of Arizona and Kennedy's degree from Harvard paralleled the differences in their family backgrounds. Goldwater was not exactly born in a log cabin, and his home in Paradise Valley did not exactly resemble one. In common with many westerners, he had retained, even so, a bit of a sense of awe about the more worldly and sophisticated trappings of the East. Savoir faire was not part of his working vocabulary. He preferred bourbon to a martini.

The years 1962 and 1963 revealed a movement only gaining strength. In the final days of 1961, the national Republican chairman, William Miller, later to be Goldwater's choice as a running mate, declared Goldwater to be the front-runner for the 1964 nomination. The criticisms in the press began to escalate. In a famous cartoon published in the *Washington Post,* Herblock drew Goldwater speaking to a woman and two children huddled in the cold in a doorway. "If you had any initiative," Herblock had Goldwater saying, "you'd go out and inherit a department store." As the din increased, Goldwater considered his options. A politician at the beginning of 1963 could still say—and be believed—that he wanted to take the year to think about it before making a decision about whether or not to run.

The more Goldwater thought about it, perhaps the more vulnerable Kennedy appeared to a challenge in 1964. And, even though the two men differed tremendously in their political philosophies, they liked each other. They had served in World War II, arrived in Washington, especially in Kennedy's case, at a relatively young age, and knew how to make fun of themselves. Goldwater enjoyed telling the story of taking Kennedy's photograph and reading the autograph on the print, advising Goldwater to pursue his real talent—photography. As a Kennedy-Goldwater matchup appeared more probable in the summer of 1963, the two men imagined a campaign that would reflect mutual respect if contrasting viewpoints. Perhaps they could campaign together, barnstorm the country a little, show Americans that the process did not have to begin with character assassination.

Kennedy's murder in Dallas abruptly ended such reveries. During the latter part of 1963, Kennedy had rallied considerably in the public eye and appeared at that time as a tough person to defeat at the polls. However, political pundits gave Goldwater more than an outside chance. His strength in the more conservative South and West could not be denied. With the right kind of campaign, he might just pull off an upset. In any event, it did not seem impossible. Then, overnight, the picture changed. Kennedy was gone and in his place entered Lyndon Johnson.

Johnson had never been a Goldwater favorite, and his prospective candidacy worked to Goldwater's considerable disadvantage. Goldwater hoped to win in the deep South, but the border states now would be much tougher to capture. Even with his considerable following in Texas, the state could hardly be expected to turn against one of its own. To make matters worse, Johnson could count on an enormous sympathy vote in a country still grieving for a fallen leader. A contest that had appeared engaging and possibly winnable crumbled into a duel with an unworthy opponent, one Goldwater believed would stoop to conquer.

He seriously considered withdrawing from the race for the Republican nomination. Peggy Goldwater did not relish the prospect of the kind of eternal spotlight that would always shine on her in the White House. And by running for president, he faced the prospect of losing his Senate seat. Even though he could legally be on the ballot for both president and senator in Arizona, he did not want the people of Arizona to have to deal with such a scenario. If he did gain the GOP nomination and lost to Johnson, he no longer would be a member of the Senate.

Goldwater also had to confront the price to be paid if he did not continue the quest. His withdrawal would disappoint all the people who had worked hard to this point on his behalf. Not only would they be unhappy with him, but he also would be letting down the conservative cause. If he dropped out, to whom would the Republicans turn? In all likelihood it would be in the direction of someone like Rockefeller or Pennsylvania governor William Scranton. Thus, his abdication threatened to forfeit conservative ascendancy; it promised to return the reins to the kind of people whom Goldwater did not want to maintain their previous stranglehold over the direction of the Republican party. Moreover, Rockefeller's divorce and remarriage in 1963 had weakened his standing in the polls. Goldwater knew that in the wake of Rockefeller's fall in popularity, he could succeed in winning the nomination.

Barry Goldwater did not like to let down his friends or forsake a cause. He decided to run, even if the ostensible goal now seemed impossible. Within his immediate circle of colleagues and amidst the conservative faithful, of course, the prospects did not seem dim. Blessed with the energy and zeal of the converted, they knew they could carry the day. Justice would triumph; Goldwater would win. If the rest of the country came to know him as they knew him, how could victory be denied? But that, it soon became all too apparent, represented a problem.

Political activists of whatever stripe struggle with the idea that politics are not as important to the average citizen as they are to them. It is almost inconceivable to the person who invests more than a little of himself or herself in the crusade of each election that fellow Americans do not share this enthusiasm. Yet the hard reality clearly indicated that an enormous number of folks did not start their reading of their morning newspaper by turning to the editorial page or even the front page. They followed the Green Bay Packers rather than Goldwater; they preferred Charlie Brown to Charles Percy. They might eventually become slightly interested in the presidential contest once the Democrats and Republicans finally figured out whom they wanted.

When the conventions had concluded, the vast majority of Americans might begin to add the presidential race to the baseball pennant race. When Americans started to pay more attention, then the images of the candidates came to the forefront. More than three decades after the 1964 campaign, it is worth noting that this was a very different era in mass communications. Cable television, let alone C-Span, had yet to enter the picture, but television had become much more important in the coverage of political campaigns and the shaping of images. Just four years before, the dour Dick Nixon in one night surrendered his status as the seasoned leader, while the previously boyish Jack Kennedy instantly had been elevated to Nixon's equal, thanks to the impact of the first of their televised debates. Nixon had looked ill at ease; Kennedy had appeared in command. Nixon had perspired; Kennedy had been cool. Nonetheless, far more than they did at the end of the twentieth century, the print journalists had considerable influence over how average Americans perceived national political figures.

The story of how Barry Goldwater seized his party's banner for the presidency in 1964 has been told many times. So, too, has been his star-crossed campaign against the Lone Star State's Lyndon Johnson. After the November election, indeed, a small army of his backers turned the defeat into a cottage industry in which one soldier after another explained how the battle had been lost. The end result of the contest resembled the Battle of Little Big Horn, but this time some of the enlisted men survived to tell their tales. Other somewhat less partisan observers rushed to judgment. The contours, at least, of the drama remain familiar, and we do not need to recreate this play, whether we dub it comedy or tragedy or—perhaps most accurately—melodrama, line by line.

However, because these months of 1964 provided the fundamental yardstick by which Goldwater became measured by most Americans, quite apart from their intrinsic interest, they merit concise review. Goldwater in his memoir called the gauntlet he ran "a wild, magnificent, screwy, splendid undertaking." He wanted to remain faithful to his conservative ideals. If he were to lose, and he doubted all along his chances, he did not wish to deviate from the path he had followed.

Combined with his readiness with a quip for inquiring reporters, it meant for quite a ride.

The Republican nomination in 1964 would be decided in
part through the primaries but to a much greater extent
through the traditional means of courting the favor of political activists whose service to the party had gained them the
opportunity to cast votes for the candidate of their choice at
the convention. On this latter score, Goldwater enjoyed a
tremendous advantage. F. Clifton White of upstate New York
had been active in the Young Republicans and had worked on
the Nixon campaign in 1960. As early as October 8, 1961,
White had assembled twenty-two like-minded political associates at the Avenue Motel in Chicago to discuss the possibilities
of a Republican conservative's gaining the presidential nomination. He had met with Goldwater after that initial session
and had not received much encouragement. Undeterred, White
plowed ahead, seeking additional support for a movement to
draft Goldwater. From his headquarters in Suite 3505 of the
Chanin Building in New York City, White orchestrated an extended effort to bring Goldwater the nomination. By the end
of 1962 it began to be apparent how much success he and his
colleagues had already realized. In the summer of 1963, Goldwater not only acknowledged their travail but also indicated a
willingness to seriously consider a run for the presidency, even
if it meant not seeking reelection to the Senate in 1964. At
year's end, White had achieved more significant results than
perhaps anyone other than he had thought possible. If Goldwater could do even nearly as well in the primaries as the
draft-Goldwater operation was faring in the nonprimary states,
the nomination could be his.

However, the primary season began badly for Goldwater.
Steaming into New Hampshire, buoyed by a strong early
showing in the national polls, he quickly encountered both the
fabled independence of Granite State voters and the intense
scrutiny of the national media. Journalist Theodore White
noted that Goldwater would "shake with fury" when the press
actually quoted what he said. His speech writers labored over

the fine details of an address only to discover that their candidate had gained headlines the next day not for his speech but for offhand remarks at some other point in that twenty-four-hour period. For example, at a press conference in Concord, he proposed that Social Security should be voluntary rather than required; if individuals could make better arrangements on their own, they should be able to do so. Although he had voted in favor of increasing Social Security benefits in 1958 and 1960, he worried about the actuarial soundness of the existing system. Time would eventually prove Goldwater had ample reasons for his concerns, but at the moment reporters promptly wrote stories indicating Goldwater wanted to abolish Social Security. He also echoed the official American position in regard to tactical use of nuclear weapons; Goldwater said the commander of the North Atlantic Treaty Organization forces should be able to order their employment if deemed necessary in the case of Soviet aggression in western Europe. Although the NATO commander already had this authority since the days of the Eisenhower administration, Goldwater came across in the media as a zealot eager to provoke nuclear confrontation. More and more voters in New Hampshire grew alarmed.

Goldwater's emphasis on victory in the cold war, moreover, further unnerved New Hampshire residents. In a speech given in San Francisco on February 12 at the Commonwealth Club, he had chastised Lyndon Johnson for but fleeting mention of foreign policy in his state of the union address. Foreign policy, Goldwater contended, was the primary responsibility of the president. In emphasizing his own views on foreign policy, Goldwater seemed determined to cause anxiety attacks from Kidderville to Contoocook. In the Commonwealth Club speech, for example, he compared the Russians to Nazis and suggested that the blockade of Cuba ought still to be in place. In Manchester and elsewhere in New Hampshire he argued for victory in Vietnam and indicated a willingness to employ a great deal of additional force to achieve that goal.

Remarks made before the New Hampshire campaign also surfaced to haunt him. The Rockefeller staff had done its research; one stray comment after another found its way into the public dialogue. What had Goldwater meant when he advocated abolishing the Tennessee Valley Authority? One voter in New Hampshire later retorted that she was not going to vote for Goldwater because he wanted to take away her TV. When informed that she had misunderstood—it was TVA not TV—she said that she had already made up her mind, and in any event, she was not going to take any chances.

Long-time political ally John J. Rhodes, Republican congressman from Arizona, had feared just this kind of problem. Writing to a Tucson resident on January 24, he said in part: "Barry will never change. I hope he doesn't. I do hope, however, that in the bigger arena in which he now finds himself, he will be able to develop a little better sense of timing and follow through." Rhodes added: "A statement which is classified as 'shooting from the hip' today, with adequate preparation, could be the utterance of an oracle tomorrow. . . . I do not disagree with his philosophy or the points he makes, but it is my hope that the technique used will be smoother."

The day before the vote in New Hampshire, Goldwater stressed individual initiative, individual dignity, and individual responsibility. New Hampshire Republicans exercised their own individualism on March 10, handing the senator from Arizona his first electoral defeat. Goldwater received a thousand more votes than his rival, Nelson Rockefeller, but twelve thousand votes less than Ambassador to South Vietnam Henry Cabot Lodge. This constituted a landslide in New Hampshire. Even though Lodge's candidacy seemed unlikely to travel well outside of New England, it represented a stunning setback.

At the same time, the defeat was not a fatal blow. In 1964 candidates for the party's nomination confronted relatively few primaries, and the Goldwater operatives continued to make substantial progress in states where primaries would not take place. There they continued to gain momentum in winning commitments from GOP members who would cast votes at the convention. The 1964 primary campaign ultimately pointed toward California. Goldwater bowed out of the Oregon primary scheduled for mid-May to concentrate his energy and funds on California. Rockefeller took Oregon, in the process dispatching Lodge to the sidelines, but California represented a more difficult challenge. Although Rockefeller appeared likely to carry the San Francisco Bay area, the majority of the state's voters lived south of Santa Barbara. In the conservative Republican surroundings of southern California, Goldwater found himself on more familiar ground. Southern California has always cast a long shadow over Maricopa County—architecturally, financially, and otherwise—and Goldwater must have felt more at home in a place where his family had often vacationed and where his message resonated. When he spoke of wanting a country where "men can govern themselves, set their own goals, find their own solutions," he spoke a language recently rooted suburban Californians both understood and endorsed.

As the vote in California neared, pollsters suggested either Rockefeller or Goldwater might win. Knowing the importance of the outcome in the state, Rockefeller had severely criticized Goldwater on his stances in regard to Social Security, nuclear weapons, and other issues. He seemed to be cutting steadily into what had once appeared to be a sizable Goldwater lead. Then, on May 30, three days before election day, Rockefeller's wife, Happy, gave birth to Nelson Rockefeller, Jr. In increasingly conservative southern California, the Rockefeller divorce and remarriage had hurt the New York governor. The arrival of Nelson, Jr., did not occur at the most politically propitious time. Some wavering voters swung into the Goldwater camp; others who might not have voted took the time to go to the polls. In any event, Goldwater carried the day.

The vote on June 2 offered a margin rather than a mandate, yet 51.6 percent of the vote was enough. With his victory in California, Goldwater would not be denied. When coupled with the unflagging commitment of White and his operatives to gain delegates in states where primary elections had not been held, it helped encourage the final pieces of the puzzle to come together. Establishment Republicans could barely be-

lieve it and could hardly mask their horror at the prospect of
Barry Goldwater as the nominee and could not let disaster go
unchallenged. They launched a last-minute crusade for a substitute. If Rockefeller were unacceptable, what about William
Scranton? Showing more resolve than wisdom, Scranton
finally capitulated to those who had clamored for months for
him to enter the fray. In retrospect, he really had little chance.
Clifton White had seen to that. But in a month's time he could
score some points. Or, to put it another way, he could draw
blood. Lyndon Johnson must have enjoyed every minute of it.

Before the Republican convention began on July 13 at the
Cow Palace in San Francisco, the Scranton brigade must have
realized that the cause had been lost. Yet when you work for a
candidate, even for a short period (and the Scranton-for-pres-
ident effort resembled more an aria than the entire opera), it
is hard to admit the campaign is over. Some ill-advised Scranton operatives composed a letter, and Scranton compounded
the problem by allowing the epistle to go to Goldwater as the
festivities in San Francisco were about to begin. "You," it
charged Goldwater, "have too often casually prescribed nuclear war as a solution to a troubled world." It continued,
"You have too often allowed the radical extremists to use you.
You have too often stood for irresponsibility in the serious
question of racial holocaust." The letter concluded with a
nasty flourish: "Goldwaterism has come to stand for a whole
crazy-quilt collection of absurd and dangerous positions that
would be roundly repudiated by the American people in November." Through this missive Scranton challenged Goldwater to a debate. Goldwater had the cards; he refused the offer,
all the while furious at Scranton's action. How could this
man, whom he had respected even as the two had disagreed,
whom he had considered a leading possibility to be his running mate, endorse such an incendiary document? Scranton
later claimed lamely that he had not looked at the letter. Such
a disavowal, of course, did not necessarily make him look any
better; the ex post facto explanation came after the damage
had been done. The Democrats loved the language.

Although much attention has been given to the line from the Goldwater acceptance speech as the sentence that began the free fall of the presidential campaign, "Extremism in the defense of liberty is no vice, and . . . moderation in the pursuit of justice is no virtue," at that point it furnished the proverbial icing on an already sizable cake. As Theodore White commented, the line surely must have been aimed as much at William Scranton and friends as at the American people. Goldwater later stated the words were meant only to emphasize the importance of freedom, a theme he wanted to be paramount in his campaign. "It was a hell of a good speech," he later observed. "I didn't write it, but I approved it." Characteristically, he never lost any sleep over it, then or since.

Nixon inquired in early August about the offending phrase's meaning and an unperturbed Goldwater wrote in return: "If I were to paraphrase the two sentences in question, in the context in which I uttered them, I would do it by saying that wholehearted devotion to liberty is unassailable and that half-hearted devotion to justice is indefensible." But he did not apologize, to Nixon, or to anyone else. The sentences reinforced doubts; they surely did give many journalists a kind of bone on which they kept chewing and which they refused to let go. Nevertheless, the cartoon had been drawn before the Republicans had gathered in San Francisco.

The Republicans had their team for the run for the White House. Goldwater had chosen a relative unknown: Representative William Miller from upstate New York. Miller symbolized geographical but not ideological balance. He was a good soldier in what turned out to be a hopeless war. Although Goldwater suggested in his autobiography that Miller was not quite as obscure a figure as he later had been portrayed in the American Express commercial in which no one could recognize him, one flounders in trying to find another vice presidential nominee in recent years so removed from political prominence. Perhaps Thomas Eagleton and Dan Quayle come the closest, and the comparison in itself is telling.

Even before their convention, the Democrats wasted no

time in starting to use their rather considerable supply of ammunition. In fact, they began to employ it before the Republicans had vacated San Francisco. For example, Democratic National Committee chairman John M. Bailey responded in this fashion to the draft of the Republican party platform: "It is evident that the extremists and warhawks are in full control of the Republican platform committee and have dictated the composition of a document whose vague phrases and weasel words can be extended to every irresponsible position taken by Senator Goldwater." Bailey labeled the foreign policy endorsed by the Republicans "at best . . . reckless" and predicted it "would condemn every American to live in fear and uncertainty that one small miscalculation could send us all into oblivion." But "at worst" the document, Bailey alleged, "proposes a war policy, recommending actions that would blindly court disaster in every corner of the world."

And that was before Goldwater's acceptance speech, clearly indicating that the Democratic strategy had been established before the nominee's remarks. After the speech, California governor Pat Brown cried, "The smell of fascism is in the air. . . . By stating that political extremism is not a vice, Senator Goldwater encourages the bigot, the Ku Klux Klan, the Bircher."

Tradition had the two major-party candidates officially beginning their efforts in early September; Democratic nominees had linked Labor Day and Detroit as a means to emphasize their support for working people. If one candidate had established a considerable advantage over the other by Labor Day, then the person who trailed had a scant two months to rally. If the public opinion polls of the era were even close to being accurate—and there is no reason to doubt them entirely—then the 1964 presidential election may be judged over before the fall campaign had started.

Nonetheless, the official opening of the Goldwater campaign in Prescott was not shrouded in doom and gloom. Tan and relaxed after some vacation time in California, Goldwater returned to the Yavapai County home base of the Goldwater clan to inaugurate officially the effort to elect an Arizonan as president of the United States. On the north steps of the county courthouse, Goldwater's familiar voice resounded down Montezuma Street: "We stand together in this historic square today, as we have stood twice before, to launch a campaign in a good and noble cause. Twice before we have won that campaign. We shall win again."

The Republican choice for the White House attempted to portray the vote in November as a real choice between two very different alternatives. Electing "this present administration," he declared, endorsed regimentation, bureaucracy, "mobs in the street, . . . unilateral disarmament and appeasement in foreign affairs." It encouraged an America "unarmed and aimless in the face of militant Communism around the world." But a new administration would offer "peace through preparedness, progress though freedom, purpose through constitutional order." Goldwater called for other Americans who shared his values to rally behind the GOP banner. Each man, he said in a time when to men it did not seem odd to omit women from such generalizations, should be responsible for his actions, the best judge of his own well-being, have "an individual conscience to serve and a moral code to uphold," and be "a brother to every other man."

Such values, of course, had been learned from the cradle by the speaker. His mother had taught him how to live, and now he had the responsibility of trying to teach the nation. These beliefs, he knew, were embraced by the people of the community in which he had been raised and, he thought, by the people of his native state. They had influenced the lives of Arizona pioneers. They had been cherished by his uncle Morris, the mayor of Prescott, and by Morris Goldwater's good friend George Ruffner, the Yavapai County sheriff. Sixty-six years before in this very square they had carried out judgment against Jim Parker, a murderer and a horse thief. Goldwater and Ruffner hanged Parker on June 3, 1898.

Now Ruffner's nephew, Lester W., or "Budge," as he was universally known, introduced Morris Goldwater's nephew on this historic day. Prescott area rancher Gail Gardner thought it might have been the biggest day in the history of the town. However, Gardner concluded, one had to recall the fire of '04 and the campaign visit paid by William Jennings Bryan during that same year.

The Goldwater campaign, according to some observers, indeed resembled the doomed crusades of the orator from the Platte. Like Bryan, Goldwater had a clear message. He, too, came from a part of the country little known and less appreciated and understood by much of the rest of the United States. He, too, inspired a fierce allegiance among his followers and encouraged a persistent hope that somehow, against all odds, their collective voices could be heard by other Americans who had somehow moved on to other places and other perspectives. Joe Medina spoke for many in his August 26 letter to the *Arizona Republic* in issuing a plea: "I say to all America, and particularly to those of you who speak with little knowledge of the facts, do not enter the battle full of prejudice and scorn, but arm yourself with knowledge and stand alongside the man who respects, honors, and cherishes the heritage that is America."

The man Joe Medina supported was not the man a majority of Americans perceived. Most people saw Goldwater through the lens created not only by his own statements but as well by Rockefeller and others in the Republican party who had opposed him and then polished by the Democrats in the final months before the election. These voters read about Goldwater not in the pages of sympathetic Arizona newspapers but through newspapers that overwhelmingly backed Lyndon Johnson. Many of them still grieved for Jack Kennedy. They refused to make distinctions between Goldwater and the most radical of his supporters. By Labor Day the polls showed Johnson with a two-to-one margin.

The polls also demonstrated why Goldwater had too high a mountain to climb in two months. A Gallup poll asked voters in early September to respond to "word pictures" which might describe Johnson and Goldwater. The disparity could not have

A campaign rally at Phoenix College, 1964. Many of the signs say "Arizona's Barry, America's Future." Photograph by Dave Davis. Barry Goldwater Photograph Collection, courtesy of the Arizona Historical Foundation

been more striking. To the description "well qualified," Johnson received 63 percent and Goldwater, 24 percent agreement. "Experienced": Johnson, 62 percent, Goldwater, 18. "Intelligent": Johnson, 56 percent, Goldwater, 33. And perhaps the most damning of all, "good judgment": Johnson, 46 percent, Goldwater, 13; "poor judgment": Goldwater, 26 percent, Johnson, 5. It is hardly surprising that Democratic strategists seized upon these perceptions and hammered on related themes the rest of the way home to election day.

As Goldwater had long anticipated, it emerged as a different campaign than he had hoped to be involved with in the company of Jack Kennedy. He had to confront "that jackass," as he described Lyndon Johnson years later to a group of students at Arizona State University. "Lyndon," he told reporter John Kolbe, "used every dirty trick in the bag. He was a powerful man who used powerful ways to get his will." By contrast, one of Johnson's biographers, Paul Conkin, called the election "the highlight of Johnson's life." As Johnson himself "put it," Conkin wrote, "he had lived his whole life for just that moment."

If one group applauded the personal attacks that permeated the campaign, it had to be the folks who produced bumper stickers and buttons. The response to "In Your Heart You Know He's Right" became "In Your Guts You Know He's Nuts." Another read, "Goldwater for Halloween." A button, emblazoned with a mushroom cloud above the words, suggested, "Go with Goldwater." Somehow, "Part of the Way with LBJ" as a rejoinder to "All the Way with LBJ" did not have quite the same ring to it.

The mushroom cloud found its way onto more than buttons. In a one-minute television advertisement that ran but once, on September 7 in prime time on NBC, a young girl in a field of daisies began to take the petals off one of the flowers, one by one. A countdown commenced, from ten to zero, and at its end the bomb exploded. A mushroom cloud replaced the girl. One heard Lyndon Johnson's voice: "These are the stakes. To make a world in which all of God's children can live, or go into the dark. We must love each other, or we must die." Another man added: "Vote for President Johnson on November 3. The stakes are too high for you to stay home."

Just in case such artifice had been missed, Bill Moyers, in charge of Johnson's advertisements, authorized the firm of Doyle, Dane, and Bernback to formulate another message to appear ten days after the first. This time a young girl ate an ice cream cone, with a female voice now in the background reminding voters of the dangers of radioactive fallout and the vote Goldwater had cast on a nuclear test ban treaty. Goldwater had supported the measure in principle but wanted it augmented by what he later called necessary safeguards. The male voice repeated the warning—the stakes were too high for voters to stay home.

Moyers also approved an advertisement which ran many times in which a hand tore apart a social security card. Thus, whether in regard to foreign policy or domestic policy, these commercials presented Goldwater as man to be feared. This kind of negative campaigning was not unknown in American politics, but in its intensity it reflected just the kind of emotions Goldwater and Kennedy had hoped not to kindle. The Democrats knew their attacks were succeeding, and they did not relent. The success of their appeals may be ascertained in the conclusion of one devout Catholic voter who determined it a mortal sin to vote for Goldwater.

Well before election night, Goldwater could read the political tea leaves. He pressed gamely on, preaching mostly to the already converted. Goldwater advocated reducing taxes, balancing the federal budget, and investing heavily in military defense. Mary C. Brennan, in *Turning Right in the Sixties: The Conservative Capture of the GOP*, concluded that "although many Americans agreed that the federal government had become economically and bureaucratically bloated, they suspected that Goldwater's emphasis on military superiority would lead to increased governmental expansion and create a garrison state antithetical to his ideal of a free state." She added: "His oversimplified economic policies ignored the complexities of the world market and the power of the modern corporation and focused on a balanced budget as a cure-all. The emphasis on education and individual initiative as answers to the problems of the poor overlooked the realities of their lives and their place in the social hierarchy."

Brennan judged Goldwater as handicapped by appearing negative rather than positive. Voters saw more what he wanted to excise rather than what he wanted to substitute. In addition, Goldwater's interest in turning back the legacy of the New Deal alarmed those who still remembered the federal government of the 1930s as one that helped people when they needed assistance.

Goldwater was handicapped additionally by a campaign staff with whom he felt comfortable but who were ill equipped to wage a successful national effort. He wrote to his campaign director, Denison Kitchel, on January 1, 1987, that he "wanted to be surrounded with people I could trust, people I knew, and people who would react to the problems I would face pretty much the way I would react to them myself. . . . If I had to do it all over again, I would choose the same people and we would have the same kind of luck, probably gotten our tail ends beat off but we would have done the country a lot of good, which we did."

In regard to his staff, Goldwater once again displayed a characteristic loyalty that superseded a more discerning judgment. The key figures in the group had become known as the "Arizona Mafia" because of their ties both to the senator and to the state. They included attorneys Denison Kitchel and Dean Burch. Kitchel gained the nod to direct the campaign, and Goldwater chose Burch instead of, as anticipated, Clifton White to chair the Republican National Committee. Goldwater stated in his autobiography that Kitchel "had no political background" and "knew no one on the national political scene." Burch had worked as an aide to Goldwater but lacked national seasoning. Another major figure, William Baroody, head of the American Enterprise Institute, a conservative think tank, was noteworthy more for his eventual influence on

Kitchel than his practical political talents. People such as Clifton White and Stephen Shadegg, political pros, had been effectively shunted aside, although, of course, they both labored on Goldwater's behalf. In the end, Goldwater had the worst of both worlds: a staff characterized by indecision and inexperience. In a race where the odds were long at the outset, choosing a staff more on the basis of companionship than competence proved to be a serious error. Too often these men refused to listen to experienced people in the field.

At the same time, as the campaign appeared to be falling apart, many prominent national Republicans chose to distance themselves from what appeared to them to be a lost cause. Nelson Rockefeller and George Romney, for example, steadfastly refused to lend a hand to the party's nominee. Dwight Eisenhower and Richard Nixon despaired about Goldwater behind the scenes, but their common concern for the party as well as Nixon's interest in his own political future prompted them to campaign for the Republican nominee. And William Scranton moved on from the Cow Palace to toil for Goldwater in Pennsylvania and the middle Atlantic states. The most cohesive Republican effort would not have salvaged the election, but division in the ranks contributed to the final margin at the polls. The Democrats, in turn, urged GOP voters not to support an individual who had highjacked the Republican ship and set it on a dangerous course. In an effective tactic of creating guilt by association, they successfully linked Goldwater with the real extremists of the far right. They also tied him with equal success to racist white southerners who saw the growing Republican strength in the South as a means through which they could resist the demands of African Americans for equality.

Although Goldwater's opposition to the 1964 Civil Rights Act (a law prohibiting discrimination in public accommodations and in employment) had offered reason to suspect his commitment to civil rights, Goldwater contended his vote on the legislation had been dictated by his commitment to states' rights. He became angry when his decision was perceived as political opportunism, as part of a carefully considered strategy to sweep the white vote in the South and elsewhere, during a summer marked by the death of civil rights workers in Mississippi and riots in urban centers of the North. Goldwater worried about the employment of race as an issue in the campaign in a way that would fuel fires already burning across America. He contacted President Johnson, and the two agreed to steer clear of the issue. But in the process, Goldwater's silence was interpreted as assent to reactionary white intransigence against long-standing African American grievances. Even though he was a national figure, Goldwater had rarely dealt directly with the small African American community in his home state. This inexperience did not help him confront effectively one of the major issues of the day.

Lyndon Johnson and Hubert Humphrey could not have asked for a more pleasing scenario in which to use their considerable talents as campaigners. Theodore White portrayed Johnson as one who succeeded in being perceived as for "Peace and Prosperity . . . the friend of the farmer and the worker, of the businessman and the teacher, of the black and the white. . . . He was Mr. Responsible, Mr. Get Things Done, Mr. Justice-for-All, Mr. President." The enthusiasm of the crowds nourished him. As the campaign moved toward election day, Johnson and Humphrey rode a triumphant tidal wave. With each stop on the trail during the final weeks, their confidence escalated, their mood grew more expansive, and their knives became more sharp.

On October 2, Hubert Humphrey pictured the Republican party as a captured ship on which Goldwater had "nailed the battle flags of nuclear adventurism and domestic tumult to the mast." Goldwater, in fact, said Humphrey, in what had become a continuing refrain, was a radical, not a conservative. He was "not in any real sense a Republican." Two days later, not coincidentally, Lyndon Johnson labeled Goldwater "the new and frightening voice of the Republican party." In his closing speech of the campaign in Madison Square Garden, Johnson hammered away for one last time: "In this campaign we face those who are interested in destroying things as they are. They are not conservatives in the American tradition. They are interested in tearing down institutions, not preserving them. They are dedicated to extreme ideas, not to old values. . . . Conservatism may be written on their banner, but 'radical' is written in their hearts."

Goldwater had ended his campaign in the tiny Mormon community of Fredonia in northern Arizona, speaking to the faithful, knowing what tomorrow would bring. "We were ahead of our time," he told his wife, as they flew back home to Phoenix to await the returns. The results even disappointed those who had feared the worst. Lyndon Johnson captured 61.0 percent of the vote to Goldwater's 38.5 percent, with the final margin 43,126,218 to 27,174,898. Goldwater carried but six states: Alabama, Arizona, Georgia, Louisiana, Mississippi, and South Carolina. Even in Arizona he barely squeaked by, 242,536 to 237,765. Idaho, Florida, and Nebraska gave him from 47 to 49 percent of the vote; the totals dwindled rather precipitously after that. In the states boasting the largest electoral vote totals—California, Illinois, Michigan, New York, Ohio, and Pennsylvania—Goldwater received barely 40 percent in but two, California and Illinois. The Johnson margin of votes exceeded that even of Roosevelt in 1936. It was one of the most one-sided results in the history of U.S. presidential elections.

Goldwater's success in the deep South, the one seemingly encouraging note for Republicans desperate for any glad tidings from the rout, had been less dramatic than it initially appeared. As Mary C. Brennan has argued, Goldwater's victories actually had been realized because the days of the so-called "Solid South" were long gone. A new middle class had emerged in the region, and its members discovered the national Democratic party appeared to be more concerned about other groups than themselves. Johnson's presence on the Democratic ticket in 1960 probably saved the election for his running mate from Massachusetts, but Nixon had far surpassed Eisenhower in the South, winning Florida and Tennessee and coming very close in Arkansas, Louisiana, and even Texas.

Election day, 1964. Cartoon by Reg Manning. As the cartoonist for the Pulliam newspapers, Manning chronicled many developments in Goldwater's rise to national prominence. Barry Goldwater Editorial Cartoon Collection, courtesy of the Arizona Historical Foundation

Texas elected John Tower to the Senate in 1961, and Republicans added four of their own from North Carolina, Florida, Texas, and Tennessee in the congressional elections of 1962. "Aside from the racists and other extremists who disliked the liberalism of the national Democratic party," Brennan commented, "many southerners who joined the GOP embraced the classical liberal ideals embodied in the Republican Party's opposition to high taxes, federal spending, and government centralization." These "neobourbons," she concluded, "clung to their rural values while practicing corporate capitalism." Of course they embraced Barry Goldwater, as they would clasp other conservatives in the future. Goldwater had moved through a door that was already open.

The night before the election, political commentator Eric Sevareid, for one, could not see any lingering or eventual influence of the Goldwater foray other than one injurious to the conservative cause. In Sevareid's judgment, Goldwater had not emerged "as a true conservative, but as a negativist, as a kind of radical reformer of the right who seemed to wish to undo what had been the status quo in our domestic life." Sevareid scorned the notion that the American people were "being crushed by the 'dead hand' of governmental bureaucracy." If the Republicans really wanted to adopt a more potent political philosophy in the future, it should be, he argued, "at least moderately liberal." Who might lead the way? Sevareid mentioned the "bright prospects" of George Romney and John Lindsay.

The political stars of Romney and Lindsay, however, soon plummeted, and after the troubled interlude of the Nixon years, Ronald Reagan gained the presidency in 1980. Some of Goldwater's ideas, ridiculed in 1964, began to gain wider currency after he had been crushed by Johnson. Goldwater personally started to enjoy a kind of unlikely political renaissance in the 1970s, aided in part by the unhappy legacies of Lyndon Johnson and Richard Nixon. One of the bitter jokes of the mid-1960s said: "You know, they told me if I voted for Goldwater, the war would escalate out of control in Vietnam. Well,

I did, and they were right." Given the patent dishonesty of
Johnson's successor, unveiled by the Watergate scandal, Goldwater's stock rose substantially a decade after the fall of 1974.

Johnson and Humphrey had run a powerful, merciless campaign, but in the aftermath of the election many Republicans
appeared less angry with Johnson than with members of their
own party, or as they often labeled them, "Me Tooers," who
had opposed Goldwater in the primaries and then been less
than enthusiastic in backing the GOP choice for the White
House. A sampling of letters to prominent conservative congressman Charles Halleck of Indiana is instructive. Charles E.
Lucas of Knox, Indiana, contended that Lodge, Rockefeller,
"and their bedfellows" had done more to defeat Goldwater
than they did to help Nixon in 1960. Walt Hadley wrote from
Logansport, Indiana, to tell Halleck that he and others believed that Republicans more than Democrats had caused the
defeat. Stephen Weld of Milton, Massachusetts, blamed "a
smear campaign of unprecedented viciousness conducted
against Senator Goldwater by most of the press and radio."
Lucas doubted that "any other candidate, even Christ himself,
could have defeated the money and political patronage Goldwater had arrayed against him."

In an interview with *U.S. News & World Report* conducted
in December 1964, Goldwater himself echoed these com-
plaints. Responding to a query about what he might have done
differently to erase what Goldwater termed the "caricature" of a
trigger-happy fellow who was going to drop the bomb and tear
up Social Security cards, he emphasized the split within the
Republican party created by Rockefeller and Romney and, to a
lesser extent, Scranton. They had made it "virtually impossible for us to retain Republicans influenced by the bomb scare
and Social Security scare." Goldwater concluded, "Frankly, I
think I was beaten July 15." The media had not helped, either
in its coverage during the campaign or at the end, by announcing early election returns from one part of the country
before polls had closed in other time zones. Time did not particularly heal this wound. Goldwater wrote on January 10,

1973, to former NBC television anchor Chet Huntley: "I am convinced that there was a determined effort on the part of a majority of the major press representatives and the press to misrepresent me."

As the years passed, as some of the self-inflicted miseries of the debacle began to recede from memory, Goldwater and others emphasized some of the longer-term benefits yielded from what had been, in their eyes, an impossible battle. Control of the party had been wrested from the East. Goldwater believed he had kept the faith; he had remained honest and spoken from the heart, despite the invective heaped upon him. Only quite some time later would it become apparent that the Goldwater candidacy had inspired young Republicans who spearheaded a conservative resurgence in the 1980s and 1990s. Perhaps most clearly, he had demonstrated the potential for continuing gains for the Republican party in the South. Charles Lucas spoke for others who knew their time would come: "As that wonderful conservative and party worker, Ronald Reagan expresses it," he wrote to Halleck not long after the 1964 election, "'we only lost a battle, not a war.'"

CHAPTER 6

Returning to the Senate

THE loss of his seat in the U.S. Senate constituted an important part of the price Barry Goldwater had to pay for seeking the presidency in 1964. His friend Paul Fannin ran successfully for the vacated position. Carl Hayden remained as Arizona's senior senator, with four years remaining in his term. Goldwater had little interest in any other political office. The Senate suited him. It provided a forum through which he could address the national issues he cared about, and it still afforded him the opportunity to do something for the people of Arizona as well as the people of America. He had been crushed in the presidential race and only narrowly had escaped the embarrassment of losing his home state in the balloting. Nonetheless, he remained generally a popular figure in Arizona. The talk soon began about his potential return to Washington.

By June 1965, Goldwater had announced publicly that he intended to run for the Senate in 1968. He no doubt hoped he would not have to run against Hayden, now an old man as well as an old family friend. In fact, as Goldwater told political scientist Ross Rice in an interview conducted in 1973, the Haydens and the Goldwaters had been "very close friends" since before the turn of the century. "My wife's father and mother lived in the Hayden home at the Phoenix Country Club," he added, "and that's where I first started going with my wife, and later we had several visits, just to be alone, at the Hayden ranch east of Tempe." Goldwater crossed party lines to support Hayden. He raised money for his campaigns and, of course, got to know him as a fellow senator in Washington. They were thus part of the old Arizona, and it perhaps should not have been surprising that "the same people that backed me backed Carl Hayden."

Regardless of his affection for Hayden, Goldwater reminded a Phoenix reporter in 1967 that the Republicans had to run a candidate. "We just can't say that Carl Hayden, an old man approaching 90 years of age, is entitled to a free ride for another term." Goldwater labeled himself the "logical candidate" for the GOP nomination. And he gave notice that he did not intend to take it easy on his friend, for they differed on many issues. Moreover, although Hayden had not needed to return home to campaign for reelection in 1962, this time it promised to be different. Arizonans deserved to know where Hayden stood on the issues. In addition, Goldwater emphasized to the interviewer that Hayden could be defeated: "Keep in mind," he stated, "that there are literally hundreds of thousands of people in this state who have never seen or heard Carl Hayden." This remark reflected not only Hayden's absence but also the continuing migration of new people to Arizona.

Goldwater respected Hayden. "His family and my family," Goldwater commented in 1966, "are amongst the oldest families in the state." That mattered a lot. So, too, did the fact that Hayden's wife had supported him in previous races. Nonetheless, he wanted to be back in the Senate: "I miss it," he told journalist David Broder. "Anyone would miss it." He cherished "the intimate day-to-day comradeship," but even more, he valued "the platform it offers." Writing his political column was all well and good, but in the column you could say something "till your hair falls out, and nobody ever sees it."

The impending conflict between the two men did not occur. Hayden decided to call it quits and deferred to his long-time aide, Roy Elson. Elson had sought Goldwater's seat in 1964, and buoyed by Lyndon Johnson's showing, he had given Fannin a reasonable race. The earlier effort offered some name recognition, and Elson had little difficulty in gaining the Democratic nomination in 1968. Facing Goldwater, he soon discovered, provided a different challenge than running against Fannin.

Early polls conducted in Goldwater's behalf indicated that
Elson had an outside chance. Goldwater, of course, was far better known than Elson, and few voters had not formed some
kind of opinion about him. The Arizona electorate tended to
be somewhat polarized about the recent presidential candidate; some residents gave him highly favorable ratings, others
highly unfavorable marks. Goldwater did best among older
voters and Republican voters. The initial polls suggested the
possibility that Elson could give Goldwater a race, but only if
those traditionally less likely to vote showed up in droves on
election day.

"Honest," "sincere," "saying what he thinks" represented
the qualities many voters in Arizona most approved in Goldwater. At the same time, Goldwater came across to some as
"impulsive/outspoken/radical." In other words, some of the
same characteristics that appealed to one voter caused another
concern. The pollsters advised: "Goldwater seems most vulnerable in the area of being impulsive, rash, and quick to comment and judge. Every precaution must be taken to keep
Goldwater out of controversy and from making controversial
statements that can be pounced upon by the press." Such
counsel, if well-intentioned, also looked to be futile. Telling
Goldwater to steer clear of controversy was like advising the
thermometer in Phoenix not to climb over one hundred degrees in July.

Goldwater did not seem to be held particularly accountable
in 1968, or, for that matter, in his two subsequent elections, for
his stances on various issues. Opponents barked about his lack
of congressional achievements. That did not matter in the eyes
of most voters, even those who had been in Arizona for more
than a decade and could recall the era when Goldwater had
previously served in the Senate. When asked for specific examples of his attainments, voters tended to say that he had
"put Arizona on the map."

That identification with Arizona marked a key element in
the strategy for the 1968 campaign. Goldwater's television advertisements showed him in a cowboy hat peering out toward

the horizon—a sort of Marlboro Country look. The tag line in the ad asked: "Senator Barry Goldwater—doesn't that sound great?" The Goldwater stationery included the same kind of image, with Monument Valley in the background. In the newspaper and over the airwaves voters received the message that linked him with his native state. He was, above all, an Arizonan, the advertisements declared. Even if America had erred in rejecting him for the presidency, the people of Arizona would not make the same mistake:

There is a great message in this beautiful land.

Barry Goldwater is, above all else, a product of the land he loves.

He has unrolled his bed on Arizona's wind-chilled mesas. Roamed her forests and valleys. And explored the yawning depths of her sheer canyons.

And he learned. There was a great message in that beautiful, raw-boned land. From Tombstone to Marble Canyon . . . from Kayenta to the Kaibab . . . the words rang strong and true.

Self-reliance. Hard work. Rugged, determined, stick-to-getherness.

These are the words Barry Goldwater has taken to the nation. The lessons of a great State that still remembers its fierce struggle for survival.

Arizona's lesson is America's lesson. But much of America has forgotten. That's why Barry Goldwater must be returned to the U.S. Senate.

From Tombstone to Boston . . . from Kayenta to Detroit . . . Arizona's strong true words are needed now, more than ever before.

It may have been the first time Kayenta and Detroit had ever been associated with each other. It is hard to measure the impact of such overwrought campaign rhetoric, but it did underscore the image of "Mr. Arizona" that served Goldwater well. Elson did not have a chance. He harped upon Goldwater's legislative record, charging that Goldwater had been so busy running for president he had not taken care of Arizona's

interests. When Elson challenged Goldwater to debate, Goldwater found no more need to debate this upstart than Lyndon
Johnson had to debate Goldwater in 1964. Goldwater's national stature, Dean Burch later recalled, made fund-raising
"no problem at all. It was sort of like running the Yellowstone
Park or something because he was sort of more of an artifact
than a person." On election day, Yellowstone won, with over
58 percent of the vote.

Goldwater's return to Washington signaled a new stage of
his career. Former manager of the Salt River Project, Jack
Pfister, recalled in 1995 that Goldwater became "a different
senator after 1968 because of his national prominence." He
remained interested in Arizona concerns, but national matters
appropriated an increasing percentage of his time. Thus Goldwater became progressively more involved in military issues
through his work on the Armed Services Committee. Such
work was not irrelevant to Arizona, given the state's military
bases and contractors and firms which had a vested interest in
national defense. He certainly worked to bring home the military and electronics bacon to Arizona. When he journeyed
back to the Salt River valley, he dutifully met with bond buyers rounded up by the Salt River Project and encouraged them
to invest in the area's future. He was a man admired, even li-
onized, by the financial community, and Pfister remembered
Goldwater's effectiveness in promoting investment in regional
economic development. However, some of the traditional issues confronting a western senator, including those related to
natural resources, did not receive the same degree of consistent, firsthand attention.

Goldwater probably did not agonize over the choices he inevitably had to make about how to allocate his time. His colleague, Paul Fannin, served on the Natural Resources Committee. The two men agreed on the issues, and Goldwater
could count on Fannin to represent Arizona. When Democrat
Dennis DeConcini gained the other place in the Senate, the
two men were somewhat more likely to differ, but DeConcini
was a moderate Democrat from another old Arizona family,

and more often than not the two shared similar perspectives on matters directly affecting the state. Goldwater had a particular fondness for those who hailed from other pioneer families, and throughout his career this affection allowed him to reduce partisan considerations in working with politicians graced by such names as Babbitt, DeConcini, Hayden, and Udall.

Goldwater's papers also indicate that regardless of his choices about committee assignments, his constituents demanded a lot from him. Indeed, because of his renown he received far more mail than the average member of the Senate. Goldwater's secretary for many years, Judy Eisenhower, and such key staff members as Twinkle Thompson helped him time and again to deal with issues large and small. Goldwater entrusted considerable authority to them; their notes to him in turn suggest they mastered the art of communicating directly and effectively with him.

Even his friends in Washington acknowledged that sponsoring legislation did not rank as Goldwater's foremost priority. Goldwater may have been somewhat sensitive on this score, probably in part because the matter kept being brought up by those who ran against him. More than once his staff sent out a list of the measures he had sponsored in the Congress. Nevertheless, John Rhodes's judgment in 1986 about Goldwater's lack of affinity for legislative detail is difficult to deny. "That was not his thing," Rhodes asserted. "Barry has always painted with a broad brush, and I say that without criticism. All of us have to do what we are best at. He has never been known as a detail man." Morris Udall similarly suggested Goldwater "was bored by details. He always focused on the big picture."

Goldwater could focus a lot of his attention on a bill if it really mattered to him. Given his sentiments about the Grand Canyon, for example, he proved more than willing to marshal support for legislation increasing the size of the national park; Goldwater's devotion to this issue is delineated in chapter 8. But even on a matter that concerned him considerably, such as the ongoing struggle between the Hopi and Navajo tribes over lands both claimed in northern Arizona, Goldwater's attention to detail ultimately could flag, causing considerable political fallout. This example is analyzed in the next chapter.

Nevertheless, if the situation demanded it, he could invest considerable energy and attention on something that loomed as truly significant. Goldwater returned to Washington in time to witness the trauma of Watergate and played a central role in dealing with the crisis that led in due course to the resignation of President Richard Nixon. Goldwater, of course, had supported Nixon against Hubert Humphrey in 1968. After reviewing Nixon's performance during his first two years in office, however, Goldwater was "amazed at the ineptitude that President Nixon has shown in the operation of the government." Even though Nixon had to be the most "politically astute animal in American politics," he had "allowed himself to be surrounded by people who really aren't too smart in the field and he is not allowed to know what is going on."

Goldwater first met Nixon after his election to the Senate in 1952, the same year that Nixon had been elected vice president. He admired Nixon's penchant for hard work as well as his "delightful" family. They both labored for the Republican cause during the 1950s, trying their best to increase the GOP representation in the House and the Senate. In retrospect, Goldwater realized he should have recognized a major character flaw in Nixon by his behavior at the Republican convention in 1960. Nixon had promised Goldwater that he would advocate the controversial right-to-work provision in the party platform. Then Rockefeller persuaded Nixon to go back on his word, and right-to-work was opposed in the platform. "I should have learned at that time," Goldwater said, "what a two-fisted, four-square liar the man is."

Nixon supported Goldwater fully in the lost cause of 1964 and then methodically labored to gain the nomination for himself in 1968. The break-in at the Watergate took place on June 17, during his bid for reelection in 1972. For quite some time Goldwater disregarded the rumors. After all, the *Washington Post* took the lead in writing stories about what Watergate meant, and the *Post* was not exactly his favorite newspaper. He wanted to remain loyal to a Republican president and had no desire that his party be tarnished by rumors. The stories persisted, however, and by the end of 1972 Goldwater asked a friend at the newspaper if there really were something to all the tales. After being reassured that the accounts represented something other than fabrications, he began to grow increasingly alarmed. On April, 11, 1973, he urged Nixon, through an interview with Godfrey Sperling, Jr., in the *Christian Science Monitor,* to "speak up now and come out in the open and get rid of Watergate once for all," for the affair was "beginning to smell like Teapot Dome." But within three weeks, Bob Haldeman and John Ehrlichman had resigned, John Dean had been fired, and Attorney General Richard Kleindienst, an old Goldwater ally from Arizona, was on his way out.

Goldwater also worried about Nixon's continuing isolation from Congress. He issued a press release on May 17 again calling on Nixon to take charge of the situation and provide the necessary leadership. Goldwater continued his efforts through a letter he typed personally to Nixon on June 20, 1973, in which he urged the president "to stop living alone, . . . to tear down that wall that you have built around you, . . . [to] emerge from the cocoon." Goldwater declared, "No one I know feels close to you." But if "Nixon the cold" emerged, then Watergate probably would have only "a minor effect in the next election."

This optimism proved short-lived, for the very next month White House aide Alexander Butterfield reluctantly admitted to the investigative committee chaired by Senator Sam Ervin of North Carolina that the Nixon administration had secretly tape-recorded conversations in the White House. By late July, Goldwater had decided the only way Nixon could be saved would be through an appearance before Ervin's committee; Nixon understandably did not want to appear before the man who referred to himself as just a country lawyer. Goldwater advised Nixon that regardless of his preferences, without such an appearance his reputation might not be redeemed, regardless of his personal complicity in Watergate.

In the meantime, Kleindienst's replacement, Elliot Richardson, had hired Archibald Cox as special prosecutor. Cox asked for certain tapes from Nixon, who refused; Nixon demanded Richardson fire Cox, and Richardson refused; Nixon then fired Richardson. The wheels obviously were coming off the Nixon wagon. Goldwater attended a truly memorable December dinner with an apparently drunk president that provided just another signpost that Nixon's days might indeed be numbered. Several months later, little hope remained that his presidency could be salvaged.

On May 8, 1974, Goldwater met with House Minority Leader John Rhodes to discuss what should be done. Goldwater had resisted the notion that Nixon should resign, but he had come to recognize that if Nixon remained in office the two-party system could be destroyed. The July 24, 1974, Supreme Court ruling that Nixon must relinquish subpoenaed tapes to Leon Jaworski, the special prosecutor, hastened the final hours of his presidency. The Judiciary Committee of the House of Representatives moved swiftly toward impeachment, with three articles passed by a 27–11 vote. The House itself scheduled a vote for late August.

Then, on August 5, the dam broke with release of a tape that confirmed Nixon had lied. This June 23, 1972, conversation, immediately after the Watergate break-in, revealed that Nixon had known all along about the cover-up and in fact had urged it himself. Goldwater valued honesty above all else, and he simply could not tolerate Nixon's transgressions. He stated in his own notes of August 7 that he had tried to excuse Nixon's dishonesty through the years as "mere lapses"; now he found himself "appalled that I could put up with it as long as I did." He added: "I guess it was more respect for the office than for the man and the grave feeling on my part that the office should not be injured but I was wrong in protecting him as long as I did."

Allegiance to Nixon had evaporated in the Congress, but could the president be persuaded to resign immediately and spare the country the specter of not only impeachment but

Facing the press the day before Nixon resigned as president, August 7, 1974. *Left to right:* Hugh Scott, Barry Goldwater, and John Rhodes. Barry Goldwater Photograph Collection, courtesy of the Arizona Historical Foundation

also conviction? Members of Congress caucused to select the right people to call upon Nixon. In the end, Senator Hugh Scott of Pennsylvania accompanied two Arizonans, Goldwater and Rhodes, to the White House. Goldwater informed the president that he "doubted if he would get as many as fifteen votes and that most of those would be older southerners who would cling to the constitutional process of impeachment rather than resignation." Rhodes contended perhaps only ten votes remained in the entire House. After the half-hour to forty-minute conversation had come to a close, Goldwater, as spokesman, faced the onslaught of the press. Later he returned to his office for a conference call that Judy Eisenhower had organized for the Arizona media, followed by twenty minutes over radio station KTAR in Phoenix, and then he "was ready for a drink."

Nixon resigned the next day. Goldwater had agonized over

his role in the process, but his blunt nature, his willingness to tell Nixon the truth about his situation, had helped forestall the president's wishful thinking that there might somehow remain some way out. And Goldwater did not absolve Nixon after Nixon left Washington or after he had received a pardon from Gerald Ford. On January 30, 1975, Goldwater wrote to Nixon and advised him "to waive your pardon and offer to appear before any court in the Capital City, to, in effect, stand trial for whatever charges might be brought against you, keeping in mind none have." Goldwater argued, "This would accomplish several things, . . . it would show you as a man of courage, as a man of decency, as a man of respect for the law and as a man who is determined to allow justice to clear his name." This kind of offer Richard Nixon refused.

In Goldwater's judgment, Alexander Haig merited the country's thanks for his role during the crisis. As chief of staff, Haig had kept the White House from falling into total disarray; he had made sure that Goldwater and his associates knew that Nixon had to be told in no uncertain terms that he must resign. In *Goldwater*, the senator phrased it this way: "He put his butt on the line when many of the most powerful men in Washington went into hiding." Goldwater wrote to Haig in September 1987: "I have always said that thanks to you, we have a republic. What you did to save this country, during the hectic days of that lying president we had, Dick Nixon, allowed us to go ahead without interruption." Haig, in turn, praised Goldwater for his support of due process and his influential role in resolving the crisis. Goldwater, Haig noted, would be viewed by history "as one of the good guys."

There can be no doubt that Goldwater's stature was enhanced by his part in the final year of the Nixon presidency. He began to be perceived and portrayed differently than he had a decade earlier. A *New York Times* story by James M. Naughton spoke of Goldwater's political renaissance. A Gallup poll elevated him to the tenth most admired man in the world. Columnist Garry Wills wrote of his "deep residual admiration for Barry Goldwater," calling him "the last man since Adlai

Stevenson to run for the presidency without losing his hold on the basic decencies." Although Goldwater "never knew tactics from his elbow," he had remained "a gentleman" in the face of the campaign waged against him in 1964. Goldwater's urging of Nixon to give up the tapes mattered, Wills observed, "because his appeal cannot be ideological, mean or petty, aimed at hurting the Nixon cause in any large or principled sense. He speaks only for decency and honor." Another liberal columnist, Mary McGrory, concluded that Watergate had made Goldwater "what he has longed to be, the patriarch of his party."

One may also conclude that Goldwater drew from this wrenching experience some lasting lessons that helped influence and shape the remainder of his career. He would remain, to be sure, a loyal Republican, but his affiliation with Richard Nixon had taught him something about the limits of loyalty. A generation after Joe McCarthy, this time Goldwater knew when to draw the line and move beyond partisan considerations and personal associations. He understood more completely the terrible price the nation could pay for dishonesty in politics, and he appeared thereafter to be all the more determined to hold others, regardless of party or ideology, to this fundamental standard. During the generation after Richard Nixon's resignation, Barry Goldwater would not hesitate to live up to the legacy he hoped to offer through example. Interviewed in 1994 for "Barry Goldwater: Photographs and Memories," a retrospective produced by KAET of Arizona State University, Goldwater responded to the question about how he wanted to be remembered: "Well, he may not have been much of a politician, but by God, he was honest."

And he remained determined to mix in lighter moments with more serious business. Goldwater may have particularly enjoyed a chili cook-off in 1974. Senator John Tower of Texas challenged Goldwater after the senator from Arizona instructed listeners at the National Press Club that "a Texan doesn't know chili from leavings in a corral." After hearing of Tower's attempt to reestablish the good name of Texas chili, the *Phoenix Gazette* could not resist a slightly biased evaluation of this concoction: "It isn't fit for human consumption. That isn't to say it can't serve a useful purpose, though; the runways at the new Dallas–Fort Worth airport have an odd red tint to them, because Texas chili has just the right greasy consistency to serve as a substitute for asphalt."

In the April 1974 contest, individuals labeled as professional chili tasters judged entries not only from Arizona and Texas, but also from New Mexico, Oklahoma, Louisiana, and, improbably, Ohio. The judges selected Goldwater's chili as the best, with New Mexico finishing second and Texas third. Gleefully reporting the results, the *Phoenix Gazette* heaped an additional helping of scorn on Texas chili, calling it "one of the great environmental hazards of our times." The newspaper warned, "A bowl of it dumped into the Gulf of Mexico could poison marine life as far away as the Straits of Magellan."

Amidst such rising political as well as culinary fortunes, Goldwater had to decide about whether to seek reelection to the Senate. He had hesitated about the prospect of six more years in Washington, for he had promised Peggy, in writing, that he would not run for another term. Goldwater told Stephen Shadegg in October 1973 that Peggy's health prompted that promise; it was "good at times and not so good at times, and added to it all, she's losing her hearing and she hates Washington." Moreover, the prospect of getting out and campaigning again "rather nauseates me." However, he waffled on the matter and by late in 1973 had decided to run even though it would mean "one hell of a mess in the Goldwater household." Watergate helped change his mind. He suggested to his old friend Bert Holloway on May 1, 1974, that he owed it to the two-party system to keep going. "One of us older bastards," he wrote, "better hang around to help the young ones." Goldwater pledged to "do my damnedest. . . . I will continue to sound off as I think sounding off should be done. At least I can sleep at night."

Five days after that letter, Scottsdale newspaper publisher Jonathan Marshall announced his candidacy for the Demo-

Peggy Goldwater. Photograph by Herb McLoughlin. Barry Goldwater Photograph Collection, courtesy of the Arizona Historical Foundation

cratic nomination for the Senate. Born in New York City, the fifty-year-old Marshall had moved to Arizona in 1963. Speaking from the observation platform of the "North Star," a railroad car used by Harry Truman in his whistle-stop campaign in 1948 and now conveniently residing in the Scottsdale Railroad Park, Marshall contended that Arizona needed "a working senator and representation in the majority party in Congress." He accused Goldwater of having the worst absentee record in the Senate and of not having introduced a single major bill in the past three years. "If you will pardon the expression," Marshall could not resist saying, "Arizona needs a choice, not an echo."

Two decades later, Marshall remembered that the campaign had not experienced an auspicious beginning. He had purchased a new suit, had worn it once, and had taken it to the cleaners so that he would look his best on this special occasion. On the morning that he would announce his candidacy, Marshall went to the closet only to find that the cleaners had not returned the pants. He resorted to wearing what he labeled an "ancient" suit, desperately hoping that it would not split at the seams as he offered his first political speech.

Marshall had stepped into the race after Mo Udall had decided not to seek the Senate seat. He won the primary handily but encountered major difficulties in the two months between the primary and the general election. Marshall had anticipated help from labor, but organized labor used the occasion to try to pressure the publisher into having workers at his newspaper belong to a union. When Marshall balked, asserting he had taken a leave from his duties and that in any event that decision remained with the employees themselves, most labor unions refused to provide sorely needed financial assistance. The national Democratic party did not pay much attention, either, and as a result the Marshall campaign foundered. By the end of September, he had to cancel his ads and fire his campaign manager.

Marshall had to resort to a low-budget campaign, and an election that might have been competitive turned out otherwise. Goldwater ignored him, refused to debate him, and coasted to a comfortable victory at the polls. Marshall discovered to his chagrin that regardless of his attacks on Goldwater's voting record, most voters in the state had decided that they simply liked the incumbent and weren't overly concerned about how he had voted on a particular issue. Eugene Pulliam at the *Arizona Republic* may have respected Marshall as a publisher, but his newspaper's coverage of the campaign made evident that as a Democrat Marshall could not count on even-handed reporting. At times Marshall probably did not know whether to laugh or cry. As he made the taxing trip from Kingman to Wickenburg on a particularly warm day, his car's air conditioning broke down. During the time mechanics attempted to revive the aging vehicle, Jonathan and Maxine

Marshall and their children stepped into an ice cream parlor. They were initially encouraged by the response of an older woman who appeared to be quite critical of the incumbent. Then she said, "Well, I just don't like Senator Goldwater. He's too liberal."

It was a clean, civil campaign. Even if Marshall disagreed strongly with many of Goldwater's positions—from foreign policy to the role of the federal government in regard to social issues—he attacked the record rather than the man. Although Marshall lost, he did begin to raise questions about Goldwater's absenteeism and perspective on issues that could be seized upon if the senator chose to run one last time in 1980. Following the election, Goldwater no doubt assured his spouse and family that this would be the final installment of his tenure in Washington. And the term seemed to pass quickly; the accolades kept mounting. Senator James Buckley of New York emphasized in 1976 that he could not have been elected "but for the political forces you unleashed." He went on, "Nor do I know anyone who has spoken more consistent good sense on the floor of the Senate, year in and year out, than you." Senator Jesse Helms of North Carolina in 1979 stressed that if it had not been "for the terrific fight you've waged down through the years, there would not today be any 'conservative cause,'" and he never would have run for the Senate.

Many on the other side of the political aisle had joined in the chorus. Mo Udall in 1978 wrote to tell Goldwater that he considered him "one of the most decent, kind, and patriotic people I have ever known. All of us in Arizona are proud of you. I'm honored to be your friend." Andy Rooney, who became famous through his commentary on *Sixty Minutes* and whose politics defy categorization, informed Goldwater in 1978 that the senator had "become of all the unlikely damn things in the world, beloved by most Americans. As a matter of fact," Rooney conjectured, "I guess there isn't a man alive with whom so many people disagree so often and like so much."

Goldwater observed his seventieth birthday in 1979 and began to go through by now what had become a somewhat

predictable ritual. Should he run again? Many people encouraged him to go just one more round. Church of Latter-day
Saints leader and former secretary of agriculture Ezra Taft
Benson urged him to try for another term. Benson offered the
services of his grandson, Stephen, whom he called a "strong
conservative, as are all of our 34 grandchildren," and a "great
cartoonist." There is no record of what young Steve Benson,
who went on to become a Pulitzer Prize–winning cartoonist
for the *Arizona Republic* and who was not always kind to Goldwater or to anyone else, thought of the option.

However, by the end of the 1970s some storm clouds had
started to gather on the horizon. Goldwater had been flayed by
the *Arizona Daily Star* for his part in the dispute between the
Navajos and Hopis. In addition to contending with his own
health problems, he had to confront his own family's feelings.
His wife no longer came to Washington; emphysema coupled
with her continuing distaste for life inside the beltway made
Arizona her permanent residence. Her husband had promised,
once again, that this would be the last term. When Goldwater
began, inevitably, to make noises about the needs of the country and the needs of the party, the family held a conference on
the occasion of his seventy-first birthday. The Goldwaters
agreed to one last go-around on the condition that he would
spend more time at home in Arizona.

The family assumed, naturally enough, that he would win.
But that result was not a given in 1980. The year before, the
Arizona Republic's Bernie Wynn had warned that if Bill Schulz
sought the Democratic nomination, Schulz could pose problems for the incumbent. A West Point graduate, the forty-
nine-year-old Schulz had made a fortune in the lucrative
Phoenix real estate market, primarily through his ownership of
more than sixty-five hundred apartment units. He had been a
registered Republican but had switched to the Democratic
party in 1974. Schulz spent more than nine hundred thousand
dollars of his own money in the Democratic party. He won
handily, gaining 97,550 votes to 59,220 for Jim McNulty and
19,244 for Frank DePaoli. With Arizona's late primary, only

two months remained until the fall election. At first, Goldwater did not appear worried. Publicly, he stated that he did not care who won the primary: "There's not a Democrat in this state who can win." He discounted the Schulz vote totals, suggesting that "at ten dollars a vote you ought to be able to win something." An early poll, sponsored by the *Arizona Republic* and television station KOOL, gave Goldwater 50 percent and Schulz 34.5 percent, with the remainder undecided. In addition, many in the Goldwater camp personally disliked Schulz and could not imagine that the voters would feel otherwise.

Goldwater and his associates discovered somewhat belatedly, however, that they had a real battle on their hands. The win over Marshall in 1974 perhaps gave them more confidence than they should have possessed, and Goldwater's recent hospitalization because of complications following an operation on his artificial right hip had imprisoned him in his Washington apartment during nearly all of July and August. Goldwater literally hobbled into the autumn campaign. His appearance did not bolster the faith of a considerable number of Arizona voters, many of whom had arrived in the state during the latter part of the 1970s. The presidential election of 1964 had receded from memory, and Goldwater did not represent as dominating or familiar a figure as he had been a decade before. Moreover, Schulz realized, as Goldwater initially did not, that one did not have to invest as much time in personal appearances in 1980, as television could relay one's message far more efficiently and effectively. Schulz hit the airways, while Goldwater and his associates, Goldwater recalled, "were fooling ourselves by in effect talking to nothing but the choir in Sun City and Fountain Hills."

Schulz sounded some of the same alarms that Elson and Marshall had in the past, but in a far more critical way. This time more people heard them. Of Goldwater, Schulz declared: "He has served this state with honor, but Arizona needs a working senator for the '80s, not one who is resting on his laurels." Schulz calculated that Goldwater had the ninety-fifth worst attendance record in the Senate. When Goldwater ac-

knowledged that his attendance had been poor, partly because of physical ailments that had required hospitalization,
the explanation did little to project a man vigorous enough to
withstand the demands of the next term.

Lashing back at the insinuation he was now too old, Goldwater said he did not think age made that much difference
"unless you become senile." Referring to Carl Hayden, he
noted that "the best senator Arizona ever had quit at 92" and
observed that "some of the best men we ever had in the Senate are well over 70 and some of the dumbest bastards I've
ever run into are young ones."

A month before the election, Mike Hellon, active in the
state Republican party, smelled trouble. Writing for the *Yuma
Daily Sun,* he remarked upon the presence of new young voters as well as those new to the state. These people "knew
Goldwater only by reputation and from their history books."
They did not remember Goldwater had served on the Phoenix
City Council; in fact, a lot of them did not remember he had
run for president. Nearly half of these individuals had not even
lived in Arizona when Goldwater returned to the Senate in
1968. Hellon did not think much of Goldwater's campaign
slogan—"Goldwater, now more than ever," noting wryly that
"now more than ever" had been the slogan of Richard Nixon
in 1972. It seemed to Hellon that Goldwater so far had been
waging a defensive campaign. He might not lose, but "nothing is a leadpipe cinch."

Even Goldwater's vaunted credentials as an expert in military affairs came under attack. After an accident involving
Titan II missiles at Damascus, Arkansas, Goldwater suggested
that all of them should be deactivated. Schulz criticized the
idea, and as a graduate of the U.S. Military Academy he appeared to the public like someone who might know what he
was talking about. After meeting with the secretary of the air
force, Goldwater retreated from his earlier position, clearly
suggesting he had overstated the case.

Frustrated by Stephen Shadegg's handling of the campaign
to date and unhappy that he had relied on Shadegg's faulty es-

timate of Schulz's appeal, Goldwater knew he was in trouble. A tracking survey taken the week of October 15–19 indicated that Schulz had narrowed the gap. Although Goldwater fared very well with older voters, especially those over sixty, Schulz now appeared to have more support from voters aged eighteen to thirty-five. Newer residents of the state, those who lived outside of Maricopa County, and working-class people seemed much more inclined to vote for Schulz. Goldwater turned to pollster Richard Wirthlin for advice. Wirthlin told him in essence that this was 1980, not 1952, and he had to rely more on television and his ads had to be much better. New television advertisements released in the waning days of the campaign began to turn the tide. Goldwater also consulted Tom Sullivan, a local who knew well the Arizona political landscape. Sullivan had already advised Goldwater on ways to improve his image with Jewish voters by emphasizing his support for Israel as a way of counteracting the negative press he had received by his frequent opposition to foreign aid. In addition, he had given Goldwater solid suggestions about ways to battle the main problems the senator confronted in the campaign: his voting record, his age, and his limited mobility.

During his first venture into politics, the Phoenix City Council election of 1949, Goldwater had sought the counsel of Tom Sullivan. As he stated in the foreword to Sullivan's autobiography, *My Life and Times,* Goldwater then did not know much about politics, but Sullivan's "deep and thorough knowledge" of Phoenix and Arizona politics "became one of the most valuable assets" of that first campaign; Goldwater credited Sullivan with helping him to avoid "foolish mistakes" and ultimately in winning the election. Born in 1914, Sullivan knew families with names such as Goldwater, Kleindienst, and Jennings; when Renz Jennings was appointed to the Superior Court, he picked Sullivan as his probation officer. After Goldwater and the other Charter Government slate gained their places on the Phoenix City Council, Sullivan became city clerk. Over the next three decades, including a fifteen-year stint as a political consultant for the Salt River Project, Tom

Sullivan developed an intimate knowledge of Arizona politics. When Goldwater called on him again in 1980, he was delighted to lend a hand.

Jack Pfister is not alone in believing that Sullivan made a difference in the outcome of the 1980 election. Sullivan developed a fifteen-minute television program, "Democrats for Goldwater," which aired widely and frequently before the election. He also understood the absolute necessity of using visual images. The Goldwater campaign had not taken sufficient advantage of television early in the campaign, whereas Schulz had used television advertisements to his advantage. The voters were deluged with pictures of an active, effective senator in the closing moments before November 4. Goldwater filmed new commercials, emphasizing, just as he had in 1968, his long-standing ties with Arizona. Either for the first time or once again voters saw the cowboy hat and open spaces. Goldwater had heard the message in the nick of time. Much as he personally disliked what he once labeled "professional packaging," he realized he could not avoid it. His campaign matched Schulz's in its expenditures when it mattered most—as the race headed toward the wire. As Sullivan had reminded him in no uncertain terms, he had almost pulled a McFarland: he had underestimated a younger opponent and had come home too late from Washington. It nearly proved fatal.

Schulz defeated Goldwater in eleven of Arizona's then fourteen counties, and before the absentee ballots were counted he led in the count. On election night it appeared to many that Goldwater had lost. Knowledgeable campaign participants, such as Elsa Mulhern, an attorney who cochaired the Goldwater effort in Pima County, remained confident. Interviewed by a Tucson television station at two in the morning, she assured viewers that Goldwater would win. The absentee voters, traditionally Republican, swung the election to Goldwater. In the end, the presidential election and the Senate election had captured the interest of an unusually high percentage of the electorate. Eighty percent of the registered voters cast their ballots. Goldwater carried Yavapai and Maricopa counties, as one would have expected; he also eked out a win in Mohave by slightly more than 100 votes. However, Maricopa made the difference, yielding a margin of 49,667 votes in an election decided by about 9,400 votes out of almost 875,000 cast. Arizona's enthusiasm for Ronald Reagan, Goldwater freely admitted, also did not hurt; Reagan led the Republican ticket in the state and probably pulled some additional voters into the Goldwater column.

Still smarting from the scare thrown into him by a man he obviously regarded as a newly arrived political upstart, a grumpy Goldwater did not exactly pull out all the stops to charm the media in a press conference conducted after the election. He resented the probing questions of the interviewers; he was tired and he did not feel well. Goldwater retorted sharply to several of his questioners, including an ill-advised comment that he wasn't going to break his back to show up more often for votes in the Senate. After several days, his emotions had cooled and his back probably felt better. He expressed his regrets about his comments.

Two weeks after the election, in a letter to former governor Howard Pyle, Goldwater delineated what an ordeal it had been: "Going through a campaign, hearing your age, your physical ability, your mental ability, your general sanity and honesty questioned day after day on television and radio is enough to drive one up the wall." He continued: "I don't mind telling you that I have come out of this campaign feeling worse than any experience I have ever gone through." Goldwater worried about the ability of one man with a lot of money to alter the course of an election. "That may be the pattern of the future" in Arizona," he said, but "I hope not."

The narrow victory remained an unhappy memory. Writing to Sullivan on June 22, 1981, he called the election "the most discouraging, disheartening thing that ever happened to me." Goldwater did take it personally. "To think that after I have lived all my life in my state, done all I could to help it, I can only win an election by one percent," he noted. One can imagine him shaking his head over changing times. He remained steadfast in his loyalty to and love for Arizona, but Arizona had changed, filled now to overflowing with people who had just arrived, who were not part of the old order, who lacked perspective on individuals and families who had built the state. Even the *Arizona Republic,* "the paper that has always backed me . . . is no longer controlled by the people who feel kindly toward me"; such a turnabout represented "another source of trouble."

In any event, Goldwater did not intend to undergo such a trial again. "I only have another five years to go," he emphasized to Sullivan, "and then I don't care whether *The Republic* goes upstairs, downstairs, or sideways." He worried about Peggy, who "has been terribly sick," and "toyed with the thought that maybe I would be of better help to her by going home and giving up this job." Yet he and she knew he would not do such a thing. There remained work to be done, and a Goldwater did not quit. Regardless of how trying the circumstances, he knew "there is always that old idea drummed into me by the military, you can always take one more step."

That work, the final installment of a thirty-year career in the U.S. Senate, inevitably encompassed moments of satisfaction and frustration. Particularly in regard to the Indians, land and water use, and the military, Goldwater continued to confront issues of ongoing concern. His involvement in these areas is described in the next three chapters. This part of the man's story properly ends here, at the end of his final campaign. He and Peggy both knew no more promises were necessary, to be made or to be broken. He looked forward to saying farewell to Washington and to coming home.

CHAPTER 7

Native Arizonans

THE next two chapters examine in detail two of the central dimensions of Barry Goldwater's life and career. His status as a native Arizonan and his associations with the Native Americans of Arizona mattered a great deal to him, and the link between native and Native is an important one. This subject is considered here. The following chapter analyzes Goldwater's part in building Arizona. His desire to promote economic growth and development of Arizona's resources helped guide his actions. In both realms, Goldwater's perspectives generally mirrored those of other white Arizonans and thus reveal crucial elements of popular sentiments and priorities.

Throughout the twentieth century, most people who resided in Arizona had been born elsewhere. Eight of ten people who lived in Pennsylvania in 1990 were natives of the state. Louisiana ranked second with 79 percent. The other states with 75 percent or more of their residents claiming such status included Iowa, Kentucky, Mississippi, West Virginia, Wisconsin, Alabama, and Michigan. By contrast, a scant 34.2 percent of Arizonans had been born in the state. Only three other states, Nevada (21.8 percent), Florida (30.5 percent), and Alaska (34.0 percent), surpassed Arizona in their percentage of migrants. This significant demographic statistic helps us understand the divided loyalties and mixed emotions about different terrain that have seemed to characterize so many Arizonans. From territorial days Arizona's growth and development have been charted to a significant extent by outsiders: companies headquartered elsewhere or newcomers looking to make a quick profit—and often, a quick getaway. There have been ex-

ceptions: "pioneers" who came, stayed, and grew to appreciate this unique place increasingly on its own terms. Some of
them prospered, and their descendants until recently have
played a disproportionate role in the leadership of the state.
They are people with names such as Babbitt, Udall, and Goldwater. And, to be sure, the character of Arizona has also been
leavened by the arrival of Asian Americans, by the earlier pioneers, Mexican and Hispanic, and by the earliest pioneers, the
Indians.

The Mexican and Hispanic presence historically has been
most significant in the southern third of Arizona. It has not
been unimportant in the Salt River valley, but less so, relatively
speaking, than in the country between Phoenix and the border with Mexico. The Asian American and the African American communities remained small and were primarily situated
in metropolitan Phoenix. "Anglos," to employ a common if
not entirely accurate term, centered early in the center and
near north—in the mining towns such as Prescott, in the Mormon communities of the White Mountains, and along the
Santa Fe railroad. Of course they migrated throughout the
area even in territorial days, and by the early twentieth century their growing presence in the Salt River valley, combined
with the valley's economic promise, signaled the future direction of Arizona's development. The far south retained more
fully its Mexican, Hispanic, and Indian character, and the far
north its Indian heritage.

When one reviews Goldwater's association with the peoples
of Arizona, it is evident that although he invested considerable
attention to the Indians of Arizona—especially the Hopis and
Navajos—he was much less engaged by the Asian American,
African American, and Mexican American communities. He
became acquainted with prominent individuals from these
communities but all in all had relatively little involvement in
the daily concerns of less prosperous persons. In this lack of engagement, he mirrored nearly all Anglos of his economic class
and political persuasion. "Minority" politics remained largely
Democratic through the course of Goldwater's career. The

antigovernment stances of Republicans did not endear them to poorer members of these communities who needed federal or state assistance in regard to their social well-being. Thus, Goldwater knew someone such as Walter Ong, a prominent Chinese American businessman who, like Goldwater, had been voted Phoenix Man of the Year, and supported his right to live in the upscale residential area near Camelback Mountain at a time when many residents protested his arrival. Ong credited Goldwater's comment, "I think we ought to ask Walter if he wants us as neighbors," for removing residual resentment. And Goldwater knew Lincoln Ragsdale, a wealthy African American businessman who shared Goldwater's interest in aviation.

Given the size of the Asian American and African American populations in the state, it is not entirely surprising that Goldwater's contact with these groups appeared limited. Goldwater's reduced involvement with Mexican Americans appears more puzzling, given their more substantial demographic presence in Arizona. However, other than offering praise for Mexican American contributions to military service or similar endeavors, Goldwater does not seem to be consistently occupied with their concerns.

During Goldwater's career, few Latinos registered as Republicans. A native of the mining town of Miami, Bob Reveles graduated from high school shortly before Goldwater first ran for the Senate. After a stint in the air force, Reveles enrolled at Georgetown and found employment in the offices of Stewart and Morris Udall. He recalled the sense of intimidation experienced by the Chicano community during elections of the era, observing that many worried that those who held power in the mining towns monitored who ventured to the polls. Those who ran the towns were Republicans; Mexican Americans who voted Democratic believed that in so doing they might endanger their social or economic status; people worried about losing their job or facing problems with immigration authorities if they became politically active. The resulting anxiety reduced the turnout of Mexican American voters at the polls.

"Most of my friends," Reveles said, "believed that Goldwater was insensitive to Mexican American concerns." The issue of farm workers played a key role in the creation of this image. Another native of Arizona, Cesar Chavez, had tried to organize farm labor and for his troubles had encountered bitter resistance from growers in the state. The United Farm Workers began in 1972 an ultimately unsuccessful drive to recall Goldwater's friend, Governor Jack Williams, who had angered the UFW by signing into law House Bill 2134, which favored agribusiness interests and sought to curtail union efforts to organize farm labor. In addition, other friends were engaged in agricultural concerns which frequently employed migrant Mexican or Mexican American labor. Goldwater's brother, Bob, together with the Arthur Martori family of Scottsdale, had formed Goldmar, Inc., a large development and investment company with real estate and agricultural landholdings. For many years, Harry Rosenzweig also served on its board. Goldmar holdings, such as Arrowhead Ranch in Glendale, employed undocumented workers, who harvested lemons and grapefruit under poor working conditions. When asked by a member of the farm workers' union about this matter in 1972, Barry Goldwater responded: "My brother is over 21 and he knows what he is doing. If you people would get off your butts and go to work he wouldn't have to hire nationals." In 1977 the Arrowhead work force, entirely composed of undocumented workers, went on strike for better pay and improved conditions. The strike brought on both the border patrol and an eventual settlement for a 20 percent pay raise from the seven to eight dollars a day the workers had been receiving, as well as improvements such as shower facilities, drinking water, and bathrooms.

This incident received considerable publicity, and the sensitivities involved with it no doubt encouraged a certain distance between Goldwater and many Mexican Americans in the state. Among the emerging Mexican American middle class as well as those Democrats who admired Goldwater's "independent streak and his patriotism," Reveles suggested, Goldwater certainly won some adherents. This comment suggests, again, that class as well as ethnicity entered into this political equation. Nonetheless, it is not inappropriate to conclude that though Goldwater connected native Anglo Arizonans and Arizona's Native Americans, native Mexican Americans remained largely outside of this recognition of commonality.

Goldwater grew up in a time when few native Arizonans were Anglo. He took pride in being a member of that select minority. And while he embraced all of the state, his ties to the northern portion of it remained the strongest. Given the Goldwater family heritage in Prescott, he looked naturally to the north from Phoenix. And when one recalls the interest of his mother and family friends in exploring the country to the north of Prescott, it is not at all surprising that he quickly became attached to northern Arizona, or what is called the Colorado Plateau. This is red rock country—*Arizona Highways* country—Indian country. For Goldwater, as a native Arizonan, this land and this sky, and the people who called it home, held from earliest memory a particular fascination and appeal. Its residents, primarily Navajos and Hopis, were, of course, also native Arizonans. Whether one spells the word as "native" or, as we frequently do today in referring to Indians, as "Native," there is a certain link between the people who share this identity. The tie exists even though they have often fought, and continue to fight, over lands that Indians have occupied, non-Indians have coveted, and both have claimed. It exists even though they have not always gone to the same church nor always spoken the same language nor always wanted the same things from the land.

In the midst of confrontation and conflict, it has been easy, at times convenient, to overlook some degree of common ground, of overlapping experience. Whether as second- or third-generation Arizonans or, as in the case of the Navajos and Hopis, people who did not necessarily even recognize Arizona as such, there remained a clear sense of family, of evolving or established tradition, of growing or deeply embedded knowledge of a particular territory one called home. Regardless of language, this emotion translated into a kind of attachment to this particular country and an undercurrent of feeling about it. Such individuals could not imagine living anywhere else. Even if others—people who could be classified as newcomers, foreigners, intruders, or simply individuals who had lost their way—did not appreciate, understand, or respect this region, these natives/Natives believed they did. They took great pride and pleasure in their surroundings. How could they not? From their vantage point it was beautiful, and all the more beautiful because it had been invested in by the efforts and dreams of other family members who had gone before.

Such a description fits Barry Goldwater. It fits as well other native Arizonans, and it underscores the kind of bond Goldwater believed he had with Indian Arizonans. Writing a draft of the foreword for a book he had contracted to put together for Macmillan with the working title "Arizona the Beautiful," Goldwater said: "This concerns my love affair with the State of Arizona—a passionate affection which began over half a century ago at my Mother's knee and which will last as long as I am privileged to live on God's earth." He added: "I am convinced that this love will continue to be a deep and abiding and consuming affair until the very last day when I see the sun come up in glory over Camelback Mountain, to spend the day baking and blistering my beloved desert only to die in the lavender and purple and gold of a White Tanque sunset." Goldwater continued, "Perhaps my love and affection is more akin to the feeling of the Indians than it is to the casual regard with which most men hold the place of their youth."

Why? He answered his own question: "I suppose the answer is to be found in the fact that I feel very close to the things of nature in Arizona because they exist in such profusion and such variety and beauty in that section of Arizona." Goldwater noted that for the Hopis, "their feeling for their home ground is intertwined with many of their religious beliefs." And the Navajos had "their sacred mountains and believe these mountains are the residing places of their Gods." For Goldwater, these two Indian nations represented the Indians of Arizona. Navajo and Hopi country came to symbolize "Indian country."

On the occasion of his presentation of his kachina "doll" collection to the Heard Museum in 1969, Goldwater mentioned another significant connection between himself and this area. He spoke of his traveling to the Hopi mesas as a child as being "in a vague, symbolic way for me . . . almost like a return to an ancestral homeland." He observed:

> Streams heading in Tusayan washes flow out from Black Mesa, which is Hopi country, onto the barren northern plateau, eventually reaching the Little Colorado River, which then joins its mother stream, the Colorado. Lower down on the Colorado, at La Paz and Ehrenberg, my grandfather, Big Mike Goldwater, had established his first stores in Arizona. Somehow I have always felt a close association with the Colorado and its drainage basin within my native state. . . . This feeling of kinship with the Colorado River country played a significant role in interesting me in the people and artifacts of Black Mesa.

In reminiscences he penned in April 1940 for the Arizona Pioneers Historical Society, Goldwater recalled: "My first trip to the Indian country was in 1918, with the Kingsburys of Tempe, Reardons of Flagstaff, and Rink Kibbey of Phoenix. I recall we got many valuable pieces of turquoise for items such as razor blades, tooth paste, and etc." He observed, "This is a far cry from today, when the Indians are half-spoiled by too many white people visiting the reservation." Later, he placed the date at 1916. At an early age, then, Goldwater was introduced to this world by, among others, an architect named John Rinker Kibbey, who traveled specifically to Oraibi to purchase Hopi art. The son of a businessman, Goldwater even as a child recognized a bargain when he spied one. He watched Kibbey purchase a Mudhead kachina nearly two feet high for about three dollars. Goldwater credited Kibbey with creating through their friendship "one of the warmest chapters of my boyhood." Over the years, Kibbey acquired a great many kachinas, and he thus "instilled and nurtured" Goldwater's interest in such collecting. Kachinas were fashioned by Hopi carvers to replicate not only the spirit beings who appear from the underworld, but also their clowns and their *koyemsi* (Mudheads), beings who serve as clowns as well as undertake other responsibilities.

In a variety of Hopi ceremonies, Hopi men impersonate the kachinas. In their masked impersonations of both male and female beings they carry out important responsibilities in helping the ceremonies achieve their desired goals. A kachina "doll," or, in the Hopi language, *kachin tihu,* is a miniature of this figure, carved from cottonwood root and painted. Originally dancers in the Hopi ceremonies presented these figures as presents to children, who in turn learned from them about the many different kachinas. As the tourist trade grew in the Southwest in the twentieth century, a market developed for these miniatures, and some Hopi carvers began to create additional dolls to meet that demand.

Therein, of course, resided difficult questions. Should, in fact, such a demand be met? A kachina was not a pot, and although the new money would be welcome, would not these outsiders inevitably intrude on Hopi life? Were there some kachinas whose sacred qualities should prohibit them from being replicated and sold for commercial purposes? Could the kachinas remain vital and effective in the ceremonies even while their likenesses were being peddled to foreigners? The future revealed that for most Hopis the answers to all of these questions were in the affirmative.

The impact of white patrons upon Native American art encompassed all of the Indian communities of the Southwest. The coming of the railroad and the rise of tourism encouraged revivals of ancient designs and the development of new patterns. But for the Hopis, among the most conservative and isolated Indian peoples of the region, the questions surrounding kachinas especially reflected larger quandaries the new century had brought in the form of schools, Christian churches, government agents, and other innovations the people had not sought but with which and whom they now had to contend.

Even as federal emissaries and Christian missionaries sought, in the unconsciously ironic words of one commissioner of Indian affairs, to make Indians in the United States "at home in America," even as they sought to change the languages the Hopis, the Navajos, and other Indian groups spoke, the gods they worshiped, the houses they constructed, the games they played, and the values they shared, many such intruders did not see all Indians as alike. As they became even slightly more acquainted with these communities, as they did about everything else, the newcomers formed opinions about the different people they encountered. And as one would suspect, they tended to be more favorably disposed to the individuals and the groups who seemed most like themselves.

Thus the Hopis, who lived in compact villages, carried out successful farming rather against the odds in a harsh environment, were clearly devout (even if, to the Christians, the nature of their devotion appeared misdirected), and had been in place on and near the three mesas which dominated the landscape of their home country, generally gained a positive image among such onlookers. The Hopis were perceived as peaceful. How could one not admire such a religious, agrarian, settled, well-mannered community which could well be said to reflect virtues and qualities the Anglo-American experience itself had taught one to respect?

The foil to the Hopis came in the Athapaskan Indians who had migrated into the Southwest. To Anglo eyes, these come-latelies had proven themselves to be aggressive, at times militant. They had fought against the Mexicans, the Hispanics, and the Anglo-Americans, and it appeared they had always initiated conflict and war against more sedentary Indian communities. These linguistically related people were the Apaches and the Navajos. Their leaders—Geronimo, Cochise, Manuelito—earned the wrath of the armies and the "settlers" who sought to contain and corral them. General James Carleton had masterminded his own civil war in the 1860s against the Navajos, driving many of them to incarceration on a reservation hundreds of miles eastward at the Bosque Redondo near Fort

Sumner in east central New Mexico. Such imprisonment, Carleton proclaimed, had to occur. Only "away from the haunts and hills and hiding places of their country," he argued, could their children be schooled, could they learn "the art of peace" and "the truths of Christianity." Carleton pledged to inculcate new habits, new ideas, new modes of life. "In the future," he concluded, peace "must rest on the basis that they move onto these lands and like the Pueblos become an agricultural people and cease to be nomads."

On one level, Carleton's experiment failed. The Navajos signed a peace treaty at Fort Sumner in 1868 and successfully negotiated to return to a new reservation established in a portion of their old home country. And yet on another level, Carleton was not entirely off the mark. If there ever were a people willing to consider and, occasionally, incorporate new habits, new ideas, and new modes of life, it would be the Navajos. If they had arrived perhaps five hundreds years before the treaty, then they had adapted well to their new surroundings. Over the course of centuries it did not seem to matter whether they learned weaving and the raising of corn from the Pueblo communities or brought such knowledge with them any more than it mattered whether they had borrowed elements from Pueblo stories to explain certain dimensions of their southwestern origins. They incorporated into their world the sheep, the goats, the cattle, and the horses the Spaniards introduced, wrapped them in their own tales, and gave them special cultural sanction and significance. Probably a relatively small group before the mid-1500s, the Navajos took full advantage of the Spanish arrival. They used more land, controlled more territory, even welcomed Puebloan refugees into their midst and over time made them Navajos. Well before the Anglo-Americans arrived in Arizona, they had moved into country previously used by the Hopis, who fanned out from their mesa settlements to employ the resources found in lands some distance from their villages. Far less nomadic and more sedentary than pictured, the Navajos, too, developed deep loyalties to lands they knew.

One could certainly suggest that if the Anglo-Americans could choose a people more than a little like themselves, that would be the Navajos. They expanded to the west; they learned from other nations; they grew in stature and authority and ambition as the centuries progressed. They were mobile (although less so than imagined), adventurous, curious, experimental. They liked a good joke. They loved to gamble, to sing, to dance, and to tell a good story. In sum, they embodied qualities to be found in other American pioneers.

Nonetheless, the die had been cast by Carleton's day. The Hopis were the model Indians: peaceful, settled, polite. The Navajos were perceived as quite the opposite: marauding, nomadic, disrespectful. The Hopis were a small group; the Navajos always seemed to be gaining in population. The Hopis had been there; the Navajos had just arrived. In their claims to country, the Hopis fit the doctrine of water appropriation adopted in the West: first in time, first in right. Barry Goldwater inherited a version of this vision, and his experiences through the years did not cause him to alter fundamentally his perspective. This is not to suggest that Goldwater saw the Navajos in as harsh a light as Carleton, but rather to argue that the foundation for his own perception had its roots in the perceptions of earlier Anglo-American migrants to the Southwest. Unlike Carleton, Goldwater liked the Navajos and did not begrudge them a place in his native state. He simply gave the Hopis a more elevated status, as people who had come first. The same kind of conclusion guided his interest in the Zunis, a Pueblo people whose village is situated in New Mexico just beyond the Arizona–New Mexico border but who had a long-standing claim to a particular site in Arizona itself. Goldwater's own sense of priority influenced his judgments in disputes that eventually erupted over Hopi, Navajo, Zuni, and other Indian land claims. In the U.S. Senate, Goldwater's views on such matters were very important because of his stature in that body as an authority on Indian affairs. For example, in 1970 Goldwater helped sway undecided senators to support a bill that returned Blue Lake to Taos Pueblo. Blue Lake was a sacred site for that community and, nationally, a symbol of Indian cultural preservation.

Goldwater extended his own involvement in Indian affairs through a variety of activities and actions. This association assumed a deep personal significance. In his autobiography he ventured that he had "probably spent more time with Arizona's Indians than any other white man" and asserted, "They'll always be my brothers and sisters." His participation in the Smoki, his part ownership of the Rainbow Lodge, his purchase of Hopi kachina dolls, and his role in the Zuni effort to obtain "Zuni Heaven" merit exploration, for they were important not only in furthering Goldwater's involvement in Indian country but also in establishing his own reputation as an authority on Native history and culture.

Goldwater's association with the Smoki is linked to his ties with the town of Prescott. The Smoki (pronounced smoke-eye) were not Indians at all, but whites imitating Indians. In 1921 the Prescott Frontier Days Association needed money. Prescott citizens created a one-day "Way Out West" celebration to raise funds. Included in the day was a kind of mock Snake Dance, performed with little seriousness or respect. Rosemary Tumber, who had resided at Hopi, suggested the idea. She and the well-known local painter Kate Cory concocted the dance and instructed the dancers. Tumber even led the dance of the all-male contingent when the men proved hesitant when the time came for their performance. The following year, the name Smoki dance was applied to the "Indian" portion of the program, with "Smoki" inspired by the name "Moqui" then commonly applied to the Hopis. Mimicking the Wild West shows of the day, the program included "Indians" attacking white pioneers en route to the West.

After the initial two years, the group from Prescott became generally persuaded that if future rituals were to be conducted, the members would have to become far more serious in their approach. They formed the Smoki People, with twenty-six individuals in the ranks, including three attorneys, a doctor, a dentist, the editor of the *Prescott Journal-Miner*,

two ranchers, and the local mortician among the more prominent enlistees. Others worked for businesses in the town.
After the initial membership had been set, the Smoki became
a self-perpetuating organization, with new members brought
in only by invitation.

Although the Smoki were all men, and indeed functioned
not unlike various male civic organizations well established in
Prescott to which individual Smoki already belonged, women
played a central role in shaping the group. In addition to
Tumber and Cory, Sharlot Hall and Grace Sparkes helped develop and promote the fledgling enterprise. Both residents of
Prescott, Hall and Sparkes saw in the Smoki a chance to promote the town and draw tourists to the area as well as an opportunity to display some of their own literary abilities. Thus
in 1922, Hall authored "The Story of the Smoki People," in
which she fashioned a kind of creation story patterned obviously after Hopi oral traditions. The secretary of the Yavapai
County Chamber of Commerce, Sparkes tirelessly promoted
the color and mystery of the evolving spectacle. She churned
out endless press releases, which paid homage to a "vanished"
Indian past and the vitality of the white present.

As the years passed, the Smoki built their own "pueblo," situated on their own "mesa," and the members became, by their
own account, increasingly fascinated by what they had initiated. The list of Native dances performed by the group seemed
to grow annually. The Smoki used Bureau of American Ethnology accounts and other sources to research what they performed. They insisted they meant to honor the Indians they
emulated. Very much in the tradition of Edward Curtis, who
photographed Indians he assumed would disappear, and of
anthropological museums which collected Indian artifacts because their officials believed Indian communities soon would
evaporate, the Smoki saw themselves as preserving rituals that
might vanish and that, in any event, were beyond the view of
the Anglo-American tourist. They bristled at the criticism
which soon came in from the outside, questioning the mo-
tives and practices of the Smoki gathering, which labeled itself

by the end of the 1920s as "the premier Indian Pageant of
America." As early as 1924, for example, the *Los Angeles Times*
called the ritual "a moronic attempt to be funny . . . a thor-
oughly offensive, objectionable and indefensible exhibition of
bad taste." A decade later, Commissioner of Indian Affairs
John Collier suggested the performances were a travesty. The
Yavapai County Chamber of Commerce countered Collier by
contending that the group sought to dramatize "in all rever-
ence, the traditions, ceremonies and chants of the American
Indians in a form that would appeal to the white man's mode
of thought." In a letter of August 3, 1934, the chamber also
noted: "If in their performances The Smoki People are able to
create in the hearts of their spectators an interest in the rites
of, and a respect for the American Indian, they feel that they
have been well paid for the many weeks of practice, and that
they are fulfilling their obligation as members of Smoki. This
obligation is as solemn and binding, and the privilege of
membership in Smoki is held as sacred as is that of any fraternal society that is known to the civilized world."

Barry Goldwater's involvement in the Smoki reflected his
interest in Indian life, his association with Prescott, his status
as a businessman, his commitment to tourism, and his general
support of fraternal organizations. Invited to join the Smoki in
1941, Goldwater accepted and received the four tattoo marks
each member bears on the side of his left hand. He often participated in his early years in the group as a dancer and later
served as a narrator and benefactor. On one occasion, when
still able to dance with the group, he flew from Phoenix to
Prescott three or four evenings a week for rehearsals. Practicing in the backyard of his home on Manor Drive, as the
Phoenix Gazette reported in 1954, he gained local notoriety for
"stomping noisily in his yard, leading neighbors to the fear he
was wrecking his home with a sledge." During his presidential
campaign in 1964 he received an unusual honor from the
Smoki by being named an honorary chief, "Flying Eagle,"
and being recognized in July 1964 through a stomp and chant
normally reserved for a new chief of the association. "We

know," said "Chief Hairlip," a charter member, "that the moccasins of Smoki braves carry them a long way from Smoki Mesa, sometimes to the greatest mesa we have which is in the center and heart of our country." Although his Senate duties often prevented him from taking part in the Smoki rituals, Goldwater remained with them in spirit, writing to express his regrets, as he did in 1969 to Budge Ruffner: "I am broken hearted that I was not able to be at Smoki this year, but we've been in debate on the floor for six weeks."

Eventually, the Smoki could not withstand changing times. During the 1960s and 1970s, Indians renewed their public criticisms of the Smoki replications of ceremonial rituals. From Prescott itself more than one dissenting voice could be heard. Jim Hills chastised the Smoki for their assumptions, which he labeled "absurd, incredibly presumptuous, and in some cases, downright sacrilegious." He came up with his own modest suggestion that "a group of entrepreneuring Indians get together and put on their own pageant depicting and perpetuating the ceremonies, both secular and religious, of the white business man." Perhaps they could be called the Whiti People. Hills waxed enthusiastic about the possibilities of substituting attache cases for gourd rattles and offering ceremonies relating to annexation, city parking, industry enticement, and water prices. When Maggie Wilson saw fit to include Hills's ideas, even without endorsing them, in her widely read column, "Maggie Wilson's Album," in the April 11, 1976, *Arizona Republic*, one could perhaps see the handwriting on the wall. Although the Smoki again counterattacked, times had changed, and it became increasingly clear in the 1980s that the performances would have to be curtailed. The Smoki let go with great reluctance, given the decades members had devoted to the association, but finally halted this dimension of their activities. Although the Smoki museum still exists in Prescott today, the annual performance is now only a memory.

Goldwater's membership in the Smoki is more than an odd footnote to his life and career. His association with the group underscored his early fascination with Indian cultures. It also

Barry Goldwater, Smoki. Barry Goldwater Photograph Collection, courtesy of the Arizona Historical Foundation

symbolized his loyalty to Prescott and to old friends such as Budge Ruffner and Gail Gardner over the decades. It indicated the kind of bridge he and other old-time white Arizonans saw between native and Native, the kind of kinship they felt with earlier residents of the region, particularly the Hopis. And it emphasized the distance Indians and others have traveled in the course of Goldwater's life—from a time when many whites assumed Indians were vanishing and when Indian peoples and their lands were seen as removed and distant, to a time when Indian nations are clearly here to stay, but when their peoples are having to confront, to varying degrees, the same illnesses, social disruptions, and associated problems as are other southwesterners. From today's vantage point the Smoki may be an easy target for ridicule, and the argument can surely be made, as the *Los Angeles Times*'s piece in 1924 illustrated it could always be made, that the whole existence of the Smoki smacked of cultural arrogance and insensitivity. It may be more useful to analyze the Smoki less in terms of arrogance and more in terms of a kind of romanticism. In attempting to re-create the rituals, Smoki such as Goldwater to some degree idealized the Indians. Goldwater often spoke of the Indians in lofty terms— as more moral, more devout, more respectful of tradition. That was certainly how he wanted to see the Native peoples of Arizona—and being a Smoki testified to that desire.

Goldwater's photographs of Indians also underlined such traits. His subjects are usually serious, dressed in "traditional" garb, timeless in their surroundings. As discussed previously, the photographs for which Goldwater is best known were taken, in fact, during an era of overwhelming economic, social, and cultural change: the 1930s and 1940s. The impact of those changes would alter customary forms of life and behavior. Indians after World War II became more and more involved in the wage work economy and began moving in greater numbers to off-reservation towns and cities as well as towns on the larger reservations. Better roads and cars and trucks broke down the old insularity; a higher percentage of children spent more years in school. These changes affected

attitudes and attire. Near century's end, Goldwater was not
the only old-timer to look back on all the changes with mixed
emotions. He did not begrudge improved living conditions,
for example, but he liked the old-style homes and the life that
went with them. Speaking of a bygone era, he said, "I miss it
and I don't miss it." But he acknowledged in 1995, "I liked the
Navajo reservation in the 1920s and 1930s when the Indians
looked like Indians. I took most of my photographs at that
time. I loved the hogans and the trading posts."

Goldwater continued to explore Indian country when the
war came to an end. His plane offered him prompt entree into
the more distant reaches of northern Arizona. Recognizing his
fondness for this rugged land and the people who occupied it,
Peggy Goldwater arranged for Barry Goldwater to become a
partner in the Rainbow Lodge on the Navajo reservation.
The lodge had been started by the Richardson family, who
figured prominently over several generations in the operating
of trading posts and other operations in Navajo country. Like
the Babbitts, who also operated a string of such posts, the
Richardson clan enjoyed the benefits of a large family, with
relatives who gained both a personal and financial interest in
doing business in far northern Arizona. Born in Tennessee in
1860, George McAdams ventured west while still in his teens.
By the 1880s he had begun to trade in the western reaches of
Navajo country, at first five miles north of Tuba City, then
at Tonalea, where he constructed the Redlake trading post.
McAdams's sister, Jane McAdams, married John W. Richardson in the mid-1870s. John Richardson's stern hand drove his
children out of the household at an early age. One son, Samuel
Irby (S. I.) Richardson, departed for Arizona and went to
work for George McAdams at the Redlake post in 1896. S. I.
Richardson worked as a trader for more than half a century.
Other members of the McAdams and Richardson clans began
to enter the trade by the turn of the century. S. I. Richardson
built the trading post at Navajo Mountain which later evolved
into Rainbow Lodge, and then Hubert Richardson owned it.
Hubert Richardson also operated the Cameron trading post,

south of Tuba City on the Little Colorado, which became a
major junction for traffic bound for the Grand Canyon.

Goldwater's first encounter with the Richardsons came at
Cameron in the 1920s, when he traveled to the Hopi villages
to observe a snake dance. Later trips into the region acquainted him with other members of the far-flung family.
Those associations over the years no doubt helped pave the way
for an eventual business transaction involving Goldwater's
own part ownership of Rainbow Lodge. The lodge had been
constructed in one of the most beautiful and remote areas of
Navajo land, where some of the Diné had hidden in the 1860s
to avoid the Long Walk to imprisonment at Fort Sumner. Hubert Richardson had explored the area from his post at
Kaibito. He dreamed of using the post at Navajo Mountain as
a base from which tourists could make their way into the region. Following the advice of a local Navajo, John Daw, work
began to expand an old trail which would allow visitors to
connect with existing trails to the west. Daw's position as a
policeman in the area helped stave off violence, for some
Navajos resisted the notion of incursion into their territory.
Once the trail had been completed in 1924, the Richardsons
then engineered a twelve-mile trail from Rainbow Lodge and
blasted out Redbud Pass to create a shortcut to Rainbow Natural Bridge, a magnificent sandstone 309 feet high, 279 feet
across, and 40 feet wide at the top. The trail to Rainbow
Bridge, as Richardson had envisioned, became an instant, natural lure for the slowly burgeoning tourist trade. Although
the post itself made money, however, the expenses of doing
business for the "dudes" who ventured to Rainbow Lodge
offset the profits to be made from them. S. I. soon surrendered
Rainbow Lodge to Hubert, who hired Stanton and Ida Mae
Borum, then brother-in-law W. W. Wilson and his wife, Katherine, to run it. The Wilsons arrived in 1928. During World War
II, Peggy Goldwater purchased a half-interest in the lodge as
a gift to her husband, who was then overseas.

The unexpected present had its own history. The Goldwaters
knew the Wilsons; Bill Wilson, who had worked at one time

for the Babbitts' CO Bar ranch, was related to former Goldwater's store manager Sam Wilson. And the Navajo Mountain
country had become a favorite spot to visit for the Goldwaters
and some of their friends. After the war, Goldwater borrowed
some equipment from the Babbitt brothers in Flagstaff and
built a two-thousand-foot runway near the lodge so he could
make the hour-and-a-quarter to two-hour flight up from
Phoenix. He also invested some money in it, including the installation of a walk-in icebox, a five-kilowatt generator, and
half a dozen one-room cabins, constructed by Del Webb.

Goldwater could never devote a great deal of time to Rainbow Lodge. The Wilsons continued to run the place, and
Goldwater flew up when circumstances allowed him to do so.
Goldwater maneuvered to spend blocks of time at this distinctive destination—a week or two, usually—when he could
climb Navajo Mountain, take tourists by mule down to Rainbow Bridge, even to sleep on top of the bridge, and get acquainted with his new neighbors. With the exception of Lisbeth Eubank, a white woman who taught school for many
years at Navajo Mountain, the neighbors were Navajos. Goldwater relished the opportunity to meet some of the local people. Isabel One Salt named two of her children after the Goldwaters. They would go to ceremonies and other gatherings.
Goldwater loved to hear the singing. But when the food became ready, his wife would take one look at the various parts
of the sheep that had been cooking in the pot and remind her
husband that it was time to go home. Goldwater smiled at the
memory. "You know," he said in 1995, "my wife was not born
on this side of the Mississippi River." The Goldwaters spent
their fifteenth wedding anniversary on top of Navajo Mountain, accompanied by old friends, a cowboy, four bottles of
champagne, a chocolate cake, and the mules.

As has been noted, this country provided the opportunity
for Goldwater to meet Ansel Adams and to take some of his
most memorable photographs. He formed enduring friendships with another fraternity, the men from families who ran
the trading posts and lodges scattered throughout the Navajo

Barry Goldwater and Billy Wilson with unidentified Navajos on the landing strip at Rainbow Lodge, ca. 1947–1948. Photograph by Herb McLoughlin. Barry Goldwater Photograph Collection, courtesy of the Arizona Historical Foundation

domain. During this generation, the traders had great power within their little realms, and the Navajos who traded at a particular post had few, if any, options where to buy, sell, or trade. In remote places such as Navajo Mountain, time almost seemed suspended during Goldwater's tenure. The local residents were particularly "traditional": clothing, weaving, housing, and language remained constant. There was not even a full-time Christian missionary who lived in the community, an unusual state of affairs by the 1940s. The Navajos Goldwater encountered tended to be friendly and yet distant, willing to offer certain forms of hospitality to the occasional white man who had somehow wandered into their world.

Goldwater flew supplies to Navajos stranded by the terrible blizzards of the late 1940s and tried to find ways to reciprocate for the hospitality he received. The lodge itself was never

profitable; in his best year associated with the operation Goldwater "lost only $1,500." But it offered a retreat; "It was heaven
to have a place like that to go to where there wasn't even a tele-
phone and to just get away from everyone." In 1951, however,
a fire broke out at Rainbow Lodge, and the building quickly
erupted in flames and was destroyed. The Wilsons almost lost
their lives in the blaze. Goldwater and Wilson chose not to re-
build the lodge. Goldwater maintained an interest in the property, with Myles Headrick operating a trading post at the site
beginning in 1958, but surrendered all interest in 1965. The fire
effectively had ended any close association he had with the
place. It had been a special time for Goldwater, and more than
forty years later he still regretted the event that ended a certain
stage of his relationship with the Navajos of that area. By 1951,
however, he had his eyes set on the race for the U.S. Senate.
Winning the election removed him from Arizona; what time
he could eke out for his native state had to be reserved almost
entirely for family and friends in metropolitan Phoenix. He
continued to return almost every year to Monument Valley, a
site he had first visited in 1928 and of which he was particularly fond, but that fondness revolved more around place than
people. His later association with the Navajos inevitably became more complicated and, ultimately, less happy.

   Goldwater's association with the Hopis, begun early in his
life, continued to be sparked by his interest in collecting kachinas. After World War II he purchased the extensive collection
of Rink Kibbey, who had suffered economic reversals and
wished to divest himself of the approximately 250 kachinas he
had acquired. Goldwater offered him all he had in his savings
account—twelve hundred dollars—and Kibbey accepted. After
placing some of the kachinas on display at the Goldwater's
store in Phoenix's Park Central Mall, Goldwater eventually donated his collection, now numbering 437, to the Heard Museum of Phoenix in 1968.

   Goldwater and Kibbey acquired the vast majority of the
kachinas at a time, in the words of Barton Wright, "when Arizona was truly Arizona." The leading non-Hopi authority on

Monument Valley. Photograph by Barry Goldwater. Barry Goldwater Photograph Collection, courtesy of the Arizona Historical Foundation

kachinas, Wright stated that Goldwater through the years became acquainted with many Hopis and purchased kachinas at modest prices, often a dollar for each inch of the kachina's height. The generous Hopis sometimes did not even ask for any money at all. Goldwater remembered: "In those days you could enter a Hopi home and if the family liked you and you admired a kachina that was in the household hanging on the wall or in the possession of one of the children, the man and head of the household would say, 'Take it! Take it! We can make some more.'"

Over time Goldwater became more knowledgeable about
the kachinas, and when he formally presented the collection to
the Heard, he spoke informally but at length about the range
and nature of his acquisitions. According to Wright, the Hopis
may also have not been beyond having a little fun with Goldwater. One of the first kachinas Goldwater collected was a
large Mudhead. This clown figure normally has a round, ball-
like object carved on top of his head. Wright took a long look
at this particular Mudhead and noticed something unusual
about the nature of the carving. Closer inspection revealed
the balls on the Mudhead's head to be golf balls. Obviously
the Mudhead had been carved with prior knowledge of Goldwater's fondness for the sport.

Goldwater's interest in kachinas resembled his interest in
photography. Just as Ansel Adams described Goldwater as an
amateur photographer, with no insult intended, Wright explained that Goldwater should not be considered an authority
on kachinas. He never kept formal records about the individual kachinas, and as a result, the Heard Museum has few details about provenance. At the same time, he had a good eye,
money, and access, and the collection is an extremely valuable
one, perhaps especially for its earliest examples, obtained by
Kibbey. At least fifty of the kachinas date from before 1900.

One of the more intriguing dimensions of the Goldwater
collection involves the role of Oswald White Bear Fredericks.
A Hopi who had left home before he reached the age of seven,
Fredericks lived in the East, taught archery, married, and eventually returned to Arizona, where he resided in the Salt River
valley. He and Goldwater became acquainted, enjoyed each
other's company, and played golf together. Although Fredericks learned how to carve, according to Wright his early departure meant he had not been initiated into the kachina cult
and lacked the kind of background to be fully informed about
the meaning and significance of the kachinas. Nonetheless,
Goldwater turned to Fredericks to repair or redo some of the
kachinas, and occasionally Goldwater himself participated in
the process. In addition, Goldwater commissioned Fredericks

to make one hundred of the more obscure and more sacred kachinas to round out the overall collection. Fredericks thus not only altered the appearance of some kachinas but also carved many on his own. In the process he sometimes offered poetic interpretations for the names of the kachinas rather than the names the Hopis themselves employed. Wright clearly believes Fredericks's role to have been ill-advised. His assessment becomes all the more interesting when one recalls Fredericks as the aide to Frank Waters when Waters resided at Hopi in order to obtain information for *The Book of the Hopi*. This volume remains highly controversial to this day among the Hopis for its interpretations and public disclosures about Hopi ceremonial life.

Goldwater's avid, genuine interest in the kachinas introduced him to both traditional leaders as well as younger men who played roles on the tribal council that the Bureau of Indian Affairs had created at Hopi in the 1930s. The Hopi world, centered on the three mesas, encompasses different villages, but in its entirety the population numbered only several thousand before the 1940s. Goldwater gained an understanding of this community and in the process also a special affection for the people themselves. Writing about the building of his collection, Goldwater commented: "In 1964, as I traveled widely in the national political campaign, within a period of months I saw from sky and ground more of our nation than most citizens ever are privileged to see. Nowhere did I see any section of the United States as beautiful or more enchanting than the Hopi country; at no time among the many native groups that I met did I see any that could compare in sincerity or steadfastness with the Hopi."

Earlier associations with the Hopis and the Navajos naturally influenced Goldwater's actions on issues relating to the two tribes during his tenure in the U.S. Senate. Even though Goldwater had enjoyed his relationships with individual Navajos, he had not formed the same kind of bond with the Navajos in general as he had with the Hopis. Navajo country extended into New Mexico and Utah, places where Goldwater

Barry Goldwater with Kachinas, April 9, 1974. Barry Goldwater Photograph Collection, courtesy of the Arizona Historical Foundation

spent relatively little time. Within the vast Navajo reservation in Arizona, Goldwater traveled widely but could not possibly have known the area in the same depth nor forged the kind of friendships he had at Hopi nor focused the same degree of attention on the nature of Navajo history and culture.

When Goldwater was elected to the Senate, he promptly sought action on a long-standing Hopi grievance. The Hopis and the Navajos were being administered through the same area office of the Bureau of Indian Affairs. In his campaign for governor, Howard Pyle, accompanied by Goldwater, had stood on a truck at the airport at Polacca and promised the Hopis that he would work to place them in a separate administrative office. By March 1954, Goldwater was able to write to Pyle that this goal had been achieved: "We have just, as you know, taken the Hopi Reservation from under the domination of the Navajos." Goldwater's sensitivity to Hopi concerns was demonstrated as well in the stance he assumed on the disagreements between the Hopis and Navajos over their overlapping land claims. The problem dated back at least to 1882, when President Chester Alan Arthur signed an executive order establishing a reservation of almost two and one-half million acres "for the use and occupancy of the Moqui and such other Indians as the Secretary may see fit to settle thereon." The Hopis (Moquis) had resided in the affected region for hundreds of years, but their villages occupied only a small portion of the area; more recently Navajos had continued their westward movement into and beyond this territory. Scholars debate the length and depth of their tenure; some hold that Navajos had occupied much of this land for generations before the 1882 order. In any event, by 1901 additions to the Navajo reservation permitted it to completely surround Hopi land.

Within the 1882 reservation, both Hopis and Navajos used the land for sacred and secular purposes. In the New Deal, the Navajos experienced the trauma of the ill-advised federal policy of livestock reduction that struck at the heart of their culture. They also came to realize that in the future their reservation would not expand. By 1943 the lands used exclusively by the Hopis had also become designated as livestock district number six. The Hopis protested against being limited to this portion of the 1882 reservation; the Navajos vowed to protect their occupancy of remaining lands. The Diné resolve had been heightened by the memory, nourished through stories, of the forced relocation to Fort Sumner in the 1860s and the more recent tale of urban relocation in the 1950s. The Navajos who occupied the remainder of the 1882 reservation were among the least acculturated of all in the Navajo Nation. These people generally did not speak English fluently, relied upon subsistence livestock herding, and feared greatly the prospect of being uprooted from lands their families now had occupied usually for several generations or more. Despite the size of the Navajo reservation, its remaining lands had been claimed fully through traditional use rights, and so there remained no available acreage for occupation by any Navajos evicted from the 1882 area.

The Hopis and Navajos disagreed about how to resolve this matter, yet relations between the two peoples had not always been entirely problematic. Individual Hopis and Navajos had traded with each other, teased each other, attended school with each other at Keams Canyon; others had largely or entirely avoided contact with members of the other tribe. Of course, Navajos who resided nearest to the Hopi mesas had far more reason to deal with their neighbors; sometimes these relations were congenial and at times they were charged with disagreement, particularly over use of the land.

In the 1950s, when Goldwater went to Washington, quarreling over boundaries and the tendency of each tribe to impound the others' wandering livestock entered a new stage. Considerable credit for raising the stakes of the issue must go to the attorneys now employed by the Hopis and the Navajos. Before World War II, neither had hired lawyers to represent them, but the advent of the Indian Claims Commission in 1946 and the growing number of matters facing the tribal councils encouraged the Hopis to hire John Boyden, a Salt Lake City attorney, and the Navajos to hire Norman Littell, who hailed from Washington, D.C. Boyden's and Littell's words and actions escalated the argument. Congressional representatives from Arizona, including Goldwater, also started to become increasingly enmeshed in this matter.

Public Law No. 85-247, passed by Congress in 1958, permitted a lawsuit to decide the rights in the area. Through *Healing* v. *Jones* in 1962 the tribes were deemed to have joint and equal interests and subsurface resources, thus establishing the notion of a joint-use area for the portion of the 1882 reservation outside of district number six. Finally, in 1974, Public Law No. 93-531 authorized the District Court of Arizona to divide the joint-use area on an equal basis and established a relocation commission to carry out the process of removing any individuals who could not continue living in particular locations after the partition had been achieved. Neither side applauded the outcome. Many Hopis believed that they had lost half of the land rightfully theirs. The law set the stage for the protracted battle by Navajos residing within the contested territory to avoid being relocated from the lands they occupied and used. Despite a variety of efforts by parties both well-meaning and otherwise to "settle" this dispute, the altercation continued through the end of 1995. By July 1987, 1,185 Navajo families and 14 Hopi families had been forced to move; in the intervening years some Navajos have successfully resisted resettlement, while still others have had to find new homes. This quite complex, tragic, and highly emotional story defies quick or adequate summation here, but Goldwater's role in the altercation was both significant and revealing.

Goldwater sympathized with the Navajo families in the affected area but supported from the beginning the Hopi position, which called for the prompt carrying out of partition and any necessary relocation. As he phrased it in 1976 in a letter to Secretary of the Interior Thomas S. Kleppe: "My feeling has always been that the Hopis are probably 95 per cent right and the Navajos about 5." The Hopis had been there first and thus had first claim. Goldwater pointed to the relative size of the two Indian nations, arguing in a letter to Bess Arviso, a Navajo, in 1973 that it was "wrong for the Navajos because of their gigantic majority to use so much of the joint use lands." He emphasized the differences he perceived, writing, for example, to Ronald Reagan in 1982: "The Hopi Tribe is a poor tribe, a small tribe, while the Navajo tribe is the biggest in the nation, and, by far, the wealthiest."

Goldwater also may have pushed for a timely solution to the land dispute because without some kind of definitive court or legislative decision, as provided in *Healing* v. *Jones,* the resources within the joint-use area could not be developed. In particular, the vast coal reserves on Black Mesa could be mined only after the way had been cleared to seek formal approval from both tribal councils. Following *Healing* v. *Jones,* the councils agreed to a proposal from Peabody Coal to lease the coal over a thirty-five-year period in exchange for a fixed royalty and the promise of jobs for tribal workers. On the Navajo side, council representatives later said they did not understand the kind of environmental damage strip mining would create. The deal stirred up a hornet's nest of environmental protest; one critic in Santa Fe labeled it "like tearing down St. Peter's to get at the marble."

The coal from Black Mesa was either slurried from Black Mesa over 273 miles to the Mohave power plant in Clark County, Nevada, or hauled by a new railroad over 80 miles to the Page, Arizona, power plant. Goldwater, along with other representatives from the Southwest, strongly supported this arrangement. He did so in part because of the needs for electrical power in the growing region and because he believed that Peabody could succeed in its plans to restore the land. On the latter point, Goldwater wrote on December 19, 1972: "It is my feeling that the Mesa will be left in better condition than it was found in, because it will be developed into usable land where it has formerly been nothing but rocks and brush." In addition, Goldwater had long sought to develop such mineral resources on Indian lands because he believed them to be centrally important to reservation economic development. As early as March 16, 1953, Goldwater wrote to Pyle arguing that "one of your first and most important measures should be to unlock the natural resources known to exist on the reservations. . . . In mineral wealth alone there is enough in reserve within the reservation boundaries to make our so-called Indian problem simple enough."

Goldwater's position on the land dispute ultimately cost him dearly in Navajo country. He ruefully remarked in a letter in 1977 that "I think I'm the oldest and probably the best friend they ever had but politically they rather hate my insides." Invited in 1978 to visit Big Mountain, a much publicized community within the contested area, he attempted to speak in a conciliatory manner to local residents and other Navajo onlookers. Goldwater was especially concerned about the Big Mountain Navajos because he believed they had, in fact, been on their lands longer than other Navajos had been on the Navajo reservation. However, Goldwater was skewered by many for not only his basic stance on the controversy but also, as they perceived it, not being fully informed on current developments. Goldwater apparently grew angry at the implied and more direct criticism, and left abruptly. According to a *Navajo Times* reporter at the scene, he retorted as he departed, "I've lived here fifty years, and I probably know this land better than most of these Navajos here today do."

Goldwater's anger may be traced to at least three causes. He became irritated when people questioned his authority on Indian matters, and he truly wanted to reduce the amount of suffering that attended impending relocation. His reaction also probably could have stemmed from believing that he had been set up. Who had orchestrated this confrontation? Who had encouraged Navajos such as Daniel Peaches to show up and give incendiary speeches? Goldwater later wrote to Caleb Johnson, a Hopi, that "the people who were sent there, presumably by the Navajo government, seemed to know so little about the framing of that law and the consequences of the law that I didn't want to get into it too deeply." By the Navajo government, he meant Peter MacDonald, then tribal council chairman. Animosity between Goldwater and MacDonald poisoned relations between the Congress and the Navajos and affected Goldwater's standing among the Diné.

MacDonald had grown up on the Navajo Nation, graduated from the University of Oklahoma with a degree in electrical engineering, and worked for Hughes Aircraft in the Los Angeles area before returning in 1963 to work for the tribal government. In 1965 he was appointed to head the newly established Office of Navajo Economic Opportunity (ONEO). This position catapulted him to political prominence, and by 1970 he had gained election as chairman, a post he held for three terms until his defeat in 1982 by Peterson Zah. MacDonald used the unresolved land dispute as a key issue in 1986 in a successful bid to return to the chairmanship. However, charges of corruption forced him from office, and conviction on these charges sent him to prison.

Although MacDonald voted for Goldwater in 1964 and remained in the Republican ranks until the early 1970s, his post as ONEO director may have encouraged a cooling of the relationship between the two men before their more publicized split during the 1972 presidential campaign. The ONEO-funded legal services program on the Navajo reservation, known colloquially as DNA (Dinébe' iina Nahiilna Be Agaditahe, or "Lawyers Who Contribute to the Economic Revitalization of the People"), came under the ONEO administration. MacDonald's predecessor as tribal chairman, Raymond Nakai, despised DNA, in part because of the flamboyant personality of its first director, Theodore Mitchell, and in part because it became increasingly apparent that the operation constituted part of MacDonald's growing political base. Goldwater acknowledged the need for some kind of legal assistance for individual Navajos but detested the zeal with which the young, white, often Ivy League–trained attorneys attacked individuals and institutions they perceived to stand in the way of meaningful social change. In particular, Goldwater was extremely unhappy with DNA's constant barrage against the traders on the reservation, who had already declined markedly in number and power. The United Indian

Traders Association, for example, in February 1970 compared DNA attorneys to "babies with a power drill," charging them with "playing tax-supported fun-and-games in creating discord and distrust and inflaming old and outworn suspicions." Goldwater agreed, stating in a letter written at that time: "It is true that young, inexperienced lawyers have infested the Navajo Reservation, and it is also true that they had sent back a number of stories relative to Indian traders. I happen to have held a trader's license for many years and I would be the last one to say that we didn't have one or two obnoxious ones, but, on the whole, these men were fair and honest and dedicated to helping the Navajo."

Goldwater informed OEO head Donald Rumsfeld in October 1969 that he was "going to continue to complain and use every other source at my command to stop some of the things going on at DNA." He called the year's allocation to DNA "ridiculous." That same month he took to the floor of Congress to complain publicly about both DNA's independence from tribal government and its actions. Goldwater thus saw DNA as causing instead of solving problems. By contrast, before he became chairman MacDonald saw DNA as a necessary means to correct long-standing problems, including some of the business dealings of many traders and bordertown merchants.

MacDonald's strong defense of Navajo self-determination launched him on an assertive campaign that continually challenged non-Indian interests in the Navajo area. He was also fiercely protective of the traditional Navajos in the joint-use area as well as politically indebted to voters in the region who had played a significant role in his victory over Nakai. Frustrated at Goldwater's unwillingness to deviate from his support of the Hopi position on the land dispute, MacDonald concluded he had no choice but to switch party allegiance. In 1972 and 1974 he supported Democrats at the local and state level and even backed George McGovern against Richard Nixon. Thanks in part to MacDonald's efforts, Navajo voters cast their ballots overwhelmingly for Democrat Raul Castro in the Arizona governor's race in 1974; in a tight contest, those votes provided the margin Castro needed to win over incumbent governor Jack Williams, Goldwater's old friend. And in a stunning reversal of their past voting behavior, Navajos gave an almost identical endorsement of Jonathan Marshall's candidacy against Goldwater. In Navajo County, for example, Navajo voters on the reservation voted for Castro 3,225 to 476 and for Marshall 3,112 to 468. On the other hand, Hopi voters preferred Goldwater by 171 to 37. Navajo County included voters most directly involved in the land dispute issue, but Goldwater fared little better in Coconino and Apache counties. The rejection rankled; Goldwater charged that a political alliance MacDonald had made with the AFL-CIO had bought off Navajo voters by promising them money for mileage to get to the polls and beer coupons if they voted for Democrats. MacDonald responded in part by noting, without needing to name any names, that certain politicians had taken the Navajo vote for granted and had expressed appreciation for the Navajo way of life as long as Navajos had been content to play the centerfold role for *Arizona Highways.*

After Goldwater and MacDonald had been reelected in 1974, their relationship continued to deteriorate. In February 1976, Goldwater demanded a General Accounting Office audit of Navajo tribal governmental expenditures, and a scandal was soon revealed within the administration of the Navajo Housing Authority. Although MacDonald was not found guilty of impropriety, rumors continued to swirl about him. A federal grand jury in Phoenix in February 1977 indicted him on charges of mail fraud, obtaining money by false pretenses, and filling out a fraudulent income tax return. MacDonald blamed one person for his problems: "Of course Goldwater is behind these indictments. He has tried several times before to embarrass me and the tribe and this has been another attempt." At the trial, a deadlocked jury refused to convict the chairman.

Rather like two rams locked in combat, the two men continued to fight, with the echoes of the clash reverberating through the remainder of their respective terms in office. In the wake of the indictment, MacDonald announced he al-

ready looked forward to the 1980 election, when Navajo votes
would help defeat Goldwater in his bid for reelection. Goldwater saw MacDonald as something of an upstart in Navajo
political affairs; in 1976 he alleged, "I've probably spent more
time on the reservation than Peter MacDonald." And he
blamed MacDonald for the failure to resolve the land dispute.
Writing to Duke Tully, publisher of the *Arizona Republic*, on
July 16, 1982, Goldwater said: "MacDonald's testimony before
our hearings last week was as totally wrong and false as testimony can be and I think that unless we begin to put the political muscle on him, which he understands, we are going to
see the Tribal Chairman's feet dragging the dust on this thing
for year after year after year." On the same day, Goldwater reiterated his position in a letter to Bruce Babbitt, charging that
MacDonald "alone is responsible for the plight of hundreds of
Navajos who might have to be moved and he is also responsible for the extreme worry of ranchers who live around the pe-
riphery of the reservation as to what his political mischief
might do to their businesses." Things had not improved in his
final year in the Senate. Goldwater sent a note to his aide,
Twinkle Thompson, in April 1986 complaining that MacDonald had expressed "some of the meanest, unkind, untrue
things about me that have ever been said."

To the very end of his time in Washington, Goldwater
hoped against hope that somehow persons of good will could
find a way to resolve the land dispute with the least possible
harm to the fewest number of people. Despite those who, in
his judgment, had obstructed progress in the negotiations—
people such as MacDonald and South Dakota senator James
Abourezk, a man whom Goldwater once described in a letter
to Hopi chairman Ivan Sidney as a person "who thought he
knew something about Indians"—he persisted in his belief
that it could be worked out. When Peterson Zah defeated
MacDonald in 1982, Goldwater's hopes rose, for Zah and Sidney had gone to school together, and Zah hailed from Low
Mountain, a community in the heart of the contested landscape. Zah and Sidney remained on good terms, but their as-

sociation did not allow them to forge a solution to the issue.
As he prepared to leave Washington, Goldwater held fast to his
judgment, as he wrote to Oneita Tootsie of Keams Canyon in
November 1986: "It is Hopi land historically and legally and
the Hopi Tribe is entitled to occupy it."

The passage of time, the removal of both Goldwater and
MacDonald from political power, and, in a perverse tribute to
the enduring nature of the land dispute, the fact the conflict
still has not concluded contributed slowly to some degree of
reconciliation between Goldwater and the Navajos. In 1988 the
Navajos agreed to a long-cherished wish of the senator's that
an arch on the reservation be named in honor of Peggy Goldwater. The sandstone arch near Navajo Mountain had been
spotted by Goldwater in the old days in a locale where he and
his wife had spent some happy times. Peter MacDonald had
regained the chairmanship at that point, but even he did not
stand in the way of calling the site Margaret Arch. The symbolic gesture by the tribal council, of course, meant a great
deal to Goldwater. He called it "one of the great thrills of my
life." Writing to thank one of the persons who had assisted in
gaining approval for the name, he mused: "You know, Peter
and I got along like a million dollars until I took the side of the
Hopi, and I often wanted to ask him what he would have done
in my position, would he take the side of the gigantic Navajo
Tribe with all their resources or try to help the little Hopi
Tribe who do not have much? I don't know, now that I am out
of politics, I will probably see Peter and I hope we get along.
He does a great job." Later Goldwater numbered among
those who requested a presidential pardon to free MacDonald
from prison. In November of 1996 the sixty-eight-year-old
MacDonald, suffering from diabetes and chronic arthritis,
had served four years of a fourteen-year sentence.

In later generations the Navajos will probably remember
Goldwater with mixed emotions and the Hopis will likely recall him as one who supported their fight against the odds. As
we will see in the next chapter, at Fort McDowell the Yavapais
will not relate entirely positive tales. There can be doubt about

how the Zunis of New Mexico will tell their stories about him. They will say how Goldwater championed their rights to sacred ground in Arizona. The battle over what is often called in English, Zuni Heaven, or, more properly in Zuni, Kolhu/wala:wa, concluded in the closing moments of Goldwater's tenure in the Senate and marked an especially satisfying chapter in his work relating to Native peoples.

As historian E. Richard Hart has explained, the Zunis tried since the 1800s to safeguard their rights to Kolhu/wala:wa, for it is a particularly important sacred site. It is "where all Zunis go after death and where the supernatural Kokko reside under a sacred lake fed by the waters from a precious spring." Every four years Zunis undertake a religious pilgrimage, a distance of more than one hundred miles, to the site "where their religious activities are aimed at bringing peace, order and prosperity not only to the Zunis but also to the entire world." Prayers are offered to bring rain so that crops may grow for the Zunis and their neighbors.

This site is not on the Zuni reservation but in Apache County, Arizona, and the people from Zuni endured looting of Kolhu/wala:wa and the sale of sacred objects from there since anthropologist Frank Hamilton Cushing's intrusion in the late nineteenth century. They attempted in vain to enlist federal help in order to buy the lands around Zuni Heaven. The American Indian Religious Freedom Act of 1978 gave new momentum to their efforts, yet an Arizona rancher, Earl Platt, resisted allowing access to Kolhu/wala:wa. Finally, in 1984, Public Law 98-408 passed Congress, turning over some of the lands to the Zunis and permitting them to purchase others in order for them to be in trust status. In all, the act encompassed almost twelve thousand acres, creating, in effect, a new Zuni reservation in Arizona. Although Platt subsequently fought against providing access to Zuni Heaven, in 1990 the Zunis' ability to follow a traditional path to the site was reaffirmed by the courts.

Late in 1984 the Zunis held an all-day celebration and feast to commemorate their success and to honor Goldwater. He flew in for the occasion, enjoying the accolades, delighting in the goal that had been achieved. Goldwater regarded it as one of the "happiest things" he had accomplished in the Senate, "getting that hallowed property back for the tribe."

According to Hart, who worked for the Zunis throughout this long process, Goldwater's support for the tribe's objectives made the difference. In a letter of August 9, 1995, Hart emphasized that the successful legislation "would not have been possible without Senator Goldwater." He added: "He has a genuine empathy for tribes and a clear understanding of their constitutional rights. So he was a very important advocate for the tribes in general, and Zuni in particular, during his tenure in the Senate. . . . He would listen, quickly synthesize, and come to pragmatic conclusions. Then he would explain what had to be done, and if it was done, what he would do."

"Whatever one's politics," Hart concluded, "when you get to Capitol Hill, you quickly learn that the real test is whether the politician is honest, forthright and will deliver." Some politicians would "equivocate when you ask for their promised response." Goldwater, however, was "direct, honest, and forthright. . . . He always delivered." There is nothing that Richard Hart could have said that would have more pleased Barry Goldwater.

CHAPTER 8

Building Arizona

IN one of the countless interviews conducted during the 1964 presidential campaign, Barry Goldwater tried to explain why Arizona mattered to him, how it had changed and not changed, and the part he had played in its maturation:

> It's home to me—where my family is, where my heart is, where I belong. Very few people my age have had the opportunity of seeing a country transformed the way I've seen Arizona. . . . Once it was wild land and desert and open spaces—and there's still plenty of that. But I've seen this land transformed into productive land, with great industry and great people and great promise of a great future. Take Phoenix. I get the greatest thrill thinking that in a small way I helped it grow, that I had something to do with its growth. And yet I can go home, get away from the city itself and get out where there's plenty of space and sunshine, and great fresh, pure air. I love walking in the desert, especially at night. Out there at night, the stars just saturate the sky. You feel close to God.

Over the course of a long life and career, Goldwater has been directly involved in the process through which Arizona has been altered. Born in territorial Arizona, growing up in a town named Phoenix that certainly could not be mistaken for a city, he contributed his energy and imagination to those of other leaders to help Phoenix and Arizona grow. With growth came prosperity; with development came opportunity. Such remains the conventional wisdom that has nourished the evolution of America's forty-eighth state in the twentieth century.

Arizonans saw many examples of such development. The

world of sports presented some obvious instances in Maricopa County. In late January 1996, Super Bowl XXX took place in Sun Devil Stadium, the current home of both the Arizona State University football team and the much maligned Arizona Cardinals. Earlier in that same month, the site hosted the Fiesta Bowl, where Nebraska crunched Florida to gain the mythical national title in college football. The Winnipeg Jets migrated south to become the Phoenix Coyotes; the franchise shared the new America West Arena with the Phoenix Suns of the National Basketball Association. An expansion major league baseball team, the Arizona Diamondbacks, anticipated opening play in 1998. The arena and the forthcoming Bank One Ballpark (the latter known as "BOB" to those who couldn't stomach its formal name) combined with the Arizona Center, Symphony Hall, the Herberger Theater, an impressive new city library designed by the innovative architect Will Bruder, and other establishments to create what had been deemed impossible: life in downtown Phoenix after 5 P.M. At the same time, new home construction kept prompting more life at all hours north of Bell Road and in other corners of the sprawling metropolis.

Nor were signs of growth limited to Phoenix. The once sleepy little Mormon community of Mesa now boasted over three hundred thousand citizens. Scottsdale continued its inexorable march northward toward the previously remote communities of Carefree and Cave Creek. A generation before, Guadalupe had been separated from metropolitan Phoenix; now it was hard to remember when it had not been surrounded. The residents of Tucson continued an ancient tradition of hurling insults at the colossus to the north of the Gila River, but more objective observers in the self-styled Old Pueblo could observe their own parade of tile roofs, golf courses, and other indices of the contemporary Southwest. Elsewhere in the state, towns such as Flagstaff, Yuma, Sierra Vista, Sedona, Prescott, and Lake Havasu experienced significant development. Retirees and telecommuters did their part to contribute to sprawl. Firms specializing in high technology still found the welcome mat generally out in Arizona. The *Arizona Republic*'s 1996 list of the dozen companies with the largest number of full-time employees, shown in the table below, proved revealing about the driving forces in the contemporary economy.

**Arizona Companies with the Largest
Number of Full-Time Employees**

Rank	Company	Business in Arizona	Full-time Employees	1995 Rank
1	Motorola	Electronics, computers	19,350	1
2	Wal-Mart	Discount stores	7,929	9
3	Allied Signal	Aircraft engines and parts	7,872	2
4	Pinnacle West Capital	Parent of Ariz. Public Service	7,335	3
5	American Express	Travel and financial services	7,200	5
6	Bank of America Arizona	Banking	7,100	10
7	America West Airlines	Airline	6,841	4
8	Bank One Arizona	Banking	6,608	7
9	Honeywell	Electronics, aviation systems	6,575	8
10	Hughes Missile Systems	Missile systems	6,500	6
10	US West	Telecommunications	6,500	11
10	Intel	Semiconductors	6,500	18

Critics in various forms emerged late in the century to protest the path Arizona had been following. Edward Abbey penned trenchant essays bemoaning the choices that had been made by the combined, overlapping forces represented in the civic, business, and political leadership of the state. As Prescott expanded, javelinas organized their own protests about this invasion. New human residents on the outskirts of town had to contend with these animals "trespassing" on and damaging their property. Environmentalist organizations decried the priorities possessed by state legislators, who generally hailed from the private sector and who usually subscribed to the credo that had informed public policy throughout most of Arizona's history.

Some of the manifestations of growth provided tempting targets for these latter-day nay-sayers. As developers fashioned lakes and golf courses, they began to have to contend with skeptics who grumbled about Californication, about the foolishness of luring people to live on Whalers Way in The Lakes district of central Tempe, or about substituting putting greens for saguaros. These critics remained a minority, for newcomers to the state still tended to bring their cultural baggage with them and thus wanted to re-create the well-watered surroundings they had left behind, and most old-timers, including Goldwater, still liked to believe in the beneficent power of science and technology to tame a harsh desert.

Nonetheless, the cultural politics of Arizona have only quite recently arrived at this point of disputation. When Goldwater came to maturity in the 1930s and inaugurated his political career in the 1940s, the prevailing perspective regarding growth and development was of quite another sort. This viewpoint, shared with residents of the other interior western states, held that only through the prompt and thorough use of available natural resources could the state develop its economy, attract new residents, and eventually obtain a more equitable status with older, more established states east of the Mississippi. If westerners today are weary of the condescending attitude of outsiders who assume there is little of value between San Francisco and Chicago except, perhaps, an occasional mountain, then westerners fifty and sixty years ago bridled at the thought of second-class citizenship. The leaders of these states wanted to build for the future, wanted to leave their mark on the land.

They embraced technological change, for it seemed to offer a more expeditious route to advancement. They cherished growth for its own sake, for it appeared to nourish the kind of fledgling urbanism necessary for a state to be taken at least somewhat seriously.

Only long after the wheels of progress had been set in motion did second thoughts surface. Only after patterns of building had been established did doubts emerge. Goldwater himself lived long enough and stayed in one place long enough to experience eventually those second thoughts and doubts. In his own shifting sense of benefits and costs, one sees what Jack Pfister termed a "native's remorse." In this instance, as Pfister explained it, that meant wanting Arizona to prosper but worrying that it was losing the qualities that caused one to fall in love with it in the first place.

The story of building Arizona centers on the story of water. Water was the necessary ingredient for growth. Contrary to popular understanding, that growth was centered for decades in agricultural, not urban, expansion. The social and cultural power of agriculture in the workings of state politics would be reflected long after farming interests began their economic descent.

Roosevelt Dam starts this particular story. Shortly after Barry Goldwater celebrated his second birthday, Roosevelt Dam was completed. There are few definable turning points in the history of a region, but the construction of the dam definitely signaled the start of a new era in the Salt River valley. Regulation of the river's flow, generation of electricity, and the use of the water stored in the lake behind the dam stimulated the local economy. As historian Karen Smith noted, Phoenix and the other towns in the valley may not have had yet a significant railroad connection; they did not have a navigable river, and barring a miracle, they were unlikely to have a harbor other than the one they would later create in their airport. Nevertheless, the assured availability of water made the difference in starting Phoenix on its way to becoming a major American city.

Goldwater learned the lesson in his childhood. Water held the key to the development of Arizona. He always remembered the Phoenix of his childhood—the dirt streets, the absence of sidewalks, the street cars and ice wagons—and he recalled the time with great fondness. However, he knew that without sufficient water the agricultural economy which buoyed the general expansion in the years before World War II simply could not have existed. Water made it possible for the pioneering spirit to be employed. A reliable water supply meant that Phoenix could live up to its name; it could become a new civilization built upon the bedrock of pioneer values brought by its early residents.

To gain a full appreciation of the impact of water, residents of the Salt River valley did not have far to look. Through its aggressive policies, including the usurpation of water from the Owens Valley more than two hundred miles to its north, the greater Los Angeles area had experienced a period of extraordinary growth. And with that growth had indeed come prosperity. If Los Angeles could be a magnet for migrants, if it could attract an array of commercial developers, then why could not Phoenix, even on a much smaller scale, meet with a version of this success?

Where would the water come from and how would it get to the people of Maricopa and Pima counties? Arizonans knew they could tap only one source and that they did not have sole claim on it. The Colorado River represented their only possibility. Nevertheless, the river began well to the north of Arizona and flowed south out of the United States into Mexico. Wyoming, Utah, Colorado, New Mexico, Nevada, and California also had plans for the Colorado; even before the construction of Roosevelt Dam, schemers and dreamers imagined ways to move the water from the great river to destinations of their own choosing. The bickering and fighting over the river obviously symbolized a fight for the future, with California determined to exert its dominance over the region. This struggle had prompted the various states to engineer an agreement in 1922 regarding how much water the upper basin and lower

basin could receive. The framers of the Colorado River compact meant well, but in their division of water they made two
important miscalculations.

First, they overestimated the amount of water in the river itself. Choosing Lee's Ferry, just south of the Arizona-Utah line
as a point of measurement, they figured an average flow and
divided the proceeds. Unfortunately, they based their numbers on a wet cycle, and in time state officials realized that the
water had been allocated beyond the ability of the river actually to provide it. In addition, they could not possibly have
computed the kind of unbelievable growth that would characterize the region and thus accelerate the demands that
would be placed upon a finite supply of water.

And so, almost inevitably, the compact did not prevent ar-
guments, even small wars, between and among the states over
access to the Colorado River. The completion of Hoover Dam
in 1935 and other impending projects suggested to Arizona
governor B. B. Moeur and other Arizonans that California
might well be determined to deny its neighbor to the east its
appropriate share of water from the Colorado. In a move that
thrilled newspaper headline writers, Moeur launched his own
little brigade to defend the rights of Arizona; he ordered Major
F. I. Pomeroy of the 158th Infantry Regiment of the Arizona
National Guard, one sergeant, three privates, and one cook to
safeguard the sacred shores of the state by proceeding without
delay to the river. According to author Marc Reisner, this band
had been instructed specifically to inform Moeur of "any attempt on the part of any person to place any structure on Arizona soil either within the bed of said river or on the shore."

Pomeroy and his men resembled mice trying to roar, but
they proceeded bravely to the town of Parker, obtained a fer-
ryboat—instantaneously establishing the Arizona Navy—and
attempted to power upstream to examine a cable put in the
soil by the Bureau of Reclamation as it prepared to begin work
on Parker Dam. The cable held a barge in place in the river; the
cable also captured the new naval vessel, which became entan-
gled following too close an inspection of the offending entity.

Much to the chagrin of the sailors, they had to be rescued by samaritans from the Los Angeles Department of Water and Power, who just happened to be in the vicinity.

Moeur refused to leave bad enough alone. Seven months later, hearing that the bureau had started to construct a bridge across the river, Moeur declared the Arizona border along the Colorado under martial law and commanded one hundred men to take some machine guns and eighteen trucks and hustle to the front lines. Secretary of the Interior Harold Ickes already had gained the nickname "The Old Curmudgeon," and he no doubt envisioned the outfit as Moeur's Marauders hellbent on causing trouble for one and all. Ickes called a temporary stop to work on the dam and things cooled off. In the end, Moeur made a deal. The bureau proceeded to build Parker Dam, which permitted the Colorado River Aqueduct to siphon more water to the Los Angeles area; Arizona received the Gila Project to bring additional irrigation to southwestern Arizona.

The prevailing dictum governing water in the West is "use or lose it." Arizona leaders feared that without finding means to obtain their fair share of the Colorado, Californians would drain nearly all of the river. Californians pointed out they were constrained by their own laws and a 1944 treaty with Mexico in regard to the river, but California's past actions did not reassure Arizonans. After the close of World War II, the Arizona Interstate Stream Commission began to fight for more water from the river as well as tackle other pressing contemporary concerns. As a member of the commission, Goldwater worked with his colleagues to try to get the Arizona state legislature to pass a groundwater code, a stipulation insisted upon by the federal government before more federal money would be forthcoming for diversions from the river. A twenty-seven-day special session of the legislature ended without a code, for farmers opposed its enactment. In March 1948 the legislature passed what can only be called a watered-down version of the code, with current uses of water not regulated. The battle illustrated the strength of rural interests in the state as well as the difficulty the state would continue to face in limiting employment of water by any sector of the economy.

In regard to the ongoing struggle with California over the Colorado, Goldwater's views reflected those of others in Arizona, both in regard to his state's claim and the general principle that the water from the river should be put to utilitarian purposes. "God put that river here for the service of man," he declared to the Kingman Rotary Club in late March 1948. Goldwater added that Arizona was "being cheated of its rightful share of the river water by a state that contributes absolutely nothing to the river and wastes a great percentage of the water it takes from the channel."

Arizona officials had a ready answer to Arizona's current water woes. The Central Arizona Project (CAP) could bring water from the Colorado to the heart of the Arizona economy in the central portion of the state. This massive undertaking, to be underwritten largely by the federal government, promised to move water a long way at considerable cost. Without that infusion of water, Goldwater warned in the autumn of 1948, 226,000 acres in central Arizona would go permanently out of production. That figure constituted one-third of Arizona's productive agricultural acreage, a two-hundred-million-dollar economic asset. In the absence of the CAP, Goldwater argued, Arizona faced disaster, with jobholders leaving the state, their earnings no longer funneling into Pima, Maricopa, and other counties. Their departure guaranteed injury to the real property tax base and the loss of four thousand farms. Underscoring the current place of agriculture in the state's economy, Goldwater contended that "as long as our agricultural economy is steady, no economic storm can blow us from our moorings"; however, if agriculture were imperiled, then Arizona was in "dire peril." Agriculture in the Salt River valley, for example, played a vital role in nearly all the businesses in the area. Thus, every Arizonan had a stake in farming and a vested interest in the CAP.

Goldwater's interest in the river, to be sure, had been sparked initially by his trip through the Grand Canyon. In the late 1940s he combined presentation of his film about that experience with additional commentary about the current status of the river. Goldwater quickly became acknowledged as an expert about the Colorado and gained a ready-made audience throughout the state for his perspectives. By June 1949 the *Arizona Republic* reported on a talk by "Barry Goldwater, Phoenix merchant and authority on Colorado River problems," at a Phoenix Lions Club luncheon at the Hotel Westward Ho.

"The talk," noted the newspaper, "which outlined Arizona's water needs, was accompanied by a color motion picture taken by Goldwater depicting a boat trip from Green River, Utah, to Lake Mead." The *Tempe Daily News* on April 18, 1952, informed its readers about a similar gathering of Tempe Rotarians, who heard Goldwater, "an authority on the river." To his Tempe audience Goldwater stressed the importance of creating "additional, productive irrigated farm acres to meet food-stuff demands" and the necessity of using the river for power as well as irrigation.

Goldwater's candidacy for the U.S. Senate prompted his resignation in May from the Arizona Interstate Stream Commission, but his subsequent election that fall dictated that he would continue to be very much involved in the issue of water. His first term in the Senate coincided with a time of debate and controversy in the West over the construction of new dams as well as such proposals as the CAP. Activity on the lower stretches of the river had not only worried Arizona but the states of the upper river basin—Colorado, New Mexico, Utah, and Wyoming—as well. Their concerns inspired the Bureau of Reclamation to advocate the Colorado River Storage Project, a combination of dams and power plants to be built on the upper Colorado River and its tributaries. Two major dams were sketched in as an integral part of this project: Glen Canyon, on the Colorado River in northern Arizona, and Echo Park, near the junction of the Green and Yampa rivers in Dinosaur National Monument, just east of the Utah-Colorado border. Historian Mark Harvey has analyzed in searching detail the

debate over Echo Park, seeing within the engagement the
origins of the modern conservation movement. Echo Park
brought David Brower of the Sierra Club, Howard Zahniser
of the Wilderness Society, author Wallace Stegner, and other
noteworthy figures to the area. The publicity they generated
eventually killed plans for the dam. Glen Canyon, "the land
no one knew," did not share the same fate.

Goldwater had witnessed the beauty of Glen Canyon and
Echo Park. He recognized as did few westerners the exceptional country that would be submerged if the dams were
completed. Yet if he fretted in private about the matter, his
public face left no uncertainty about what needed to be done.
The rivers were there to be used. The dams had to be built.
"I've been there by boat, plane, and horse," he said of the site
of the Echo Park Dam, "and I'm convinced the proposed dam
will not harm the scenic beauty of the area." These sentiments
had been employed by proponents of dams since the fabled
fight over Hetch Hetchy earlier in the twentieth century.
Then John Muir and others who sought to save the magnificent valley adjacent to Yosemite had been defeated by engineers and their allies, who argued that in drowning Hetch
Hetchy they were in fact creating a different kind of beauty
through the new lake.

Glen Canyon presented a dramatic example of this conflict.
Although the sandstone canyon country would be lost forever, supporters of the dam believed that in Lake Powell they
had produced something equally special. Indeed, because of
the remote nature of Glen Canyon, the Lake Powell boosters
could plead that a kind of wilderness elite wanted to monop-
olize the scenic splendors of the region. With a lake, more than
the young and the able-bodied could enjoy this magnificent
locale. Conservationists believed otherwise, but they failed to
mount the kind of successful campaign that had quashed the
Echo Park Dam. Glen Canyon Dam not only produced Lake
Powell but also affected Goldwater's beloved Grand Canyon,
situated directly to the west of the dam. "Practical" considerations for the power production and the storage of water out-

weighed concern for the ecology of the Grand Canyon. The river that flowed hereafter through the Grand Canyon had been regulated; that regulation altered the nature of the river itself and thus affected the beaches, the vegetation, and the fish and wildlife within the stretches of the national park.

Some Arizona politicians never regretted the decision to build Glen Canyon dam. Governor Jack Williams wrote from the edge of Lake Powell to Goldwater in May 1971 suggesting that "those who criticize us for creating a civilization on the Sonoran desert plain and who complain about our dams and lakes, couldn't dream of creating the view here. Michangelo, Rubin, (You name 'em)," the governor maintained, "but as men they created beauty; here is beauty on scale that would make the gods breathless." Regardless of how Williams conveyed or spelled his sentiments, he spoke for the many tourists who came from throughout the world and who truly enjoyed the odd vistas they encountered on the kind of lunar sea that is Lake Powell.

But Goldwater did have second thoughts. In 1976 he said that of all the votes he had cast in the Senate, if he could change one of them, it would be "a vote I cast to construct the Glen Canyon dam on the Colorado River." He agreed with Williams: "Glen Canyon has created the most beautiful lake in the world and has brought millions and millions of dollars in to my state and the state of Utah." He also remembered what had been lost: "I think of that river as it was when I was a boy. And that is the way I would like to see it again."

Goldwater did not always display such remorse, but his varying perspectives on growth and development naturally mirrored the matter at stake. As did any elected Arizona politician during the era, he continued to work toward the passage of federal support for the CAP. The final stage of the process coincided with Goldwater's four-year absence from the Senate; President Lyndon Johnson signed Senate Bill 1004 into Public Law 90-537 on September 30, 1968. Even though Goldwater did not hold elective office during that period, he remained engaged in the effort to gain approval for the legislation. For example, in early autumn of 1965 he appeared before a House interior subcommittee hearing on the CAP. The Tucson *Arizona Daily Star* praised him for being "an excellent witness." Goldwater testified that the project was feasible financially and could be accomplished technologically; the newspaper said he spoke "authoritatively, as he long followed such water problems and was a member of the Arizona Interstate Stream Commission prior to entering the U.S. Senate." Again, his continuing involvement came as no surprise. The project had become such an article of faith and litmus test for Arizona politicians that even if he or others had entertained any doubts about it, they could not have acknowledged them publicly. Goldwater was continuing to do what he had done as a senator, when he had carried on the tradition of western representatives to try to obtain federal aid needed to develop local natural resources. There were a few public skeptics, but they were not candidates for public office and were easily dismissed by Jack Williams and his allies as "Tories of today." Still basking in the afterglow of the bill's passage, Williams in 1970 assured one and all that "we still have the backbone to handle a few malcontents who are playing with our water future as though it were their personal jigsaw puzzle." The baffled governor said, "I cannot understand how anyone living in a desert can turn down any water, regardless of what it costs."

Goldwater's life and career exemplified fluctuating stances in regard to growth and development. In regard to his place of residence, his involvement in the campaigns to save Camelback Mountain and to expand the Grand Canyon National Park, and his support for a major new dam not far from Phoenix, we can see significant examples of these different perspectives. In the 1950s he and his family built a new home. In the 1960s, Goldwater helped lead the fight to preserve the upper portions of Camelback Mountain in Phoenix from the encroachment of new homes. In the 1970s he labored in the face of widespread resistance to add lands to the Grand Canyon National Park and the bordering land base of the Havasupais. And in the 1970s and 1980s he remained a staunch advocate of the proposed Orme Dam, which if completed would have flooded most of the lands of the Yavapai community at Fort McDowell. An examination of these four instances helps shed light on varied dimensions of building Arizona.

In the 1950s the population of Phoenix quadrupled from slightly over one hundred thousand to well over four hundred thousand. Some of that remarkable increase stemmed from annexation. Phoenix and other valley towns and cities added both populated areas and large amounts of vacant land. This strategy promoted more rapid growth, for it committed the different communities to provide services and to redefine who they would become. Scottsdale, for example, liked to continue to advertise itself as "the West's most western town," but aggressive annexation destined it to emerge as something other than a modest outpost on the frontier. The statistics from the decade also indicated the kind of stunning immigration being experienced in the Salt River valley. Phoenix continued to sprawl across the desert. Its residents preferred low-density, single-story residences, and developers promoted the process as they raced to concoct new neighborhoods more and more distant from the old downtown. Many people moved to Phoenix in the decade, but others moved within the city. The Goldwaters were among the latter.

Phoenix had remained a small city until after World War II, but it became evident by the 1950s that the old core residential area was changing. The immediate neighborhood of the Phoenix country club, where the Goldwater family had resided on 5 Manor Drive since 1936, had not lost its elegance, but it had become more of an island, increasingly surrounded by other neighborhoods that were considerably less affluent. Following a pattern common to western cities, many more prosperous residents relocated either to more recently constructed or more distant neighborhoods either within the city limits or in such adjacent towns as Scottsdale. Phoenix real estate continued to be inexpensive in the face of competition among builders and the availability of land. For those with vision and cash, there existed some very pleasant options.

In 1957 the Goldwaters made the decision to stay in Phoenix (although a later shuffle of town lines placed them in Paradise Valley) but to build a new residence. On a desert hill site south of Squaw Peak, at the north end of 40th Street, where as a boy Goldwater had ridden horses and occasionally spent the night, he planned a new home. It had been known as Scorpion Hill during Goldwater's youth, and it was situated in the area north of the Arizona Canal that his father had said would never be worth much. But Goldwater remembered in 1995 that even as a boy he had told himself he would build a house there. Barry Goldwater wanted the house to be distinctive but not ostentatious and plotted with architect Paul Yeager to make sure that the place bore an unmistakable Goldwater stamp. And there could be no doubt that the new home reflected Goldwater's interests. It also, plain and simple, demonstrated a businessman's acumen in regard to investment. Initially valued at $93,500, the house and the land on which it was constructed provided one of countless examples of Arizonans' wise decisions about homes and homesites that were destined to escalate dramatically in their worth. Goldwater purchased the land from Frank Brophy in 1950 for what now seems a pittance: $700 an acre. Over time he sold off pieces of the parcel, including three acres in 1995 for $1,000,000.

The Goldwater home featured walls of Arizona sandstone quarried near Cameron on the Navajo reservation. Goldwater hoped that his use of eighty-five tons of the deep red rock would promote a new source of tribal income, but he also obviously loved the way it looked—the color and what he called "the remarkable ripple markings of ancient beaches." The house also included a steam bath, a speaker in every room for the record player, a built-in movie projector, and a photography darkroom. Indian art and paintings of western scenes were featured prominently. Given Goldwater's passion for ham radio, the house soon sported an antenna noticeable from a long way away. Then and now, one could spot the Goldwater house without any difficulty by means of this particular signature.

The senator took great pleasure and pride in the new residence. He loved the gadgets and all the creative touches that permeated the structure. And although only one of the Goldwater children still resided at home—Joanne had married; Barry, Jr., was enrolled in college; Michael continued the family tradition at Staunton Military Academy in Virginia; and Peggy attended Judson School in Scottsdale—Barry Goldwater definitely regarded this new home as a future center for the family. He could not be at home as often as he wanted, but his house symbolized not only his affection for Arizona but also his affection for his family. He wanted all of them to share in his emotions about Be-Nun-I-Kin, which in translation from the Navajo language meant, essentially, "House on the Hill." Once, in an undated letter to his daughter Peggy—any parent will guess it was while she was a teenager—he spoke to the importance of the house. "I will beseech you," Goldwater wrote, "to be a good helper around the house—It is our home—It is a part of us and we should each in our own way contribute to its beauty—By using it—by taking care of it—to see that its loveliness is never abused."

Goldwater had an additional reason to grow fond of his home. He never grew tired of the view. One has an unobstructed panorama across the valley. Directly to the east is the dramatic sight of Camelback Mountain. He seemed especially to enjoy the vision that greeted him at night, when all the lights of the Salt River valley reminded him that this area had defied those who predicted it had no future. Goldwater had strong, vibrant memories of his youth, but he knew that just as his children had to grow up, Phoenix could not remain frozen in time and space. He reminded all the writers who trooped up the hill to interview him that one could not stand in the way of progress, that life never stands still. It all somehow fit together—his maturation, that of Phoenix, and that of his family. After his daughter Peggy was married, he wrote to her:

I can look out upon a vast valley stretching far beyond my eyesight with glittering lights, lights that cover an area that, when I was your age, was nothing but the American desert.

I think back to the days of the youth that is yours, which was mine once, and I say parenthetically which is always wasted upon the young, and I remember the admonitions of my elders who held that this place could never grow.

Well, I sit here tonight looking with my poor 20/100 vision, upon the multitudinous lights that make up the fastest growing city in the world . . . and I am reminded that life never stands still.

While Goldwater customarily announced his gratification in the ongoing march of Phoenix, there were indeed limits to his enthusiasm for the process. Camelback Mountain is a familiar landmark to Phoenicians. The impressive sandstone formation had been an isolated place to hike and climb in Goldwater's youth, but as time passed, the beauty of the mountain and the vantage points it afforded lured more and more well-to-do individuals to build homes initially at its base and then steadily up its facade. Left unchecked, the pattern of development threatened to swallow Camelback. Despite its steep incline, people dreamed of building homes at ever more perilous heights; budding entrepreneurs imagined a hotel or a restaurant at its summit or perhaps an observation tower served by a funicular railway. "Frank Brophy," Goldwater recalled in 1995, "owned the top of it and talked about building a revolving restaurant on the summit."

Camelback had been outside of the Phoenix city limits in the 1950s when concerned citizens from the valley began to voice their concerns about residential encroachment on the mountain, which many had assumed had been held by the government rather than by private interests. Through such organizations as the Valley Beautiful Citizens Council, area residents started to lobby against the denial of public access to the site, which they knew would increasingly be restricted as more and more homes were constructed. Unlike the South Mountain area, where Phoenix had been able to place acreage under city administration, Camelback had been carved up among homeowners and land speculators. The Maricopa County Planning and Zoning Commission in 1954 decided that building could not take place above the elevation of sixteen hundred feet, but that left a considerable portion of Camelback open to additional private pockmarks.

Louise Woolsey, Bonnie Upchurch, and others solicited the help of conservationist organizations to save the mountain. In 1960 the Arizona Conservation Council and the Arizona Conservation Foundation organized to promote and encourage conservation of natural resources, historic sites, and places of scenic beauty. These represented useful steps, but more clout had to be mustered at the local level before significant headway could be achieved in regard to Camelback itself.

So began the Preservation of Camelback Mountain Foundation, an offspring of the Valley Beautiful Citizens Council. Barry Goldwater accepted the challenge of serving as its chairman. Assisted by his former colleague on the Phoenix City Council, Margaret Kober, he plunged into the fray, eager to do what he could to stem the tide of construction. "This old mountain is worth the fight," Goldwater said. "A Camelback cluttered with roads and utility poles and bulldozed scars and houses would be the shame of the state. If we ruin Camelback, ever afterward people will think of Phoenix as the city that made something ugly of the most beautiful thing it had." It goes without saying that he did not deviate from his respect for private property. Goldwater did not attempt to tear down homes already completed. However, he thought if he and his allies moved quickly, they could at least save the summit and much of the uppermost portion of the mountain. He "talked like a Dutch uncle to Frank Brophy" about Brophy's ill-advised scheme for the Camelback summit. In the absence of federal, state, or local funding, his group had to raise the money themselves to purchase real estate parcels already in private hands. The foundation estimated it needed to raise three hundred thousand dollars to achieve its goals.

The campaign to save Camelback came at a propitious time in Goldwater's life. He had lost the race for the presidency, and the Senate election did not take place until 1968. What better way for him to occupy some of the time he now found on his

Camelback Mountain from Sky Harbor Airport, March 27, 1996. Photograph by Allen A. Dutton. Courtesy of Allen A. Dutton

hands in 1965 than to try to save this wonderful symbol of his home community? Goldwater backed up his determination in the best possible way. He pledged twenty-five thousand dollars, and his mother pledged the same. By putting fifty thousand dollars on the table, Goldwater then could proceed to have some amiable conversations with some of his oldest friends. He called and he wrote to wealthy people and some less endowed, reminding them all that over the years attempts had "been made to acquire the properties there privately owned on Camelback Mountain before that beautiful landmark is completely destroyed." He stated, "It is time now that we act, or in my opinion, forget all about it, so . . ." One suspects no good friend escaped. Goldwater contacted Eugene Pulliam, Harry Rosenzweig, Henry Luce, and some of the other usual suspects. The widows of Frank Lloyd Wright and Philip K. Wrigley sent checks. Luce pledged twenty-five thousand dollars. Mary Dell and John Pritzlaff (whose daughter, Ann, would marry future Arizona governor J. Fife Symington) pledged ten thousand dollars. Goldwater wrote on December 1, 1965, to the Pritzlaffs: "Your contribution has been one of the real inspirations of the campaign and we will be eternally grateful to you for having made it."

From twenty-five cents to twenty-five thousand dollars, the donations came in. Twenty-seven hundred individuals, plus many hundreds of children through school projects, forwarded their contributions. The *Arizona Republic*'s Reg Manning drew one of his patented cartoons, showing a cowering Camelback Mountain about to be devoured by a gigantic steam shovel labeled "Private Real Estate Development." The caption to the cartoon ran, "Not A Minute To Lose," with Manning's John Q. Public figure (wearing a shirt with "Uno Who" on it) completing the sentence: "—If We're Going To Save Him From Being Chewed Up Completely!" Donors received a certificate from the foundation adorned with a sketch of Camelback and two saguaros, attesting that they were "entitled to the enjoyment of Camelback Mountain in Arizona's Valley of the Sun, a portion of which was acquired with your gift, to be preserved in its natural state as a heritage of beauty for everyone."

The drive enjoyed some fine moments. Area high school students collected 15,280 pounds of cans, which added $183.36 to the foundation's coffers. Goldwater donned a Beatles wig and played the trombone in a band at a high school dance. His brother had bet him one thousand dollars that he couldn't learn to play "Silent Night." "I did," he said with a smile, "and he paid." In fact, Goldwater added, "Bob's wife, Sally, bet me another thousand dollars that I couldn't learn another song. I did, but she wouldn't pay me." He ignored his back problems and climbed the mountain and then spoke to reporters about why the mountain mattered. Goldwater took photographs and showed slides to groups all over the state. He rented a helicopter to inspect personally some of the parcels on the mountain sought by the foundation.

In 1966 it appeared that the effort had made quite a bit of headway but that donations had fallen off. Goldwater swallowed, clenched his teeth, then wrote to Don Hummel, the former mayor of Tucson and now the assistant secretary for renewal and housing assistance in the federal Department of Housing and Urban Development. He noted that the campaign had raised $250,000, but the stakes had been raised, and the city of Phoenix hoped the federal government might match this sum to put the endeavor over the top. Goldwater hastened to inform Hummel that he would have preferred not to consume any of that dreaded substance, federal aid, "but after years of effort we seemed to have hit the bottom of the barrel and because this is one of the most famous landmarks in the entire world, we do want to protect it and protect it by any means." Flattery got Goldwater nowhere. In his response, Hummel confirmed all of Goldwater's suspicions, indicating that the possibilities for aid were "rather dim." Goldwater also appealed to Secretary of the Interior Stewart Udall, indicating that by now the foundation had acquired "a very sizable part of the south slopes of the mountain" but observing that it still needed to purchase some additional acreage on the north side and that these purchases had proven to be more problematic.

This appeal eventually bore fruit. In May 1968, Udall accompanied Lady Bird Johnson to Phoenix to participate in ceremonies ending the long battle to save the top of the mountain. Udall presented the mayor of Phoenix with a check of $211,250 from land and water funds to match a like amount donated. Goldwater then entered the home stretch, cajoling the donors to make good on their pledges. He acknowledged that time remained on the pledges but emphasized that it was "most important that we get this done." He personally would pay up all of his balance slated to run over the next three years, he informed John Pritzlaff on June 19. "I notice," Goldwater remarked to Pritzlaff, "there is still $4,175.30 due on your pledge. If you make this payment or partial payment on it at this time, it would be of great benefit because of the need to convey immediately remained pledged funds to the city of Phoenix." On July 8, 1968, Save Camelback Mountain Foundation formally turned over the deeds and money to the City of Phoenix.

Due in no small part to Goldwater's personal intervention, the top of the mountain had been saved. He had convinced some landowners to donate their parcels and others to sell their lands at reduced prices. Others bargained for full value but still relinquished precious acres. Goldwater had also been able to stimulate an impressive degree of direct participation in the drive. If friendship initially failed, then the Goldwater velvet hammer descended, as it did on H. W. Cronrath of the Mountain Shadows resort. Learning that Cronrath had written to decline the opportunity, Goldwater sent the following epistle:

> Your letter turning down participation in the Save Camelback drive has me extremely puzzled. If it is the case of not being able to afford it, I shall certainly understand, but if it is a case of not wanting to participate, I would certainly like to know the reason, because this is the first such case we have had. In the many, many times I have been at Mountain

Shadows, I have always marveled at the volume of business that you do and have heard of the interest your guests have shown in the mountain. Possibly something has been done to offend you relative to this drive and if this is true, please let me know so that amends might be made.

There is no official record of whether Cronrath contributed, but one can guess how the story ended.

The enlargement of the Grand Canyon National Park ranked in Goldwater's judgment as one of his two most important legislative achievements, together with the Armed Services Reorganization Act. No one could doubt the special place the canyon had in Goldwater's heart. He liked to say that if he ever would have a mistress, it would have to be the canyon. Throughout his adult life he kept returning to it, to run the river, to hike its trails, to take photographs. In 1967 Harry Reasoner worked with Goldwater on a CBS special, "Barry Goldwater's Arizona." Goldwater kept bending Reasoner's ear about the canyon. Reasoner finally concluded that "Arizonans are as proud of the Grand Canyon as if they'd dug it themselves."

When Goldwater returned to the Senate after the 1968 election, he pondered the current status of the canyon. River rafting on the Colorado through the canyon had become steadily more popular. More and more tourists inundated the park, particularly during the summer months. Access had to be balanced with protection of the area's fragile environment. Many different groups had particular interests in the management of the region. Ranchers wanted access to public lands for grazing. Environmentalist organizations pushed for additions to the park land base without any substitutions or subtractions. The Havasupais protested the usurpation of some of their traditional territory; the park now included some of their most valuable and cherished sites.

The summer after the presidential race in 1964, Goldwater and members of his immediate family had returned to the Colorado. Experiencing again its extraordinary beauty may well have inspired him to tackle the issue of the park lands. Although Goldwater never said it in so many words, it seems rea-

Grand Canyon, 1965. Photograph by Barry Goldwater. Barry Goldwater Photograph Collection, courtesy of the Arizona Historical Foundation

sonable to conclude that for him the river was the heart of the canyon. If he could help fashion a bill that safeguarded the river, he would be making a valuable contribution to the park's future. If he could, in addition, expand the minimal land base of the Havasupais, he would be working in the best interest of an Indian community he had long admired. With the multiple, conflicting perspectives involved in the entire discussion, he knew some compromises had to be made. That, after all, was how congressional politics worked, even if emotions ran high and zealous people hated to retreat even one inch.

On March 20, 1973, Goldwater and Morris Udall introduced identical bills in the Senate and House. The measures included several key features. First, the Havasupai reservation would expand from a mere 500 acres to 169,600 acres. In order to achieve this expansion, 41,400 acres would be deleted from the current park, including Topocoba Hilltop, and 14,700 out of the present Grand Canyon National Monument on the west side of Cataract Creek on Tenderfoot Plateau. The additional 113,000 acres would be transferred from the Kaibab National Forest. The Navajos had agreed to include a mile-wide strip along the east rim of Marble Canyon, and the Hualapais a comparable strip along the south shore of the river through their reservation to the west; in each area, the tribes promised not to build tourist or recreation facilities without approval of the secretary of the interior.

Second, Grand Canyon National Park would become larger. The bill added 198,280 acres from Grand Canyon National Monument and 26,080 acres from Marble Canyon National Monument into the park itself. It also attached 331,500 acres of the lower or western part of the canyon, which extended the park to Grand Wash Cliffs, an area presently in the Lake Mead National Recreation Area, and a small amount of Kaibab National Forest land around the Lower Kanab Canyon. Third, three pieces of the existing park would also be deleted: 23,700 acres on Tuckup Point, 9,000 acres near Jensen Tank, and 5,380 acres of Slide Mountain west of Toroweap Valley.

Goldwater acknowledged that these features did represent compromises, yet they ultimately were consistent with "the principle of identifying all of the Marble and Grand Canyon within one great national park." The Havasupais, who had lobbied for years to expand their minuscule base, had ample reason to applaud the proposal. Although the bill did not add all they ideally had wanted, it came close to matching their demands. Two months before he introduced the legislation, Goldwater had arrived by helicopter in Supai and listened to the tribe's requests. He had told tribal chair Oscar Paya—who had wired Goldwater and encouraged him to visit—and oth-

ers that "we are in better shape to get land back than we have
been in many years." Goldwater pledged to fight for the Havasupai addition, which restored all the waterfalls, Hualapai Hilltop, the pack trail to Supai, Long Mesa, and some grazing
areas to tribal control.

Not all observers agreed with this component of the legislation. Environmentalists gave lip service to Havasupai needs
but gave a higher priority to federal rather than tribal control.
Joan Coaton of the Tucson Audubon Society worried that the
Havasupais did not have "the resources to control heavy public land use," while Kevin Dahl of the Arizona branch of
Friends of the Earth argued against deleting park lands when
forest service acreage could be substituted. In August, Goldwater complained publicly before his colleagues in the Senate
about the Sierra Club's unwillingness either to acknowledge
that he had tried to incorporate many features of their initial
proposals or to accept gracefully that politics represented the
art of the possible. When the Sierra Club had testified against
his park legislation at the Senate hearing of June 20, Goldwater felt betrayed as well as surprised. "I should like to remind
the Sierra Club," Goldwater admonished, "that it does not
help the legislative process a bit to make a recommendation on
one day and then to turn against it shortly afterwards without
even consulting the people who have worked with them on im-
plementing the original idea. And it similarly does not aid the
legislative process to take an attitude where it is only the other
individual and group who is expected to make any compromises." He reminded one and all that he had been "a conservationist for all of my adult life" and added that "long before
the words 'ecology' and 'pollution' became prominent in public discussions, I was known in my native state as a 'Desert Rat'
and as a 'Grand Canyon Buff' because of my concern for my
beloved desert land and my interest in the Grand Canyon."

Goldwater ducked brickbats hurled by others as well.
Hunters complained about being denied access to animals they
had customarily been able to kill. Anti-Indian individuals contended that the Havasupais did not deserve a single additional

acre. Some people decided too much land had been added, and others grumped that too little had been incorporated. Goldwater had difficulty disguising his vexation but persevered. President Gerald Ford ultimately signed Public Law 93-260 on January 4, 1975.

From Goldwater's perspective, the matter of Orme Dam would be resolved in a less satisfactory manner. The battle over Orme took place in the context of a changing national and regional perspective on dams in the West. Soon after Jimmy Carter became president in 1977, he announced a hit list of proposed water projects he wished not to be funded. Although Carter failed to gain reelection, his disappearance did not end debate over the need for every last dam westerners could imagine and propose. Orme Dam was part of the CAP. As construction on the CAP continued in the 1970s, Orme and other dams were slated for completion for the purposes of storing project water and regulating the flow of various rivers. Even opponents of Orme acknowledged that its site, the confluence of the Salt and Verde rivers, made a good deal of sense. But a somewhat unlikely alliance began to protest the planned dam. When completed, the dam would flood about two-thirds of the Fort McDowell reservation. The dam also threatened eagle habitat at Fort McDowell as well as the flow of water on the Verde, a favorite river for "tubers," who liked to float it in the endless Sonoran summer. So, for their own reasons, the Yavapais, environmentalists, and recreationists combined to complain. Earlier in the history of Arizona, their voices would have been drowned out, their objections summarily overruled. Once again, however, times had changed.

Orme certainly had its proponents. Phoenix residents' fears of flooding seemed a bit odd to the uninitiated, but the Salt had been known to cause problems, and the years of 1978, 1979, and 1980 brought unusually heavy rains and subsequent flooding to the valley in general and Phoenix in particular. The flood in 1980 damaged bridges and created massive traffic jams in the city. The *Arizona Republic* helped tub thump for Orme as a means of avoiding such inconvenience, irritation, and expense. The newspaper's editor, Pat Murphy, wailed "that high and dry Washington bureaucrats have been dilly-dallying for at least 10 years over approval of the Dam, worrying more about nesting bald eagles than the lives and property and jobs of the people of Phoenix who must endure floods." He demanded, "Now dammit, give us our dam!"

Goldwater had little patience with the environmentalist critique of Orme and other such initiatives. He admitted that environmentalists meant well, but in the end they stood in the way of progress. "They will really hamstring this country," he alleged in 1977. "It seems so much trouble comes from them." Goldwater sympathized with Murphy's plea. In a letter to Steven Johnson of Phoenix of October 10, 1980, he expressed his concern over flooding in the Salt River valley and reminded Johnson that he had "for many years urged construction of Orme Dam, which would do much to relieve the terrible problems that have occurred during the past several years."

Perhaps the most complicated confrontation between Goldwater and foes of Orme evolved between the senator and the Yavapais of Fort McDowell. Plans for Orme developed a major snag when the residents of McDowell turned thumbs down on a deal which would have compensated each tribal member a hefty sum of money in exchange for their relocation from most of their land. The balloting took place a generation before the advent of the Fort McDowell Casino; most Yavapais were poor, and backers of the dam assumed they could be persuaded to move. But when East Valley leaders such as Keith Turley of Mesa compared the reservation to a barrio and expressed surprise that the people weren't eager to move, it just made the Yavapais all the more intransigent.

Goldwater bore the brunt of much of the Yavapai ire because of his outspoken and unequivocal support for Orme Dam. He suspected outsiders of poisoning the perspectives of the Yavapais and said as much in a letter to *Audubon* in the summer of 1977, responding to a May article that had been uncomplimentary toward the CAP. Goldwater suggested that if the dam were not built, the Yavapais "will barely continue to have an existence on the lands in which they live. They are nice people, very sweet people, but they are very lazy people, and somebody has changed their minds."

Audubon subscriptions had always been rather limited in number at McDowell, but, mysteriously, the letter somehow made the rounds of the small community. Tribal leader Hiawatha Hood did not mince words: "Goldwater is wrong in everything he says. He is against the Yavapais because we refused to sell our land." Dixie Davis of Fort McDowell said her people's "bare existence . . . would be far better than living in an urban slum which we have seen happen to other tribes who have lost their reservations, and cannot survive or adjust to that kind of strange environment." She retorted, "As for not being ambitious, we have demonstrated that to be untrue by our refusal to allow our ancestral lands to be flooded and turned into a playground for wealthy people."

Goldwater did not back down. As he explained to Fort McDowell tribal chairman Norman Austin in March 1981, he could not "back away" from his support of Orme, because it represented the only way he knew to accomplish the goals of the CAP. Goldwater told Austin that he had pointed out to the tribe on his first visit with it about this subject in the 1940s that the value of tribal land "would greatly increase by having a lake located partially in a place that would touch their farming lands" and that this value "would far, far exceed any value the farmlands might ever achieve."

Goldwater remembered that leaders from that era had agreed to the idea, but he admitted he could find no records to support his memory. In closing, he reiterated his understanding of why the Yavapais might not want to move, especially given their history of having "been moved from place to place throughout your history," but in his judgment it still seemed like the best option.

Austin told Goldwater in return that it was "plain" that "you mean well, but there are facts which you do not seem to be aware of." Orme Dam, Austin argued, would not provide lakefront land. Given the acreage that had to be reserved for flood control, the water levels would vary and the shoreline would vary from month to month. Austin thought most of the area behind the dam "would be a giant mud flat of more than 15,000 acres." He said the Army Corps of Engineers and others had identified less expensive alternatives to serve Orme's purposes. As for tribal approval, the Yavapai elders had recalled to him that the tribal council had rejected the dam "around 1946 when it was proposed to them by the President of the Salt River Project" and that the tribe had remained adamant in its opposition ever since. Austin invited Goldwater to visit McDowell "as it is today and meet with us. . . . I think you will be happy and surprised to see how far we have come since the last time you visited with us. You will see why we do not wish to lose this rich land which is now making us self-sufficient."

That summer Austin renewed the invitation, noting that it was evident from Goldwater's letters that he had "some feelings for our people and you want to do what is right." He again expressed the hope that Goldwater's visit would allow him to "see the progress we have made since your last visit many years ago and you will understand why we will not give up our land now or ever." Goldwater and fellow senator Dennis DeConcini continued to support the dam, but other public officials began to reconsider the situation.

The Yavapais must have known the tide had begun to turn in their favor when Secretary of the Interior James Watt visited McDowell in September and seemed moved by their pleas. In the meantime, Governor Bruce Babbitt had appointed an advisory committee to study alternatives to Orme. When the committee members voted overwhelmingly in favor of Plan 6, which scrapped Orme Dam and called for, among other stipulations, a new Waddell Dam south of Lake Pleasant, just north of the CAP aqueduct, and a raised Roosevelt Dam, Babbitt declared the war was over. Salt River Project manager Jack Pfister had not listed Plan 6 as his first choice but had already indicated the Salt River Project could support it. Wes Steiner, the head of the Arizona Department of Water Resources, had advocated Orme in the past yet now joined in the retreat. Once

Watt approved Plan 6, Goldwater, DeConcini, John Rhodes, and others accepted political reality. For the time being, at least, Orme Dam was dead.

Goldwater may have lost the battle, but he had not been convinced that the victors had been correct. In 1987 he wrote to Stephen Shadegg to express his conviction that "we made a stupid mistake when we gave up Orme, just because a handful of people from the East were complaining about it." A year later, he still stewed over the decision. Goldwater wrote again to Shadegg and again used the same adjective to describe the decision about the dam. "The average person living in this valley or living in Arizona doesn't give a damn about water," he observed, but then in the next breath he groaned that even when he and Shadegg had been "a lot younger, the citizenry was filled with people who didn't understand the need for water."

As Norman Austin had gently underscored, Goldwater's advocacy of Orme Dam should not be construed as opposition to the Yavapais. He had wanted to remain well thought of by the people of Fort McDowell. Nonetheless, as he would have been the first to acknowledge, a life in politics sometimes meant choosing between and among your friends. For Barry Goldwater, the benefits of Orme Dam outweighed its potential or real liabilities. During the twentieth century, the process of building Arizona had begun with water. If you lived in a desert, he believed, you had no choice.

In evaluating Barry Goldwater's more general stance in regard to growth and development, it is useful to remember that throughout his public career he did want to promote economic expansion and find means for young Arizonans to remain at home and for other Americans to be able to move to and stay in Arizona. Just as those who lived through the Great Depression and the World War II took certain lessons from their experiences and applied them for the rest of their lives, Goldwater always remembered the Arizona of his youth and never deviated from a view that said prosperity is hard-earned, fragile, vulnerable. You had to keep working; you could not take water or a strong economy for granted. But you also should appreciate that the land itself is also fragile and easily scarred. The land remembered, too. You should appreciate the great landmarks—the Camelbacks and the canyons—and treat them with respect. There were limits to where and what and why you should build. You could not stop progress, but you could question what it meant.

Goldwater's perspective, thus, on building Arizona did not remain constant. Along with other Arizonans, he experienced native's remorse as he watched the air of his beloved valley become more polluted and the pristine quality of areas such as Sedona transformed. In sum, the efforts to promote and develop the state had succeeded, at times all too well. New questions had emerged for Barry Goldwater and others about progress, about quality of life, and about fulfilling the promise of Arizona.

CHAPTER 9

Coming Home

LONG before he completed his final term in the Senate in 1986, Barry Goldwater had pondered what his life might be like once he left Washington. Unlike many of his peers, he had absolutely no desire to remain in the District of Columbia. He was eager to come home to Arizona. However, he did not relish the prospect of extended vacations in California—the preferred destination of Peggy Goldwater for leisure time. As he debated whether to run for the Senate in 1980, he wrote to his wife: "I have to tell you right now that I cannot spend long, drawn-out vacations in California with you because, frankly, I just don't have anything to do. I'm not cut out to sit the rest of my life doing nothing but resting on a couch all day. . . . Retirement and sitting on my duff is not the kind of life I can live with long. I'm sure that it will be the beginning of an end for me if I had to do it."

Such sentiments, combined with his continuing concern about the financial situation of his immediate and extended family and his commitment to serving his state and nation, contributed to his eventual decision to seek a final term. Nonetheless, as his time inside the beltway came to a close, he made his peace with the prospect of some form of retirement and anticipated having more time to spend with Peggy. As they approached their fiftieth wedding anniversary in 1984, he had ample reason to reflect upon their years together. She had also been born in 1909, and he liked celebrating her birthday, in part because, for the moment, she had reached his age. Signing himself "El Viejo," he had penned a sentimental poem to her on the occasion of her seventy-fourth birthday.

Noting that she had always been ahead of him in life, he observed:

> We've loved each other
>   not for once—But
> Forever
> And Forever is just now
>   starting
> Together for days and years
>   with no real parting
> But Old Gal for once
>   you are 74
> And for once my angel—
>   I've been there
> Before

She continued to entreat him to retire and he kept reminding her that he must finish his term in order to fulfill his obligations to the citizens of Arizona as well as his responsibilities as a Republican. If he resigned early, then Democratic governor Bruce Babbitt would appoint a Democrat. If he stayed until the end of 1986, then "a Republican like John McCain" could be elected to replace him. "I must do my job," he wrote to her two days after their fifty-first wedding anniversary on September 24, 1985. "I agreed to do it; you agreed with me."

He primarily wanted to tell her "how very happy I was with you on our 51st wedding anniversary, how completely proud I am of you and what you have done for me and what you have done for our children and grandchildren, and how proud I am of you just as a plain, good woman." He added: "Coming home means so much to me. More so every time. And I don't mind telling you every time I leave the house, I look at it and wonder, 'Will I ever see it again?' Oh, I know I will, but when you get to my age, those thoughts come into your mind once in a while."

The Goldwaters had shared a dream of time together after the term had concluded, but the fates ruled otherwise. Peggy Goldwater was hospitalized on Thanksgiving Day in 1985 and underwent two surgeries to alleviate circulatory difficulties.

She had suffered from arthritis, emphysema, and heart problems. The second surgery resulted in amputation of her left leg. She lapsed into a coma for two weeks, and when the Goldwater family agreed to remove life supports, she died early in the morning of December 11 at the Good Samaritan Medical Center in Phoenix. Memorial services were conducted at Christ Church of the Ascension, a church constructed on land the Goldwaters had donated.

In addition to her family, Peggy Goldwater's legacy included her steadfast support for Planned Parenthood. On the occasion of the fiftieth anniversary of the founding of the Mother's Health Clinic on 7th Street and Adams, Planned Parenthood Executive Director Gloria Feldt recalled the role Peggy Goldwater had played in establishing this first birth control clinic in Arizona. Feldt quoted what Mrs. Goldwater had said two years before her death: "Every day that religious, political, and medical leaders fail to do something about birth by chance, they are placing themselves on the side of misery, even disaster, and against the people of the world who await their guidance for physical, economic, and spiritual salvation. Family planning is essential to each of these areas."

Her husband more than mourned her passing. Comforted by the presence of his sons and daughters, he remained in the Phoenix area until Congress reconvened in January. Then he pushed on for the final installment of a long career in Washington. There remained important work to do. He steeled himself to assume an assignment that mattered.

Goldwater had served since his return to the Senate in 1969 on the Armed Services Committee and in 1985 had assumed its chairmanship. In this capacity he had earned the admiration of his Democratic and Republican colleagues for his dedication, his plain speaking, and his common sense. He regarded the chairmanship as one of "the biggest challenges I've had in public life." He spared no one in his commitment to this task, attacking waste, corruption, and lack of productivity. Goldwater charged that the federal government "may be wasting two billion to three billion dollars a year" on military contracts.

He labeled the current system "a license to steal" and ridiculed five-hundred-dollar hammers and six-hundred-dollar toilet seats. On the occasion of Goldwater's retirement from the Senate, Howard Metzenbaum (Democrat, Ohio) spoke of the odd couple from Ohio and Arizona who had joined together "to introduce real competition into the procurement system," filing suit in federal court "to stop the Defense Department from its proposal to let a sole-source contract for the CTX airplane." Jeff Bingaman (Democrat, New Mexico) remembered a committee hearing in 1983: "I recall Barry telling a Navy witness that he could build A-6E attack planes in his garage at the same rate the Navy was proposing to build them, six a year."

Now Goldwater tackled passage of the Defense Reorganization Act, which revised the military services and their programs and procedures. The act, in the words of Chris Dodd (Democrat, Connecticut), was "designed to alleviate the chain-of-command and service rivalry problems which have dogged our military for years." As Goldwater stated it in his autobiography: "Our central aim was to have U.S. air, sea, and ground forces fight as a team through a series of organizational and command changes within the services." More particularly, it clarified the role of the secretary of defense, reinforced the position of the chairman of the Joint Chiefs of Staff in policy making, and gave much more authority to field commanders. It also confronted the problem of budgetary excess and inefficiency by establishing a new under secretary of defense for acquisition. Goldwater had the credentials to push for this legislation, given his lengthy tenure in the Senate and on this committee as well as his status as a retired air force major general who had flown almost every aircraft in the military inventory, including the F-16 (a supersonic fighter plane) and the SR-71 (a new surveillance plane). Dale Bumpers (Democrat, Arkansas) concluded: "The simple truth is that without Senator Goldwater's tireless pursuit of this landmark piece of legislation, it would never have made it," given its adversaries in the Pentagon. Members of the Joint Chiefs of Staff, including General John A. Wickham, Jr., army chief of staff; General

Barry Goldwater, with model airplanes, at home. Barry Goldwater Photograph Collection, courtesy of the Arizona Historical Foundation

P. X. Kelley, commandant of the Marine Corps; and Admiral
James D. Watkins, chief of naval operations, had initially opposed the central elements of the reform. They had argued
against placing each chief under a civilian secretary and opposed giving more authority to commanders going into combat. Goldwater and the ranking Democrat on the Armed Services Committee, Sam Nunn of Georgia, countered the men
and denied the accuracy of some of their allegations but ultimately did not convince them. All the service chiefs and the
secretaries of the army, navy, and air force opposed the key dimensions of reorganization when they were first proposed in
1982. So, too, did most in the Congress.

However, in 1986 the Senate passed Goldwater's bill by, in
Bumpers's words, "the amazing vote of 95–0"; the House
agreed by a 406–4 margin. Bumpers observed: "This legislation will be a lasting tribute to him for it will enhance our military strength while it streamlines our defense management
from top to bottom. Barry's gift to the country is best described by *Armed Forces Journal,* which calls it 'the greatest
contribution to America's security we'll see in our lifetimes.'"
Bumpers went on, "I can tell you not much legislation passed
around here gets an accolade like that." The Senate honored
Goldwater by naming the act after him.

Goldwater in more restrained moments would refer to this
act as the "hallmark" of his career. More typically, he would
use phrases comparable to those employed in his autobiography: "It's the only goddamn thing I've done in the Senate
that's worth a damn. I can go home happy, sit on my hill, and
shoot jackrabbits."

In the waning months of his last Senate term, the honors
and the applause washed over him. On September 9, 1986,
friends and associates gathered for a special tribute at the Hyatt
Regency. Cochaired by Strom Thurmond and Sam Nunn and
presided over by Dean Burch, the dinner featured remarks by
Nunn, Justice Sandra Day O'Connor of Arizona, Ted Kennedy,
Andy Rooney, and Paul Laxalt. This bipartisan coalition symbolized Goldwater's perspective on the political process. De-

spite being a loyal Republican, he could work constructively with Democrats, not always agreeing, but listening, willing to compromise if the occasion called for it. After working their way through a four-course dinner featuring Arizona Consommé, Salad Fredonia, Filet of Beef Maricopa, and Sun Devil Torte, the assemblage heard some warm tributes and a little teasing. On this occasion, Nunn spoke of the profound, indelible impact Goldwater had had on the District of Columbia, the United States, and the Senate; he informed his listeners that more and more of Goldwater's colleagues in the Senate had adopted "his creed and his motto: Ready, fire, aim!" Ted Kennedy allowed that as a member of the Armed Services Committee he had been "always very respectful of Chairman Goldwater. When I first went on the Committee, he told me we could either do things his way—or he could make a very nice submarine base out of Hyannisport." Conceding that he and Goldwater had had their ideological differences over the years, Kennedy emphasized he had admired Goldwater's "sense of principle, his character, and his courage." And Kennedy remarked: "There is another vital quality that marks him out. While Barry Goldwater takes issues seriously, he never takes himself too seriously. He is not self-important or self-righteous, and woe betide the partisan—of the right or the left—who calls legitimate dissent unpatriotic, irreligious, or un-American. Barry Goldwater is likely to threaten to kick their you know what."

In October, even the *Washington Post,* which admitted that Goldwater had not "been a particular favorite in these columns," added its commendation. Emphasizing that "his views outlived his catastrophic candidacy," it suggested that "Barry Goldwater transformed American conservatism, which in turn transformed American politics." The newspaper labeled him an original who had "made a difference in politics and in national life." And before year's end he received the Distinguished Flying Cross "for 45 years of aerial skill and distinguished service," the Department of Defense Distinguished Service Medal, and the Presidential Medal of Freedom.

Formal tributes paid to Goldwater on the occasion of his retirement from the Senate included this point, with Bob Dole
(Republican, Kansas) noting that "probably no Republican
has left a bigger imprint on the party and on the course of contemporary American politics than Barry Goldwater." Additional compliments indicated other contributions. Carl Levin
(Democrat, Michigan) remarked that Goldwater did not legis-
late by press release nor vote by party affiliation. Mark Hatfield
(Republican, Oregon) stressed Goldwater's "high degree of
integrity, strong convictions and dedication to public service."
Claiborne Pell (Democrat, Rhode Island) echoed Hatfield in
calling attention to "his integrity, his passion for freedom and
individual rights, and, above all, his candor and unsurpassed
ability to 'call them as he sees them.'"

Senators are always retiring from the Senate; their compatriots line up and bid them farewell. Five other senators also
received commendations that day, but most of the attention
focused on Goldwater. One might have anticipated the praise
offered him by conservative Republicans such as Malcolm
Wallop of Wyoming and Orrin Hatch of Utah. More telling is
the recognition provided by people with whom Goldwater
frequently disagreed, including Kennedy, Pell, Metzenbaum,
Joe Biden of Delaware, and Daniel Patrick Moynihan of New
York, who emphasized the kind of role Goldwater had played
as chairman of the Select Committee on Intelligence.

Metzenbaum declared that, given Goldwater's willingness
to say what he believed and stand up for what he said, he
looked forward to Goldwater's "continued speaking out" after
he left the Senate. It is safe to assume he has not been at all disappointed in the past decade. During the ten years after he returned home to Arizona, Goldwater spoke out on a variety of
issues, endearing himself to some people and alienating himself from others. In the process, he left a more complex legacy
than many observers would have once assumed. If for older
Americans Goldwater's image typically remains mired in the
debacle of 1964, for younger Americans, especially those who
reside in Arizona, he emerged in the decade after his retire-

ment from the Senate as a "cheerful malcontent," to employ a description offered by columnist George Will in the spring of 1994. Arizonans in their twenties remembered little, if anything, about Goldwater as a senator. His actions and words as a public citizen generated their image of the man.

Goldwater returned home to an empty house and an uncertain future. Writing to his daughter, Joanne, in October 1986, he confessed to being "terribly lonesome back here without your mother. . . . I don't know how many times I reach for the phone just to call her and then I realize she is not there. . . . I don't know how many times I think, 'I better ask her permission before I do this,' and then I realize she isn't there." Being back in his old home brought back new reminders. Triple bypass heart surgery, artificial hips, and an artificial knee curtailed inclinations to camp, fish, hike, climb mountains, or, most missed of all, float the Colorado through his beloved Grand Canyon. Not wishing to simply become an "old saguaro" on top of his hill, he grumbled about age denying him an opportunity to serve. When you approach eighty, he told Dean Burch in the fall of 1988, "people for some un-Godly reason, don't think you can do a thing anymore. You start looking for lawns to mow."

However, Goldwater cared too much about his native state not to let contemporary developments pass by without an occasional pronouncement. Although he had wanted to prevent Bruce Babbitt from appointing a Democrat to succeed him in the Senate, he admired the man. On his final day as a member of the Senate, he wrote to Babbitt to praise him for doing "a good job for Arizona." Despite not having "the cooperation you should expect from the legislature . . . you'll go down as a very fine Governor." He concluded in a telling footnote: "As a fellow native of the state, thank you, you've added a lot of luster to the name of Arizona and to that lovely name of Babbitt." Babbitt's unlikely successor, Republican Evan Mecham, had won a curious three-person race for the position in the fall of 1986, winning with less than 40 percent of the vote. The right-wing Mormon car dealer had been known as the Harold

Barry Goldwater at his desk, at home. Photograph by Leonard McCombe. Barry Goldwater Photograph Collection, courtesy of the Arizona Historical Foundation

Stassen of Arizona, always running for some office and never coming close to success. This time around he had captured the Republican nomination in a stunning primary upset of an overconfident veteran Phoenix legislator, Burton Barr. Barr struck many Republican voters as arrogant, and many of the party's newcomers were too young to remember or had not been present to behold Mecham's earlier fiascos. Running against the Democratic nominee, Superintendent of Public Instruction Carolyn Warner, and old Goldwater nemesis Bill Schulz, who jumped in at the last minute as an independent candidate, Mecham had garnered enough Republican votes to squeak through to victory.

Goldwater had dutifully backed Mecham as his party's nominee, but along with a lot of other Republicans had been chagrined by Mecham's performance as governor. Even if he would be the last person to criticize another for blunt language, Goldwater drew the line at a person who embarrassed

Arizona. Immediately after his inauguration, Mecham rescinded the state's Martin Luther King, Jr., holiday that Babbitt had declared. Through one comment after another that a great many people considered insensitive or incompetent at best, and ignorant and racist at worst—ranging from use of the word *pickaninnies* to a comment about the shape of Asian eyes—Mecham quickly became a political pariah. When a movement to recall the governor received an overwhelming number of signatures for a recall election, in October 1987, Goldwater called upon Mecham to resign. Republican National Committeeman Jack Londen called Goldwater's advice "way off base," and Senator John McCain considered it premature. Goldwater did not back down. In February 1988 he said Mecham was as stubborn as a mule and he could not govern the state. "He is a very obstinate man," Goldwater declared. "I used to drive mules and he's a lot like a mule." Two months later, Mecham had been forced out of office, impeached and convicted by the legislature. Goldwater wrote in the aftermath: "I'm glad he's out, even though many people disagree with me . . . he's a hell of a nice guy, a pleasure to be with, but he was a disaster in that governor's office."

Goldwater's part in evicting Mecham had not endeared him to the Jack Londens of Arizona, but they soon discovered that the former senator was just warming to the task. Many of them perhaps had not realized Goldwater's consistent willingness to recognize good work across party lines and to condemn ill-advised behavior within them. For example, Goldwater had written to Mario Cuomo following Cuomo's eloquent address to the Democratic convention in 1984, calling it "about the best speech I've ever heard." He informed the New York governor, "I liked what you had to say, and I think it served a real purpose." And if Goldwater were fond of a Democrat like Joe Biden, he could forgive a transgression like Biden's wholesale borrowing from Neil Kinnick's speeches and even twit him about it. After Biden had been dismissed from Walter Reed hospital in 1988, Goldwater advised him not to get so mad at people and to calm down; moreover, "if you're ever going to borrow a speech, do like I did—go way back, I stole a hell of a good one from Socrates." If the Democrat were a native Arizonan from a family Goldwater had known and respected, such as Senator Dennis DeConcini, he would advise him privately in May of 1988, well before the election in November, that "once in a while, I may have to make a statement that sounds like the old Republican I am," but reassure him in the same breath, "I know you're going to win this election and I can tell you under the cover of this envelope, I'm not going to do anything to hurt you." Goldwater also supported Morris K. Udall in his final campaign for reelection to the House of Representatives in 1990, sending him a five-hundred-dollar contribution, telling his old friend, who was battling Parkinson's disease, "to stay in the saddle," as "you've done this state more damn good than anyone I know." He reminded Udall, "I've always supported you, and I think it's time this old Republican quit hiding behind the bush."

Thus it should not have surprised Jack Londen when in 1992 Goldwater announced he could not support Doug Wead, the Republican nominee for the House of Representatives in Arizona's sixth congressional district. Wead had arrived in Arizona only two years before, and at least one native Arizonan had not been impressed by his overall understanding of his new environment. Instead, Goldwater backed State Senator Karan English, a Democrat, as one better able to serve her constituents. English won, and irritated die-hard Republicans blamed Goldwater for her triumph. Two years later, after a lackluster first term in Congress, English was easily defeated in her bid for reelection by a different Republican nominee, who this time around had Goldwater's endorsement.

Wead had also exasperated Goldwater, because as a former evangelical minister he embraced the kind of use of religion in politics that Goldwater abhorred. Throughout the 1980s Goldwater had attacked the Moral Majority for its approach to issues such as abortion and school prayer, contending that if a person did not go along 100 percent with them, "they're out to get you." He also had criticized the Republican party in

Arizona in 1989 for passing a resolution declaring the United States a Christian nation. "I don't like the party being taken over by a bunch of kooks," he said.

Those who had supported the resolution rather resented being called kooks. They also tended to be involved with or sympathetic to groups such as Arizona Right to Life. When Goldwater in 1992 also opposed Proposition 110, which called for a ban on abortions except to save a mother's life or in cases of rape and incest, he again bore the brunt of criticism. Jay Nenninger, the executive director of Arizona Right to Life, argued that given his stance, Goldwater no longer should call himself a conservative. Queried about whether his position made him less conservative, Goldwater replied, "Oh, Christ, no," reminding his questioner that conservatives did not approve of governmental interference into people's lives.

Nenninger also complained about Goldwater's "supporting gays and homosexual rights." Goldwater had supported a gay rights ordinance considered by the Phoenix City Council earlier that year and in 1993 advocated ending the ban on gays in the American military. "We need all our talent," he wrote in a column for the *Washington Post*. Disagreeing with the "don't ask, don't tell" compromise, saying it did not deal with the issue but tried to hide it, Goldwater stated such discrimination was wrong, once again speaking of the need to stay out of private lives. He reminded his readers that others in the past had opposed blacks in the armed forces or women or an all-volunteer force. That opposition had been equally ill-founded. In the kind of classic one-liner that Americans like, regardless of whether they agree with the sentiment being expressed, Goldwater concluded that it did not matter whether soldiers were straight as long as they could shoot straight.

Goldwater's endorsement of a Martin Luther King, Jr./ Civil Rights Day additionally offended those on the far right. He had been scored against during the presidential campaign for his opposition to the 1964 Civil Rights Act, and, while he insisted time and again that he did his best to end segregation in Phoenix and to promote civil rights in more recent years, as

has been noted, in comparison to his interest in the Indians of
Arizona, African Americans occupied far less of his time and
consideration. Regardless of how one judged his record, he
thought it unfair for Arizona to be seen as a racist state, an
image heightened by some of Mecham's remarks and the rejection in 1990 by Arizona voters of a paid holiday for state
workers to observe Martin Luther King, Jr.'s, birthday. In a
state where voters are called on constantly to vote on a great
many ballot propositions, they were greeted by two relating to
this issue. One created a King holiday and thus an additional
state holiday, while the other substituted the King holiday for
Columbus day. The yes vote split, and the King day lost by less
than 1 percent. The National Football League, which contributed to a backlash immediately before the vote by threat-
ening to pull the 1993 Super Bowl from Arizona if the vote
failed, promptly made good on its pledge. Civic pride and empathy for the business sector prompted Goldwater to join
those who called for Arizonans to vote in favor of a 1992 ballot proposition which created a holiday observance for King
and also combined Washington's and Lincoln's birthdays into
Presidents Day, following the national model, thus not increasing the number of paid state holidays. Proponents of the
measure used a brochure with endorsements by Goldwater
and Ronald Reagan. Granting that he and King had had their
differences, Goldwater also praised him for his "insistence on
nonviolence . . . the most decisive factor in effecting a peaceful, non-divisive, irreversible movement toward securing civil
rights for all." Goldwater urged a yes vote on Proposition 302
"because I feel it is right for Arizona and right for America."
In a state with 3 percent African American population, the
measure gained a 62 percent approval, despite a continuing
objection to any kind of recognition for King in portions of
rural Arizona and in Mesa. Speaking to an Arizona history
class at Arizona State University in December 1995, he referred
to King as "a very good man" and suggested that Mesa voters
had been primarily responsible for delaying approval of the
holiday.

This track record angered not only Nenninger but also many others in Arizona who had supported Goldwater in the past and thought he had drifted from his political moorings. What had happened? Some searched for scapegoats, trying to uncover individuals who had swayed the senator. They proclaimed Goldwater had been swayed on the matter of gay rights by a gay grandson and a lesbian grandniece. They blamed old age. But their favorite target appeared to be Susan Schaffer Wechsler of Scottsdale.

A branch manager for Kimberly Quality Care (and subsequently director of the Hospice of the Valley), Susan Wechsler had met Goldwater in 1990. Divorced and the mother of four children, she was thirty years younger than Goldwater. As the two became better acquainted, Goldwater drove her around Arizona to see his favorite places. They spent New Year's Eve in 1991 at Rainbow Bridge and were married by a retired Episcopal bishop, Joseph Harte, at the Goldwater home on February 9, 1992. In the fall of 1993, Goldwater said simply: "Every day she makes me happy." On another occasion, he noted the number of grandchildren each of them had brought to the marriage and, with a smile, observed: "I'm loaded." However, even new love had its limits. In addition to children and grandchildren, Susan Goldwater brought to the marriage a schnauzer that her husband found less than delightful, referring to it as a "one hundred year old French poodle." When Sofie's high-pitched yapping interrupted an interview at his home in the summer of 1994, Goldwater thundered: "Throw that damn dog in the incinerator and turn it on!"

Although Susan Goldwater's views may be generally more progressive on some matters than her husband's, she did not cast some kind of mesmerizing liberal spell over Barry Goldwater. For the most part she probably had little more effect on his views than he had upon Sofie. To cite but one example, Goldwater's analysis of current health care policies varied considerably from hers. Hearing him ramble on about the subject, she finally retorted in July 1994, "He's so ill-informed about it, he shouldn't even talk about it." Barry Goldwater's judgments on the issues enumerated in this chapter, in fact, appear to be quite consistent with his long-term determinations about freedom, choice, and the well-being of Arizona.

His most recent comments have not been a barrier to additional honors. At Arizona State University, Goldwater has held for the past eight years the Goldwater Chair of American Institutions. In this capacity he has made approximately 170 visits to the Tempe campus and west campus of the university, speaking informally to undergraduate and graduate students. He has enjoyed the give-and-take with the students, invariably praising their maturity and speaking optimistically about what they will contribute to Arizona's future. Arizona State University has also named a new research facility, constructed with federal funds, the Barry M. Goldwater Center for Science and Engineering.

The bombing and gunnery range near Gila Bend, Arizona, covering almost three million acres, has been renamed in Goldwater's honor. During his final term in the Senate, Goldwater fought to keep the range rather than to turn it over to private interests for cattle grazing. Given Goldwater's early experience in training pilots in the area in 1941 and his years as a pilot, he expressed pleasure at the designation of the range while acknowledging its limitations for cattle. At the ceremony announcing the appellation, Goldwater prompted laughter by saying that "if you can graze a cow on this whole damn place, I'll eat him."

Phoenix recognized Goldwater's contributions to aviation in 1990 by naming the new terminal at its airport after the recipient of the Distinguished Flying Cross. The *Arizona Republic* had suggested changing the name of Sky Harbor International to Barry Goldwater International, but Goldwater quickly scotched any effort in that direction. He did not protest the terminal's designation, however, nor did he try to dissuade the city of Scottsdale from altering 70th Street to Goldwater Boulevard in 1989. And he was flattered by the decision to call the new high school in Phoenix Barry Goldwater High and moved by the naming of its performing arts center after Margaret J. Goldwater. Heeding the memory of Goldwater's beloved Cyclone, school officials chose as a mascot a bulldog, not a schnauzer.

During 1994 and 1995 the accolades continued. One final example of recognition deserves mention. On December 11, 1994, at the Kerr Cultural Center in Scottsdale, the Arizona Civil Liberties Union held its 1994 Bill of Rights celebration. The organization presented its 1994 Civil Libertarian of the Year award to Barry Goldwater. Its March 1995 *Civil Liberties in Arizona* newsletter included a photograph of Goldwater from the celebration. He is flanked by American Civil Liberties Union national board member Alice Bendheim and Arizona Civil Liberties Union Executive Director Louis Rhodes. It is not necessarily a photograph one might have anticipated in 1964.

And it is not to imply that Goldwater and Rhodes were in full accord. For example, Goldwater agreed to serve as honorary chairman for a drive to make English the state's official language. Chairman of Arizonans for Official English Robert Park, of Prescott, noted that "Senator Goldwater is Mr. Arizona" and expressed his enthusiasm for Goldwater's willingness to lend his name to the effort. "You live in this country, you speak English; you live in Mexico, you speak Spanish; you live in France, you speak French," Goldwater stated. He had backed official-English measures as a senator, and he saw no reason now to change his mind. State Senator Jaime Gutierrez of Tucson responded that he was "a little disappointed, because Senator Goldwater has shared quite a history with Arizona, and he certainly has seen the cultural impact of different groups in Arizona's development." As it has in a number of other states, the initiative succeeded in Arizona.

Others were no doubt disappointed by Goldwater's answer to a question posed to him in October 1994 by William H. Rentschler of the *Los Angeles Times*. When asked, "What can we do to get this country straightened out?" Goldwater replied: "Well, I think we've lost the mother complex." He praised his mother: "My mother was a damn strong woman.

When I got out of hand, she'd give me a good whack. Set me straight on a lot of things. She was a great influence on my life." Goldwater stressed that "a person's mother is the most important factor in any kid's development." He added, "Mothers aren't around enough these days. They're out working or exercising or going to school or partying. Most of 'em aren't in close enough contact with their kids. We need more mothers to be mothers. That's the best way to get kids on the right track and reduce juvenile delinquency and gangs and violence."

The Sierra Club also did not consider giving Goldwater an award. On the one hand, he continued to inveigh against the encroachment on beautiful sites in the state. In 1988 he wrote to Betty Sue Ray and Wayne D. Iverson of the newly formed Northern Arizona Trust Lands, an organization trying to save open space with high scenic, ecological, and cultural values in the Sedona area, commending the group for its attempt "to perpetuate these lands. . . . God knows, this may be the last beautiful land in Arizona to withstand the thrust and deterioration of man's efforts to build bigger houses and buildings." In addition, Goldwater deplored the air pollution in the Salt River valley, complaining about "the brown crap" that obscured the view from his house. "We've got too many automobiles," he told Arizona State University students in December 1995. "I think it's a crime the way we've let the automobile exhaust mix with the dust of the desert. I hope some day we can get rid of all that." Yet when asked if there were any chance of getting people out of their cars and into mass transit, Goldwater expressed his doubts. He did not wish to deny the kind of individual freedom the car provided.

So what could be done? Goldwater still embraced technology as a panacea to solve pressing environmental problems. In this instance, he suggested: "Maybe we'll invent a new way to run cars—something other than gasoline." He insisted, "We'll work it out." Goldwater maintained a comparably sunny optimism about the question of Arizona's water supply. "I'm not worried about it," he averred. Echoing a prophecy he had made more than thirty years before, he spoke about using the Pacific Ocean. Desalinization was "beginning to cost not quite as much as it used to and so we'll just drop a hose in the Pacific Ocean and it will take a long time to drink that."

During 1995, both the *Arizona Republic* and the *Tribune* newspapers appeared to be taking a far more critical stance than they once had toward the question of growth in Maricopa County. In March the *Republic* published an article by Gail Tabor which it headlined "Developers Still Climbing Mountain." Tabor documented the ongoing struggle over Camelback Mountain. Although recognizing Goldwater's earlier role in preserving Camelback's summit, Tabor also quoted a homeowner near the Phoenician Resort, which wanted to build new homes at higher elevations and add more holes to its golf course. Shirley Odegaard asserted, "Barry thinks he did something into perpetuity, but anyone who knows Arizona politics knows perpetuity is impossible."

Goldwater would agree, and his interest in saving the mountain has not flagged, but his more general response to urban sprawl in the valley did not deviate from the persistent paean to "progress" he had offered for decades. "You can't complain about progress," he said in November 1995. "My God, in 20 to 25 years this is going to be the fourth biggest city in the U.S. There's no way to stop it." He repeated the prediction to the university students in December. Suggesting that this growth will make it "too big a place for me," he prefaced his prognostication with an affirmation of his enduring pride in development. "I'm very proud of what Arizona has done," he emphasized.

The next day the *Tempe Tribune* published the next installment in its series, "Sprawl: The Valley's Growing Dilemma." The headline on December 5, 1995, read, "Buyers, Builders Share Blame." Reporter Doug MacEachern inquired: "You can look at all the desert destruction and, perhaps cynically, but certainly with some legitimacy, ask yourself: Is the idea to make it all go away?" At the end of the 1950s Goldwater had been elated with the boom the decade had witnessed. "There's no stopping Arizona!" he proclaimed, combining a native sense of pride and an almost innocent endorsement of growth. Almost forty years later, MacEachern's story received a sub-head: "No innocents in business of sprawl." However, Arizona governor Fife Symington, for one, did not seem unduly troubled. "I think the die is cast in this valley in terms of our patterns of growth," the former developer said. "And I believe it's good. It's not bad."

In his ambivalent yet ultimately acquiescent posture toward that business, Goldwater once again mirrored the society in which he lived. He certainly expressed more mixed emotions about what development had wrought, but he could not bring himself to favor the kind of restrictions necessary to bring any kind of fundamental change to this ongoing process. In December 1995 a poll of valley residents indicated they strongly supported maintaining desert and mountain lands. At the same time, as Mesa Planning Director Frank Mizner noted, "I haven't had citizens organizing saying enough is enough." He added, "Growth is almost a religion in Mesa. Nobody, with rare exceptions, stops to think about the negative impact of the growth," including the loss of farmland, increased traffic, and the need for more schools. "People tend to ignore them or deal with them in piecemeal fashion," Mizner concluded.

Elsewhere in the state versions of the same scenario could be perceived. Those in the White Mountains treasured their idyllic surroundings yet incited inhabitants of Phoenix and Tucson to build or buy cabins or homes "in the cool pines" in order to get away from triple-digit temperatures. Old-time citizens of Prescott and Prescott Valley luxuriated in the revenues brought by the onrush of new subdivisions and commercial concerns, all the while reproaching newcomers for contributing to a variety of new urban ills. Only the existence of federal, state, and county parks preserved some degree of open space in greater Tucson, as the transmutation of private land parcels swallowed up chunks of previously pristine terrain. Pima County's population more than doubled from 1970 to 1995, exacerbating air quality and solid waste disposal prob-

lems as well as encouraging rezoning for high-density housing and the creation of projects such as North Ranch, labeled
by its critics a Disney desert.

Even the Central Arizona Project had fulfilled the old
proverb of being careful about what you wish for, as skyrocketing costs for its water and the continuing decline of farming
created what had once been unimaginable: the project actually
now delivered more water than Arizona could use. Secretary
of the Interior Bruce Babbitt commented that debt repayment
clauses had not worried anyone in the 1960s. "It was just sort
of an article of faith that we'd do whatever is necessary to get
and use the water. The premise of reclamation was that you
sign now and worry about economics later."

Later had arrived at century's end, but public officials puz-
zled over what to do next. Once again, Barry Goldwater's response to the price of progress continued to be emblematic of
the complicated, at times contradictory, impulses of the residents of America's forty-eighth state. In 1996 he persisted as
a symbol of an evolving culture in a place that combined
promise and denial. Goldwater embodied the sentiments and
aspirations of most of Arizona's populace as he had throughout a long, colorful, and full life. He could look back upon the
twentieth century and ponder the evolution of his home country. Certainly he had done his part to encourage interest in its
rich past through his photographs and his part in establishing
and leading the Arizona Historical Foundation. His photography, reprinted frequently in *Arizona Highways,* had also bolstered tourism. His enthusiasm for the Grand Canyon and the
Grand Canyon State had encouraged countless others to discover the scenic wonders of Arizona. His ties to aviation, the
military, and the electronics industry had done much to foster economic growth. He had helped transform the workings
of Arizona politics through revitalization of the Republican
party. His ability to laud individualism and yet demand federal
assistance for major endeavors such as the Central Arizona
Project reflected a kind of bifurcated approach to the needs of
the era to which most of his peers subscribed. His interest in

Indian history and culture had promoted a more general appreciation for the central place of Native peoples in the state, even as he had occasionally advocated using Native lands for the benefit of non-Native communities. He had labored indefatigably to build Arizona and had observed the complications and consequences of its maturation. If any single person can be said to have personified the character of a state over the course of a century, for Arizona that individual unquestionably had been Barry Goldwater. The words he employed in an interview following his final return from Washington remained appropriate. "Thank God I could represent Arizona," he said.

Sources

The main source for this biography is the Barry Goldwater Papers housed in the Arizona Historical Foundation in Tempe, Arizona. The foundation is independent of Arizona State University but is quartered in Hayden Library at the university. The papers reflect the senator. They are open, uncensored, and remarkably candid about his public career and private life. In addition to his correspondence and materials relating to his years in the U.S. Senate, they also contain extensive files of newspaper stories, editorial cartoons, and other pertinent matter.

The Arizona Historical Foundation also holds the papers of the Goldwater family, Hancock family, Paul J. Fannin, Bert Fireman, Orme Lewis, Jonathan Marshall, Lester W. Ruffner, and William Saufley. The papers of Carl T. Hayden, Howard Pyle, and John Rhodes are housed in Special Collections, Hayden Library, Arizona State University. Texts of interviews conducted by Ross Rice, author of a biography of Carl Hayden, are also available there. The Charles Halleck Papers are held by Indiana University in Bloomington.

In addition to notes from Goldwater's presentations to classes at Arizona State University and his remarks at the roundtable, "Continuity and Change in Arizona since World War II," held at Arizona State University on April 5,1989, I have also employed comments made by the senator in a personal interview conducted at his home in November 1995. Although this interview had been postponed for some time and took place at the very end of the process of writing this book, it nonetheless allowed me to gather additional anecdotes and perceptions that I am delighted to be able to include here. Other participants in the 1989 roundtable were Budge Ruffner, Frank Snell, and Jack Pfister. A videotape of this panel is available at the Arizona Historical Foundation. An interview with Jack Pfister in the summer of 1995 also proved especially helpful. Interviews with Gary Avey, Hugh Harelson, Richard Hart, Jonathan Marshall, Elsa Mulham, Bob Reveles, and Barton Wright also yielded valuable information and insights.

Goldwater's books are essential reading. The most important for my purposes have been *The Conscience of a Conservative* (Shepardsville, Ky.:

Victor, 1960), *Delightful Journey down the Green & Colorado Rivers* (Tempe: Arizona Historical Foundation, 1970), *Goldwater*, with Jack Casserly (New York: Doubleday, 1988), and *With No Apologies: The Personal and Political Memoirs of Barry M. Goldwater* (New York: William Morrow, 1979). For Goldwater's photography, in addition to *Delightful Journey*, see *Arizona Portraits* (Phoenix: privately printed, 1940), *Barry Goldwater and the Southwest* (Scottsdale, Ariz.: Troy's Publications, 1976), and *People and Places* (New York: Random House, 1967). Goldwater also contributed the text to accompany *Arizona*, a collection of the photographs of David Muench (Chicago: Rand McNally, 1978).

Goldwater has been the subject of a number of biographies. Most of these studies are hagiographic. They tend to focus too exclusively on the presidential race of 1964 and have been written by journalists or other freelance writers who either worked for Goldwater or sympathized entirely with his political cause, as they saw it. I have not employed such work directly. However, Burton Bernstein, "AuH₂O," *New Yorker* (April 25, 1988), 43–73, is a perceptive profile. On the occasion of Goldwater's retirement from the Senate in December 1986, the *Phoenix Gazette* compiled a special supplement, "Barry Goldwater: The Warrior Comes Home," which includes helpful glimpses of Goldwater's life and career. Although published in cooperation with the Arizona Historical Foundation and hardly an impartial view, Dean Smith, *The Goldwaters of Arizona* (Flagstaff, Ariz.: Northland Press, 1986), is based on extensive interviews and offers useful information in regard to the history of the Goldwater family. Written with the full cooperation and participation of the Goldwater family is Robert Alan Goldberg, *Barry Goldwater* (New Haven: Yale University Press, 1995). Goldberg's book is based on extensive archival research and provides a more thorough and more independent judgment than prior biographies. Published in October 1995, it appeared too late to influence my interpretation. As we used some of the same sources, particularly the Goldwater papers, Goldberg and I came to comparable conclusions in some instances; my study pays greater attention to the southwestern dimensions of Goldwater's life and career.

Bradford Luckingham, *Phoenix: The History of a Southwestern Metropolis* (Tucson: University of Arizona Press, 1989), is a valuable overview of the city's evolution. For Tucson, see C. L. Sonnichsen, *Tucson: The Life and Times of an American City* (Norman: University of Oklahoma Press, 1975). The struggle against growth in Tucson and Albuquerque (but not Phoenix) has been analyzed recently by Michael F. Logan, *Fighting Sprawl and City Hall: Resistance to Urban Growth in the Southwest* (Tucson: University of Arizona Press, 1995). Mark E. Pry, "Arizona and the Politics of Statehood, 1889–1912" (Ph.D. diss., Arizona State

University, May 1995), provides a solid examination of this phase of Arizona's political history. The quotation from the *Coconino Sun* relating to the visit by Albert Beveridge to Arizona is from Karen Underhill Mangelsdorft, "The Beveridge Visit to Arizona in 1902," *Journal of Arizona History,* Autumn 1987, p. 250. The most recent synthesis of Arizona history is Thomas E. Sheridan, *Arizona: A History* (Tucson: University of Arizona Press, 1995). On the early years of the Salt River Project, see Karen Smith, *The Magnificent Experiment: Building the Salt River Reclamation Project, 1890–1917* (Tucson: University of Arizona Press, 1986). The title for the first chapter is borrowed from Elliott West, *Growing Up with the Country: Childhood on the Far Western Frontier* (Albuquerque: University of New Mexico Press, 1989). West reminds us that those children who were born in the West or moved there when very young saw the land in a different way than parents who came from different environments.

My comprehension of western urban history in general and the history of metropolitan Phoenix has also been aided by Carl Abbott, *The Metropolitan Frontier: Cities in the Modern American West* (Tucson: University of Arizona Press, 1993); Carol A. O'Connor, "A Region of Cities," in *The Oxford History of the American West,* ed. Clyde A. Milner II, Carol A. O'Connor, and Martha A. Sandweiss (New York: Oxford University Press, 1994), 535–64; and John M. Findlay, *Magic Lands: Western Cityscapes and American Culture after 1940* (Berkeley and Los Angeles: University of California Press, 1992). For syntheses of western American history in the twentieth century, with significant attention to urbanization, I have relied upon Michael A. Malone and Richard W. Etulain, *The American West: A Twentieth-Century History* (Lincoln: University of Nebraska Press, 1989); Gerald D. Nash, *The American West in the Twentieth Century* (Englewood Cliffs, N.J.: Prentice Hall, 1973); and Richard White, *"It's Your Misfortune and None of My Own": A History of the American West* (Norman: University of Oklahoma Press, 1991).

For Goldwater's importance as a photographer, I have consulted interviews conducted with Goldwater by Evelyn Cooper (available in the Goldwater papers) as well as Evelyn Cooper, "Creating Understanding with a Camera: Senator Barry M. Goldwater," *Native Peoples* 1, no. 1 (Fall 1987): 17–22; an interview with Goldwater by Peter Ensenberger, "Barry Goldwater on Photography," *Arizona Highways,* May 1988, pp. 12–17; and Robert C. Dyer, "The Formative Years," in *Timeless Images* (Phoenix: Arizona Highways, 1990), a volume which reviews the evolution of the magazine. In addition, my involvement as a historical consultant for "Barry Goldwater: Photographs and Memories," a production of KAET, Arizona State University's public television station, also contributed to my understanding of this subject. The production first aired in the spring of 1995 and is available on videotape.

The *Arizona Good Roads Association Illustrated Road Maps and Tour Book,* originally published in 1913 and reprinted by *Arizona Highways* in 1987, offers a vivid sense of tourism and travel conditions in Arizona a year after statehood. *Arizona Highways* provides through the years a clear picture of the importance of the Grand Canyon in the overall marketing of Arizona. Don Briggs has produced "River Runners of the Grand Canyon," a two-hour survey on video of the people who have made the journey. Goldwater is interviewed for this engaging story. A contemporary guide to the Colorado River and the canyon that accompanied me from Lee's Ferry to Phantom Ranch in the summer of 1995 is Larry Stevens, *The Colorado River in Grand Canyon,* 4th ed. (Flagstaff: Red Lake Books, 1995).

Goldwater's participation in aviation and the military is chronicled in a variety of magazine articles, copies of which are available in the Goldwater papers. The impact of the war years is discussed by Luckingham and other observers. Ivan Doig, *Heart Earth* (New York: Atheneum, 1993), presents but one example of how Arizona attracted workers during the war years. Gerald D. Nash, "Shaping Arizona's Economy: A Century of Change," in *Arizona at 75: The Next 25 Years,* ed. Beth Luey and Noel Stowe (Tucson: Arizona Historical Society, 1987), 123–47, emphasizes the significance of the war years in altering the workings of the Arizona economy. Goldwater's initial campaign for the Senate is analyzed by William T. Hull, an Arizona State University graduate student, in "Candidates, Parties, and Political Change: 1952 and the Beginning of a New Political Era in Arizona." For the career of Ernest McFarland, see James McMillan, Jr., "Ernest W. McFarland: Southwestern Progressive, the United States Senate Years, 1940–1952" (Ph.D. diss., Arizona State University, 1990).

The standard source for the 1964 presidential campaign is Theodore H. White, *The Making of the President 1964* (New York: Atheneum Publishers, 1965). As one might imagine, the Goldwater campaign received somewhat different coverage in the *Arizona Republic* than it did in the *New York Times.* The Goldwater papers include a thorough canvas of how the press analyzed and reported his candidacy as well as the texts of various speeches. Biographies of Lyndon Johnson offer intriguing perspectives on the election. See, for example, Paul Conkin, *Big Daddy from the Pedernales* (Boston: Twayne Publishers, 1986). Among the many interviews conducted with Goldwater after the election, one with David Broder, published in *The New York Times* Sunday magazine, is particularly searching; see "There's No Radical Change in Goldwater," June 19, 1966.

Goldwater's involvement in the Watergate crisis and the end of the Nixon
presidency is considered in his autobiographies and detailed in his papers. The Jonathan Marshall Papers add insight into the 1974 race for
the Senate. Tom M. Sullivan, *My Life & Times* (Phoenix: Phoenix
Books, 1986), addresses Sullivan's role in Arizona politics, including
the 1980 election. For assessments of the evolving American political
landscape, I have consulted, among others, Christopher J. Bailey, *The
Republican Party in the U.S. Senate: 1974–1984: Party Change and Insti-
tutional Development* (Manchester, England: Manchester University
Press, 1988); Mary C. Brennan, *Turning Right in the Sixties: The Conservative Capture of the GOP* (Chapel Hill: University of North Carolina Press, 1995); Leon D. Epstein, *Political Parties in the American
Mold* (Madison: University of Wisconsin Press, 1986); Allen J. Matu-
sow, *The Unraveling of America: A History of Liberalism in the 1960s*
(New York: Harper & Row, 1984); Kevin P. Phillips, *The Emerging Republican Majority* (New Rochelle, N.Y.: Arlington House, 1969); Nicol
C. Rae, *The Decline and Fall of the Liberal Republicans from 1952 to the
Present* (New York: Oxford University Press, 1989); and A. James Reich-
ley, *Life of the Parties: A History of American Political Parties* (New
York: The Free Press, 1992).

Bradford Luckingham, *Minorities in Phoenix: A Profile of Mexican American, Chinese American, and African American Communities, 1860–1992*
(Tucson: University of Arizona Press, 1994), presents a helpful overview. Jose Maldonado, "3 du Octubre: The Ghost Worker Strike at
Arrowhead Ranch," an unpublished paper completed for Professor
Miguel Tinker Salas's history graduate seminar at Arizona State University in 1993, provides details about the strike and the general issue of
Mexican and Mexican American farm laborers. The Chicana/o collection in the Arizona State University library also yields considerable information about Mexican American community life in Arizona.

My perspective on the Indians of northern Arizona is grounded in three
years' residence on the Navajo Nation from 1969 to 1972, my own research on modern Navajo history, and teaching at Arizona State University from 1975 to 1976 and since 1986. I have drawn from my book,
The Navajo Nation (Albuquerque: University of New Mexico Press,
1983); from an essay, "Knowing the Land, Leaving the Land: Navajos,
Hopis, and Relocation in the American West," in *Montana: The Magazine of Western History,* Winter 1988, pp. 67–70; and from various jour-
neys, including a hike from the site of Rainbow Lodge to Rainbow
Bridge. Information about the Smoki may be gleaned from the collections of the Sharlot Hall Museum in Prescott and the Heard Museum
in Phoenix. I have benefited from copies of materials provided to me by
Robin Hunt, a student in one of my classes at Arizona State University,

and by the research of Jennifer DeWitt for her M.A. thesis on the Smoki. Gladwell Richardson, *Navajo Trader,* ed. Philip Reed Rulon (Tucson: University of Arizona Press, 1986), relates the early years of the Rainbow Lodge and the activities of an important family of traders. Mary Shepardson and Blodwen Hammond offer an informed analysis of Navajo Mountain in *The Navajo Mountain Community: Social Organization and Kinship Terminology* (Berkeley and Los Angeles: University of California Press, 1970). The Heard Museum houses the Goldwater collection of kachinas. Books by David Brugge, Catherine Feher-Elston, and Jerry Kammer relate different versions of the Navajo-Hopi land dispute and Goldwater's part in it. See Brugge, *The Navajo-Hopi Land Dispute: An American Tragedy* (Albuquerque: University of New Mexico Press, 1994); Feher-Elston, *Children of Sacred Ground: America's Last Indian War* (Flagstaff: Northland Publishing, 1988); and Kammer, *The Second Long Walk: The Navajo-Hopi Land Dispute* (Albuquerque: University of New Mexico Press, 1980). E. Richard Hart, ed., *Zuni and the Courts: A Struggle for Sovereign Land Rights* (Lawrence: University Press of Kansas, 1995), is essential reading in regard to Zuni oral history, lands, and land claims. Personal conversation with Hart and a letter from him about Goldwater's role in regard to Zuni Heaven have also added to my understanding of this matter.

Edward Abbey offered a variety of loving and devastating commentaries on Arizona; see, for example, "The BLOB Comes to Arizona," in a collection of his essays, *The Journey Home: Some Words in Defense of the American West* (New York: E. P. Dutton, 1977). For a discussion of the cultural baggage brought by newcomers to Arizona, see my essay, "The Cultural Politics of Water in Arizona," in *Politics in the Postwar American West,* ed. Richard Lowitt (Norman: University of Oklahoma Press, 1995), 22–41. The conflict between Arizona and California over the Colorado River is described by many writers, including Marc Reisner, *Cadillac Desert: The American West and Its Disappearing Water* (New York: Viking, 1986), and Philip L. Fradkin, *A River No More: The Colorado River and the West* (New York: Alfred A. Knopf, 1984). The story of Echo Park is well told by Mark Harvey, *A Symbol of Wilderness: Echo Park and the American Conservation Movement* (Albuquerque: University of New Mexico Press, 1994). During the course of my research for a biography of Carlos Montezuma, I first gained appreciation for the emotions raised by the prospect of Orme Dam. My conversations with residents of the Fort McDowell reservation and with such advocates for the Yavapais as Carolina Butler of Scottsdale taught me about these feelings, as did a paper by Paul Lowes, "Sitting on Gold: Yavapai Resistance to Orme Dam," completed for my American Indian history class at Arizona State University in 1989.

Tributes from various U.S. senators upon the occasion of Goldwater's retirement from the Senate give a rich sense of his standing among his
colleagues. Articles in the *Arizona Republic* and the *Tempe Tribune*
provide coverage of and commentary on Goldwater's participation in
Arizona life after 1986. *High Country News* of Paonia, Colorado, pays
close attention to environmental issues in the West. My residence in
Arizona since 1986, Goldwater's many presentations at Arizona State
University, and my interview with him in November 1995 also informed
the final chapter.

Index

Abbey, Edward, 191–92
Abbott, Carl, 61
Abbott, Chuck, 24
Abourezk, James, 185
Acheson, Dean, 87
Adams, Ansel, 24, 26, 45, 170, 174
African Americans: and Goldwater, 122, 152–53, 233–34; and 1964 campaign, 121–22
AiResearch, 57
Akin, Wayne M., 67
Allied Signal, 191
Alsop, Joseph, 95
Aluminum Corporation of America, 57
American Civil Liberties Union, 237
American Enterprise Institute, 120
American Express, 113, 191
American Federation of Labor–Congress of Industrial Organizations (AFL-CIO), 184
American Indian Religious Freedom Act, 187
Americans for Democratic Action, 85
America West, 191
America West Arena, 190
Apache County, Ariz., 89, 187
Apache County Independent News (Saint Johns), 79
Apaches, 83, 159
Arizona, 14, 26, 29, 40, 50, 78, 87, 93, 94, 98, 101, 105, 123, 135, 137,

223, 224, 226, 227, 228, 235, 236; African Americans of, 122, 152–53, 233–34; Asian Americans of, 50, 152–53; beauty of, 9, 19, 24, 32, 36–37, 79, 131, 175, 200, 205, 238; chili of, 139–40; early development of, 4–6; economy of, 18–19, 21–23, 35, 45, 46, 48, 57–60, 62–64, 151-52, 180–81, 189–93, 197–98, 202, 211, 219, 240–41; federal presence in, 17–18, 21, 57, 64, 77, 83, 132, 159, 201, 209–10; Indians of, 21–23, 35, 41–43, 45–46, 83, 99, 133–34, 144, 151, 152, 155–65, 167–75, 177–88, 215–19, 242; Mexican Americans of, 20–21, 152–55; migration to, 35, 57–58, 62–63, 72–73, 81, 84, 102, 129, 147, 156, 160, 192, 202, 240; photography of, 24–26, 41–42, 45, 79, 139, 167, 241; politics of, 5, 58, 60, 70, 72–84, 88–91, 99, 102, 115, 128–32, 140–43, 144–50, 152–55, 183–84, 192, 229–34, 241; statehood of, 15–16, 20–21; tourism in, 18–19, 21–23, 35, 56, 158, 163–64, 169, 211, 213, 241; water politics of, 67–68, 193–201, 215–19, 238–39, 241
Arizona, 43
Arizona Canal, 9, 203
Arizona Cardinals, 190

Arizona Center, 190
Arizona Civil Liberties Union, 237
Arizona Club, 9
Arizona Conservation Council, 206
Arizona Conservation Foundation, 206
Arizona Daily Star (Tucson), 89, 201
Arizona Daily Sun (Flagstaff), 89–90
Arizona Department of Water Resources, 218
Arizona Diamondbacks, 190
Arizona Good Roads Association, 22
Arizona Highways: evolution of, 23–24, 40–43, 46; and Goldwater, 24, 40–42, 155, 184, 241
Arizona Historical Foundation, 12, 241
Arizona Interstate Stream Commission, 67, 196, 198, 201
Arizona National Guard, 195
Arizona Pioneers Historical Society, 157
Arizona Portraits, 43
Arizona Public Service, 191
Arizona Republic, 116, 185, 191, 198; and growth in Salt River Valley, 239; and support for campaign to save Camelback Mountain, 208; and support for Goldwater, 72, 77, 89, 98, 142, 150; and support for Orme Dam, 215–16
Arizona Right to Life, 233
Arizonans for Official English, 237
Arizona State University: and Goldwater, 7, 118, 234, 236, 238; growth of, 60; as site of Fiesta Bowl and Super Bowl, 190
Armed Forces Journal, 226
Armed Services Committee, 132, 223, 226–27

Armed Services Reorganization Act, 211, 223–25
Army, U.S., 50–52, 87, 226
Army Corps of Engineers, 218
Arrowhead Ranch, 154
Arthur, Chester Alan, 96, 177
Ash Fork, Ariz., 7
Asian Americans, 50, 152–53
Atkinson, Alfred, 67
Audubon, 216–17
Austin, Norman, 217–19
Automobiles: and impact on metropolitan Phoenix, 11, 63; and role in tourism, 21–22; and travel in Arizona, 48
Avey, Gary, 23–25
Avey, George, 23–24
Aviation: and Goldwater, 47–54, 64–65, 73–74, 170–71, 224, 241; and Phoenix, 50, 55–57, 236

Babbitt, Bruce: and Goldwater, 133, 185, 229; as governor, 218, 222, 249; and water, 241
Babbitt family, 152, 168, 170, 229
Bailey, John M., 114
Baker, Mildred, 29
Baker, Russell, 98
Baltimore Sun, 95
Bank One, 190–91
Bank One Ballpark, 191
Baroody, William, 120
Barr, Burton, 230
Barry Goldwater and the Southwest, 26
Bates, Tom, 25–26
Behrens, Earl, 81–82
Bendheim, Alice, 237
Benson, Ezra Taft, 144
Benson, Steve, 144
Beveridge, Albert, 20–21
Biden, Joseph, 228, 231–32
Big Mountain, Ariz., 181

Bimson, Walter, 59–60
Bingaman, Jeff, 224
Bisbee, Ariz., 42, 90
Black Mesa, 157, 180
Blue Lake, 161–62
Bluff, Utah, 29
Book of the Hopi, The (Waters), 75
Borum, Ida Mae, 169
Borum, Stanton, 169
Bosque Redondo, N. Mex., 159
Bowie, Ariz., 22
Boyden, John, 178–79
Bozell, Brent, 93
Brennan, Mary C., 119–20, 123
Bricker, John, 90
Bridges, Styles, 95
Bright Angel Trail, 21, 38
Broder, David, 129
Brophy, Frank, 203, 205–206
Brower, David, 199
Brown, Bill, 35
Brown, Pat, 114
Bruder, Will, 190
Bryan, William Jennings, 116
Bumpers, Dale, 224, 226
Burch, Dean, 226, 229; as director
  of 1964 campaign, 120; as legisla-
  tive assistant to Goldwater, 120;
  and 1968 campaign, 132
Bureau of American Ethnology, 163
Bureau of Reclamation, 195, 198
Butterfield, Alexander, 135

California: and Colorado River,
  194–95, 197; industrial economy
  of, 57; influence of, 192, 194;
  1964 primary of, 110–11; residential pattern of, 63; as site of
  Goldwater family vacations, 7,
  114, 221; and vote for Lyndon
  Johnson, 123
Camelback Mountain: beauty of,
  156, 204–205, 220; campaign to

save, 201, 205–206, 208–11; con-
  temporary threats to, 239; resi-
  dential development near, 153,
  205–206
Cameron, Ariz., 29, 168–69, 203
Canyon de Chelly, 24, 42–43
Carefree, Ariz., 100
Carleton, James, 159–61
Carlson, Raymond, 23–24, 40–41,
  46
Carter, Jimmy, 215
Casa Grande, Ariz., 67, 73
Case, Clifford, 101
Casserly, Jack, 93
Castro, Raul, 183–84
Cataract Canyon, 27, 32
Catholics, 69, 119
Cave Creek, Ariz., 100
Central Arizona Project (CAP):
  construction of, 215; federal sup-
  port for, 197, 241; and Orme
  Dam, 216–18; passage of legisla-
  tion for, 200–201; significance
  of, 197–98
Chandler, Ariz., 17, 62
Charleston News and Courier, 98
Charter Government Committee,
  68–70
Chavez, Cesar, 154
Chicago, Ill., 7, 192; as site of Gold-
  water speech, 86; as site of meet-
  ing to draft conservative Repub-
  lican candidate for president,
  108; as site of Motorola head-
  quarters, 59; as site of 1960 Re-
  publican convention, 97–98
Chicago Tribune, 98
Childs, Marquis, 100–101
Chili, 139–40
China, 54, 78
Chinese Americans, 153. *See also*
  Asian Americans
Christian Science Monitor, 135

Civil Rights Act of 1964, 121–22
Coal Mine Canyon, 40
Coaton, Joan, 214
CO Bar Ranch, 170
Cochise, 159
Cochise County, Ariz., 89
Coconino County, Ariz., 90
Coconino Sun (Flagstaff), 20
Cohn, Bernard, 4–5
Collier, John, 164
Colorado Plateau, 24, 39–40, 83, 112, 155
Colorado River: Arizona share of, 67–68, 194–98; and Glen Canyon dam, 200; Goldwater family association with, 28, 211–12, 229; Goldwater film on, 38–40, 68, 198; Nevills trip on, 27–29, 32, 35–39; Powell trip on, 27–29, 39
Colorado River Aqueduct, 196
Colorado River Compact, 194–95
Colorado River Storage Project, 198. *See also* Central Arizona Project
Communism: American anxiety about, 96, 101; Goldwater and, 77, 96, 100, 115; Harvard and, 100; McCarthy and, 87–88; Nixon and, 92
Computers, 191. *See also* Electronics
Conkin, Paul, 118
Conscience of a Conservative, The (Goldwater), 92–93, 95
Consolidated Vultee, 57
Coolidge, Ariz., 68
Cooper, Evelyn, 26, 43
Cory, Kate, 162
Cow Palace, 112, 121
Cox, Archibald, 136
Cronrath, H. W., 210–11
Crossing of the Fathers, 32
Cuba, 103, 109

Cuomo, Mario, 231
Curtis, Edward, 163
Cushing, Frank Hamilton, 187
Cutler, Hugh Carson, 29, 32, 38

Dallas, Tex., 62, 105, 140
Davis, Dixie, 217
Davis, Wayne, 24
Davis-Monthan Field, 56
Daw, John, 169
Dean, John, 135
DeConcini, Dennis, 132–33, 218, 232
DeConcini family, 232
Defense Department, U.S., 58, 224, 227
Delightful Journey, 27
Dellenbaugh, Frederick, 29, 39
Democratic Party, 85, 93, 99; candidates for U.S. Senate from Arizona, 76–78, 80–81, 88–89, 129–32, 140–43, 144–49; domination of Arizona politics, 72, 76–77, 88; gains in 1958 election, 91; Goldwater support for candidates of, 229, 231–32; and Morris Goldwater, 5; and Navajo vote, 183–84; 1960 convention of, 97; 1964 campaign of, 112–14, 116, 118–19, 121–23; and recognition of Goldwater, 223–24, 226–28; and representation of Arizona minority groups, 152; and South, 125; and unions, 85–86
DePaoli, Frank, 144
Deppe, James, 68, 70–71
Depression, 17, 19, 219
Diamond Creek, 39
Diné. *See* Navajos
Dinébe'iina Nahiilna Be Agaditahe. *See* DNA Legal Services
Dirksen, Everett, 86
DNA Legal Services, 182–83
Dodd, Christopher, 224

Doig, Ivan, 57–58
Dole, Robert, 228
Douglas (Ariz.) *Dispatch*, 89–90
Dunn, William H., 39

Eagleton, Thomas, 113
Echo Park Dam, 198–99
Economic Opportunity, U.S. Office of, 193
Edison, Thomas, 47
Ehrenberg, Ariz., 5–6, 157
Ehrlichman, John, 135
Eisenhower, Dwight D.: bipartisan appeal of, 76; criticism of, 93, 101; election of, 81; and end of second term, 92; Goldwater support for, 76; and 1964 campaign, 121
Eisenhower, Judy, 133, 137
Electronics: and Arizona growth, 47, 55, 58–60, 65, 132, 191, 241; and Arizona politics, 72
Elks Lodge, 70
Elmer, Carlos, 24
Elson, Roy, 129–32, 145
El Tovar (Ariz.), 21
Encanto Park (Phoenix), 7
English, Karan, 232
Environment: and Arizona growth, 190–92; and Black Mesa, 198–99; and Camelback Mountain, 205–206, 208–11; and Colorado Plateau, 28–29, 36, 39–40, 42–43, 155, 212; and Echo Park, 198–99; and Glen Canyon, 198–200; and Grand Canyon, 212–15; and Orme Dam, 215–19; and Phoenix growth, 12, 190, 202; and Salt River Valley growth, 17, 63, 190, 192, 202, 239; and Sedona area, 238; Texas chili as danger to, 140
Episcopalians, 7, 68, 223, 235
Ervin, Sam, 133

Escalante, Silvestre Velez de, 32
Eubank, Lisbeth, 170

Fannin, Paul, 12, 128–29, 132
Farming, 59, 193, 197–98
Federal Housing Administration, 64
Feldt, Gloria, 223
Fiesta Bowl, 190
Findlay, John, 63
Fireman, Bert, 12
Flagstaff, Ariz., 29, 89–90, 157, 170, 190
Florence, Ariz., 22
Ford, Gerald, 138, 215
Fort McDowell Indian Community: and Goldwater, 186, 216–19; and Orme Dam, 202, 215–19
Fort Sumner, N. Mex., 159–60, 169, 178
Fortune, 80
Foster, Hohen, 69
Fountain Hills, Ariz., 145
Fraternities, 100. *See also* Smoki
Fredericks, Oswald White Bear, 174–75
Fredonia, Ariz., 123
Friends of the Earth, 223

Ganado, Ariz., 22
Gap, Ariz., 35
Gardner, Gail, 116, 167
Gates, Jay M., 67
Gay rights, 233, 235
General Accounting Office, 184
General Electric, 59
Geological Survey, U.S., 36
Geronimo, 159
G.I. bill, 60
Gila Bend, Ariz., 236
Gila City, Ariz., 4
Gila County, Ariz., 89
Gila Project, 196

Gila River, 14, 190
Glen Canyon, 27, 32, 46, 198–200
Glen Canyon Dam, 198–200
Glendale, Ariz., 17, 62, 73, 154
Glendale News, 91
Globe, Ariz., 23
Goldmar, Inc., 154
Goldwater, Anna, 28
Goldwater, Baron: birth of, 4; business activities of, 6, 7, 15; death of, 14; parental role of, 7, 9, 12, 14; personal traits of, 7, 9; and Phoenix development, 9, 203; wedding of, 7
Goldwater, Barry: and affection for Arizona, 32, 37, 39, 40, 45, 46, 90, 156, 189, 239–41; and African Americans, 121–22, 152–53, 233–34; anti-Communism of, 77, 115; appeal of, 65, 70, 72, 77, 79–80, 81, 85–87, 90, 92–96, 98, 101–102, 116, 127, 130–31, 138–39, 143–44, 227–28; and Arizona economic development, 18, 35, 58, 59–60, 62, 67, 83, 180–81, 189, 192–94, 197, 201; and Arizona history, 12, 25, 32, 35, 82, 241; and Arizona pioneer families, 129, 132–33, 152, 229, 230; and Arizona tourism, 18, 35, 164, 241; and Asian Americans, 50, 152–53; and aviation, 47–54, 56, 73, 170–71, 224, 236; birth of, 7; as businessman, 15, 18, 28, 46, 56, 64, 67, 74, 77, 82, 164; and campaign to save Camelback Mountain, 205–206, 208–11; childhood of, 7, 9, 11–12; and Clifton White, 108, 111, 120–21; and Colorado River trips, 27–29, 32, 35–39, 68, 82, 211–12; and *The Conscience of a Conservative*, 92–95; criticism of, 66, 85, 88–89, 95–96, 101, 104,

111–12, 114, 118, 121–23, 125–26, 130–32, 141–42, 145–47, 149–50, 217, 233, 235; and Cuba, 109; culinary skills of, 32, 139–40; education of, 12, 14–15, 103–104; and electronics, 47, 58–60, 132; and Evan Mecham, 229–31; family life of, 17, 29, 38, 74, 75, 144, 202–204; and father, 4, 6–7, 9, 12, 14, 38; and gay rights, 233, 235; and Grand Canyon, 27–29, 37–39, 211–15, 229, 241; and grandparents, 3–6; and growth, 55–56, 67, 204–205, 238–42; and Hopis, 155–58, 161, 167, 172–75, 177–87; and Howard Pyle, 72–73, 81, 149, 177, 180–81; and Indians, 161, 167–75, 177–88, 213–14, 242; and Joe McCarthy, 87–88, 139; and John F. Kennedy, 102–105; and labor, 82, 85–86, 184; and Lyndon Johnson, 105, 107, 109, 118, 122–23; and Martin Luther King, Jr., 234; and Martin Luther King, Jr. Holiday, 234; and Mexican Americans, 152–55; and military, 47, 50–54, 132, 223–24, 226–27; and mother, 6–7, 9, 14, 38, 94, 115, 155, 156, 237–38; and named recognition of, 226–27, 236–37; as native Arizonan, 7, 65, 75, 90, 94, 151, 155–57, 161, 241; and Navajos, 155–57, 161, 168–72, 177–87; and Nelson Rockefeller, 106, 109–11, 121; and newspaper column, 94–95; and 1980 campaign for senate, 144–50; and 1950 Pyle campaign for governor, 72–73; and 1952 campaign for senate, 70, 73–82; and 1958 campaign for senate, 88–91; and 1974 campaign for senate, 140–43; and 1964

Civil Rights Act, 121–22; and 1964 convention, 112–13; and 1964 presidential campaign, 114–16, 118–27; and 1964 presidential primaries, 107–12; and nuclear war, 109, 112, 114, 118–19, 126; and Peace Corps, 100; and Peggy Goldwater, 16, 25–28, 38, 50, 52, 75, 140, 143, 150, 170, 186, 221–23, 229; and Peter MacDonald, 181–86; and Phoenix city council, 69–71, 76–77; and photography, 24–28, 38, 40–43, 45–46, 68, 79, 167, 170, 241; and Prescott, 78–79, 115–16, 155, 162, 164, 167; as public speaker, 72, 74, 83–86, 97; and Richard Nixon, 113, 121, 134–38; and role of federal government, 17–18, 56, 77, 83–84, 119–20; siblings of, 7, 9, 11, 38, 69, 154, 209; and Smoki, 162–67; and Social Security, 109, 111, 126; and South, 121–25; and Susan Goldwater, 235–36; and Tennessee Valley Authority, 110; and uncle Morris, 4–6, 69, 115; Vietnam, 109; and William Scranton, 112, 121

Goldwater, Barry, Jr., 17, 38, 144, 204

Goldwater, Ben, 4

Goldwater, Caroline, 4

Goldwater, Carolyn, 7, 11, 38

Goldwater, Elizabeth, 4

Goldwater, Henry, 4

Goldwater, Joanne, 17, 38, 144, 204, 229

Goldwater, Joseph, 3–5

Goldwater, Josephine Williams: and campaign to save Camelback Mountain, 208; and migration to Arizona, 7; parental role of, 7, 9,
14, 49, 94, 115, 155, 156; personal traits of, 7, 9, 38, 237–38; wedding of, 7; youth of, 6

Goldwater, Leonora (Annie), 4

Goldwater, Michael (Mike), 3–6, 94, 157

Goldwater, Michael (son), 17, 28, 38, 144, 204

Goldwater, Morris, 4–6, 66, 78, 115

Goldwater, Peggy Johnson: and Barry Goldwater, 27–28, 38, 50, 52, 140, 143, 170, 221–22, 229, 236–37; death of, 223; and dislike for Washington, D.C., 140, 144; education of, 16, 26; health problems of, 140, 144, 150, 222–23; and Margaret Arch, 186; and Margaret J. Goldwater Performing Arts Center, 236–37; parental role of, 17, 75; and photography, 25–26; and Planned Parenthood, 16–17, 93, 223; and Rainbow Lodge, 168–69; shyness of, 16–17, 105

Goldwater, Peggy (daughter), 17, 38, 144, 204–205

Goldwater, Robert, 35, 58, 69–70; birth of, 7; and campaign to save Camelback Mountain, 209; and Goldmar, 154

Goldwater, Sallie, 6

Goldwater, Sally, 208

Goldwater, Samuel, 4

Goldwater, Sarah Nathan, 4

Goldwater, Susan Wechsler, 235–36

Goldwater Bombing and Gunnery Range (Ariz.), 236

Goldwater Boulevard (Scottsdale), 236

Goldwater Center for Science and Engineering (Arizona State University), 236

Goldwater Chair of American Institutions (Arizona State University), 236

Goldwater High School (Phoenix), 236–37

Goldwater's department store: beginnings of, 5–6; and Goldwater, 14–15, 28, 82, 86; legacy of, 75, 78–79; and World War II, 57

Goldwater Terminal (Sky Harbor Airport), 236

Good Samaritan Medical Center (Phoenix), 223

Goodyear Aircraft, 57

Graham County, Ariz., 89

Grand Canyon: and dams, 198–200; and expansion of national park, 133, 201, 211–15; Goldwater affection for, 28, 197–200, 229, 241; and Nevills trip, 27–39; photographs of, 24, 38, 40, 68; and Powell trip, 29, 39; as tourist attraction, 21–22

Grand Wash Cliffs, 213

Greenland, 52–53

Greenlee County, Ariz., 89

Green River, 29, 198

Green River, Utah, 27, 29, 32, 198

Green River, Wyo., 27

Guadalupe, Ariz., 190

Gutierrez, Jaime, 237

Hadley, Walt, 126

Haig, Alexander, 138

Haldeman, Robert, 135

Hall, Sharlot, 163

Halleck, Charles, 126–27

Hamann, A. P., 61

Hancc Rapid, 37

Harelson, Hugh, 41

Hart, E. Richard, 187–88

Harte, Joseph, 235

Harvard University, 100, 104

Harvey, Mark, 198–99

Harvey Houses, 21

Hatch, Orrin, 228

Hatfield, Mark, 228

Havasupais, 201, 211–14

Hayden Carl: Americans for Democratic Action rating of, 85; congressional service of, 75, 146; as family friend of Goldwater, 128–29; Goldwater praise of, 146; influence of, 99; as member of pioneer family, 129, 133; and retirement from senate, 129; and Stephen Shadegg, 93

Headrick, Myles, 172

Healing v. Jones, 179–80. *See also* Hopi-Navajo land dispute

Healy, Paul F., 86

Heard Museum (Phoenix), 40, 172, 174

Heart Earth, 57

Hellon, Mike, 146

Helms, Jesse, 143

Henderson, Esther, 24

Herberger Theater (Phoenix), 190

Herblock (Herbert Block), 104

Hermit Falls, 37

Hetch Hetchy, 199

Hills, Jim, 165

Hispanics, 152, 159. *See also* Mexican Americans

Holbrook (Ariz.) *Tribune News*, 77

Holloway, Bert, 140

Honeywell, 60

Hood, Hiawatha, 217

Hoover, Herbert, 76

Hoover Dam, 39, 195

Hopi-Navajo land dispute: and attorneys, 178–79; and coal resources, 180; evolution of, 177–81, 185–86; and Goldwater, 133–34, 179–81, 184–85; impact of, 179, 185; origins of, 177

Hopis: arts of, 42, 157–58, 162,

172–75; attorneys of, 178–79; ceremonies of, 158, 169; Goldwater interest in, 152, 156–57, 161, 162, 169, 172–75; lands of, 40, 42, 133, 155–57, 175, 177–80; positive image of, 159, 161, 167; and tourism, 22–23; and vote for Goldwater, 184. *See also* Hopi-Navajo land dispute
Hospice of the Valley, 235
Housing and Urban Development, U.S. Department of, 209
Houston, Tex., 63–64
Howland, O. G., 39
Howland, Seneca, 39
Hoyt, Ross G., 60–61
Hualapais, 214
Hughes Aircraft, 182
Hughes Missile Systems, 191
Hummel, Don, 209
Humphrey, Hubert, 122, 126, 134
Huntley, Chet, 127
Hyde, Bessie, 27
Hyde, Glen, 27

Iceland, 52–54
Ickes, Harold, 196
Indian Claims Commission, 178
Indians: changing status of, 167–68; and Goldwater, 41, 99, 151–52, 155, 162, 164, 242; images of, 21, 163; and James Abourezk, 185; and Smoki, 165; and tourism, 21–22. *See also* individual Indian communities
Iverson, Wayne D., 238

Japanese Americans, 50. *See also* Asian Americans
Javelinas, 192
Javits, Jacob, 101
Jaworski, Leon, 136
Jennings, Renz, 147

Jews, 5, 69, 147
John Birch Society, 114
Johnson, Caleb, 181
Johnson, Lady Bird, 210
Johnson, Lyndon B.: and Colorado River Storage Act, 200; criticism of, 109, 118; election of, 123, 125, 129; Goldwater dislike of, 105, 118; as potential presidential candidate, 85; as presidential candidate, 105, 107, 116, 118–19, 122–23, 126
Johnson, Peggy. *See* Peggy Johnson Goldwater
Johnson, Ray, 16, 128
Joint Chiefs of Staff, U.S., 224, 226
Judiciary Committee, U.S. House of Representatives, 136
Judson School, 203

Kachinas, 157–58, 162, 172–75
KAET television station, 139
Kahl, Lester, 81
Kaibab National Forest, 131, 213
Kaibito, Ariz., 169
Kaiser Aircraft, 59
Kayenta, Ariz., 29, 131
Keams Canyon, Ariz., 178
Keating, Kenneth, 91
Kelley, P. X., 224, 226
Kennedy, John F.: charisma of, 81; death of, 105, 116; and Goldwater photographs, 104; and potential race against Goldwater, 104–105, 118, 119; presidency of, 102–103; and televised debates, 107
Kennedy, Ted, 226–27
Kibbey, John Rinker (Rink), 157–58, 172, 174
Killian, Ray, 67
King, Martin Luther, Jr., 231, 233–34
King, Martin Luther, Jr. Holiday, 231, 233–34
Kingman, Ariz., 67–68, 73, 142, 197

Kinnick, Neil, 231
Kirk, Russell, 96
Kitchel, Denison, 120–21
Kleindienst, Richard, 135–36
Kleppe, Thomas S., 179
Knowland, William, 91
Kober, Leslie R., 69
Kober, Margaret, 69, 206
Kolb, Ellsworth, 28, 39–40
Kolb, Emory, 28, 30–40
Kolbe, John, 82
Kolhua/wala:wa, 187. See also Zuni Heaven
KOOL television station, 145
Korean War, 78
KOY radio station, 66
Kravitz, Irving, 49
KTAR radio station, 66, 137
Ku Klux Klan, 114

Labor, 82, 85–86, 142, 184
Lake Havasu, Ariz., 190
Lake Mead, 27, 39, 198, 213
Lake Pleasant, 218
Lake Powell, 199
La Paz, Ariz., 4–5, 157
Larabee, Charles W., 29, 35
Lathan, Mabel, 12
Latter-day Saints, Church of Jesus Christ of, 69, 144. See also Mormons
Laxalt, Paul, 226
Lee, John Doyle, 35
Lee's Ferry, 27, 32, 35, 195
Levin, Carl, 228
Lincoln Day dinners, 72, 83–85
Lindsay, John, 125
Lippmann, Walter, 95
Litchfield Park, Ariz., 57
Littell, Norman, 178–79
Little Colorado River, 157, 169
Lodge, Henry Cabot, 97, 110–11, 126

Londen, Jack, 231–32
Los Angeles, Calif., 47; and acquisition of water, 194, 196; growth of, 62, 194; as site of Goldwater speech, 86; as site of 1960 Democratic convention, 97. See also California
Los Angeles Times, 94, 98
Lowman, Hubert, 24
Low Mountain, Ariz., 185
Lucas, Charles E., 126–27
Luce, Henry, 208
Lukachukais, 43
Luke, Frank, Jr., 47
Luke Field, 47, 51, 54, 56, 60

McAdams, George, 168
MacArthur, Douglas, 78
McCain, John, 222, 231
McCarthy, Joseph R., 87–88, 139
MacDonald, Peter, 181–84, 186
MacEachern, Doug, 239–40
McElhaney, R. H., 67
McFarland, Ernest B.: election as governor, 88; as example in 1980 senate election, 148; and 1952 campaign for senate, 76–81; and 1958 campaign for senate, 88–91
McGibbeny, Joseph, 24
McGovern, George, 183
McGrory, Mary, 139
McLoughlin, Herb, 24
McNulty, Jim, 144
Manley, Ray, 24
Manning, Reg, 98, 208
Manuelito, 159
Marble Canyon, 27, 36–37, 43, 130, 213
Margaret Arch, 186
Maricopa County, Ariz., 147; and Central Arizona Project, 197; growth of, 54–55, 60, 62, 190, 236; and influence of southern

California, 111; planning and zoning commission of, 205–206; and role in Goldwater electoral victories, 89, 148–49. *See also* Salt River Valley

Marine Corps, U.S., 226

Marshall, Jonathan: and Navajo vote, 184; and 1974 campaign for senate, 140–43; and use of criticisms in 1980 campaign, 145

Marshall, Maxine, 142–43

Martori, Arthur, 159

Masons, 5, 70

Mecham, Evan, 229–31

Medina, Joe, 116

"Meet the Press," 84, 97

Melczer, Joe, 15

Mesa, Ariz.: growth of, 17, 54, 62, 190, 240; as home of George Avey, 23; as home of Keith Turley, 216; as home of Ray Killian, 67; and opposition to King holiday, 234; summer climate of, 22

Mesa Tribune, 89, 239

Methodists, 69

Metzenbaum, Howard, 227, 228

Mexican Americans, 20–21, 152–55

Mexican Hat, Utah, 27, 29

Mexico, 25; border of, 152; and Colorado River, 194, 196; and farm labor, 154; and Indians, 159; and Spanish language, 237

Miami, Ariz., 23, 153

Miami *Arizona Silver Belt*, 23

Miller, William, 104, 113

Mingus Mountain, 29

Mitchell, Theodore, 182

Mizner, Frank, 240

Mobile Press, 98

Moeur, Benjamin B., 195–96

Mohave County, Ariz., 89, 149

Mohave County Miner (Kingman), 68

Monticello, Utah, 29

Monument Valley, 24, 29, 42–43, 131, 172

Moore, Lee, 50

Moquis. *See* Hopis

Moral Majority, 232

Mormons, 229; and Fredonia, 123; and Mesa, 190; as pioneers, 35; and White Mountain communities, 152. *See also* Latter-day Saints

Motorola, 59, 191

Moyers, Bill, 119

Moynihan, Daniel Patrick, 228

Muench, David, 43

Muench, Josef, 24–25, 42–43

Muir, John, 199

Mulhern, Elsa, 148

Muncie, Ind., 16, 84, 95

Murdock, John, 76, 81

Murphy, Frank G., 69

Mutual Life Insurance Company, 69

My Life and Times (Sullivan), 147

Nakai, Raymond, 182–83

National Basketball Association, 190

National Football League, 234

National Press Club, 139

National Review, 92

Naughton, James M., 138

Navajo County, Ariz., 89

Navajo-Hopi land dispute. *See* Hopi-Navajo land dispute

Navajo Housing Authority, 184

Navajo Mountain, 168, 170–71, 186

Navajo Springs, Ariz., 35

Navajos: arts of, 23, 150, 160; attorneys of, 178–79, 182–83; ceremonies of, 170; and economic and social change, 45, 160; Goldwater interest in, 152, 155–57, 161, 168, 171–72, 177; Goldwater photographs of, 35, 41–43, 45–46; lands of, 39–40, 42–43, 133, 160, 168–69, 172, 175, 177–81, 186, 203,

213; language of, 204; Long Walk
of, 159–60, 169, 178; negative im-
ages of, 159–61; and tourism,
22–23; and votes for Democratic
candidates, 183–84. *See also*
Hopi-Navajo land dispute
Neilson, Earl, 48
Nenninger, Jay, 234, 235
Nevada, 151, 180, 194
Nevills, Doris, 29, 38
Nevills, Norman, 27–29, 35, 37–39
New Hampshire, 108–10
New Mexico, 224; border with Ari-
zona, 43, 161; chili of, 140; and
Colorado River, 194, 198; and
Navajo incarceration, 160; and
Navajo reservation, 175; statehood of, 20; and Zuni reservation, 187
New Republic, 96
New York Daily News, 86
New York Herald Tribune, 95
New York Times, 88, 93, 98, 102, 138
Nixon, Richard M.: anti-Commu-
nism of, 77, 87, 92; conservative
distrust of, 99; Goldwater criti-
cism of, 134, 136; and Goldwater
presidential campaign, 113, 121,
134; legacy of, 125, 139; 1972 political ambition of, 103; 1972 presidential campaign of, 134, 146,
183; 1960 presidential campaign
of, 92, 96–99, 108, 123, 126; resignation of, 136–37; in television
debates, 107; and Watergate,
134–39
Nixon Rock, 38
Nogales, Ariz., 85
North Atlantic Treaty Organization (NATO), 109
North Rim (Grand Canyon), 38
Novak, Robert, 103
Nunn, Sam, 226–27

Oak Creek Canyon, 24, 42, 51
O'Connor, Sandra Day, 226
Odegaard, Shirley, 239
One Salt, Isabel, 170
Ong, Walter, 153
Oraibi, Ariz., 157
Orme Dam, 201–202, 215–19
Orpheum Theatre (Phoenix), 40
Osborn, Sidney, 67

Page, Ariz., 180
Papago Park (Phoenix), 17
Paradise Valley, Ariz., 104, 203
Park Central Mall (Phoenix), 172
Parker, Ariz., 195
Parker, Jim, 115
Parker Dam, 195–96
Parks, Robert, 237
Paya, Oscar, 213–14
Payette Valley Standard (New Ply-
mouth, Idaho), 96
Peabody Coal, 180
Peace Corps, 100
Peaches, Daniel, 181
Peggy G (airplane), 52–54
Pell, Claiborne, 228
People and Places (Goldwater), 43
Peoria, Ariz., 86
Peoria, Ill., 86
Pfister, Jack, 132, 148, 193, 218
Phantom Ranch, 37
Phoenician Resort, 239
Phoenix, Ariz.: and aviation, 25,
47–50, 56–57, 193, 236; climate of,
56–57, 130, 215–16; downtown of,
40, 42, 48, 58, 80, 190; and fed-
eral government, 17–18, 57, 63–
64, 209, 233; government of,
59–61, 68–71, 76–77, 147, 209–10;
growth of, 11, 17, 54–56, 60–64,
67, 189–90, 193, 202, 204, 239;
as home of Goldwater family, 7,
11–12, 16–17, 78, 89, 128; and

Planned Parenthood, 16–17, 93, 223; race relations in, 122, 152, 153, 233–34

Phoenix College, 17

Phoenix Country Club, 128, 202

Phoenix Coyotes, 190

Phoenix Gazette, 82, 164; evaluation of Texas chili, 140; support for Goldwater, 70, 79, 89, 98

Phoenix Municipal Stadium, 17

Phoenix Suns, 190

Phoenix Union High School, 12, 40

Pima County, Ariz.: growth of, 240–41; and 1980 election for senate, 148; and 1958 election for senate, 89; and water, 194, 197. *See also* Tucson

Pinal County, Ariz., 89

Pinnacle West, 191

Pipe Springs, Ariz., 25

Platt, Earl, 187

Polacca, Ariz., 177

Pomeroy, F. I., 195

Potato, Charlie, 43

Powell, John Wesley, 27–29, 39

Presbyterians, 69

Prescott, Ariz.: and Goldwater family, 5–7, 78–79, 94, 155, 167; growth of, 190, 192, 240; image of, 42; as site for beginning of Goldwater campaigns, 78–79, 114–16; and Smoki, 162–65, 167; and support for Goldwater, 79, 89; and tourism, 22, 48

Prescott Courier, 89

Prescott Journal-Miner, 162–63

Prescott Valley, Ariz., 240

Preservation of Camelback Mountain Foundation, 206, 209–10

President Harding Rapid, 36–37

Pritzlaff, Ann, 208

Pritzlaff, John, 208, 210

Pritzlaff, Mary Dell, 208

Pueblo Indians, 160–61. *See also* Hopis; Taos Pueblo; Zunis

Pulliam, Eugene: and campaign to save Camelback Mountain, 208; and corporations, 59; and Phoenix city government, 60; and support for Goldwater, 70, 72–73, 142

Pyle, Howard: and correspondence with Goldwater, 149, 180–81; and gubernatorial campaigns, 70, 72–73, 75, 177; and Indian affairs, 177, 180–81; and influence on 1952 election for senate, 73, 81

Quayle, Dan, 113

Radio, 47–48, 66, 70, 126, 137

Ragsdale, Lincoln, 153

Railroads, 7, 21, 43, 152, 180

Rainbow Bridge, 26, 32, 41, 169, 235

Rainbow Lodge, 41, 162, 168–72

Ranching, 170, 211, 214, 236

Ray, Betty Sue, 238

Reagan, Ronald: appeal of, 102, 149; election of, 125, 149; and Hopi-Navajo land dispute, 180; and King holiday, 234; and 1964 presidential election, 127

Reasoner, Harry, 221

Reclamation Act of 1902, 21, 83

Redbud Pass, 169

Redlake Trading Post, Ariz., 168

Reed, Thomas Delbert, 29, 32

Reisner, Marc, 195

Rentschler, William H., 237

Republican Party, 134, 135, 146, 222–24, 227–28; anti-government stance of, 153; conservatives in, 95–97, 99–102, 106, 108, 126–27; gains in South, 123, 125; Lincoln Day dinners of, 72, 83–85; losses in 1958 election, 91;

and 1980 election results, 148–49; and 1986 election in Arizona, 229–30; and 1950 campaign in Arizona, 72–73; and 1952 campaign in Arizona, 75–81; 1960 convention of, 97–98; and 1964 convention of, 112–14; 1964 presidential campaign of, 114–16, 119–23, 126–27; and 1968 senate election in Arizona, 128–30, 132; revitalization of in Arizona, 58, 70, 72–76, 241; support for Joe McCarthy, 87–88

Reston, James, 102

Reuther, Walter, 85–86

Reveles, Bob, 153–55

Rhodes, John: Americans for Democratic Action rating of, 85; and Arizona water, 218; election of, 76, 81; as member of Arizona delegation, 99; and Nixon resignation, 136–37; and perspective on Goldwater, 110, 113

Rhodes, Lewis, 237

Rice, Ross, 128

Richardson, Elliot, 136

Richardson, Hubert, 168, 169

Richardson, Samuel Irby (S. I.), 168, 169

Richardson family, 29, 168, 169

Right to work, 86, 134

Roberts, John A., 67

Rockefeller, Happy, 111

Rockefeller, Nelson: appeal of, 106; conservative opposition to, 99; and criticism of Goldwater, 110–11, 116, 126; Goldwater criticism of, 97–98, 101; as hindrance to Goldwater candidacy, 121, 126; 1964 presidential campaign of, 109–12; political demands of, 93, 134

Rockefeller, Nelson, Jr., 111

Rogin, Michael, 88

Romney, George, 121, 125–26

Rooney, Andy, 143, 226

Roosevelt, Franklin D., 123

Roosevelt, Theodore, 21

Roosevelt Dam, 21, 193, 218

Roper, R. D., 48

Rosenzweig, Harry: and campaign to save Camelback Mountain, 208; as childhood friend of Goldwater, 11–12; and Goldmar, 154; 1950 Phoenix City Council campaign of, 69–70; and role in Goldwater decision to seek Phoenix City Council seat, 69–70

Rosner, Ann, 37

Ruffner, Budge, 115, 165, 167

Ruffner, George, 115

Rumsfeld, Donald, 183

Russia, 52, 77, 96, 109

Safford, Ariz., 73

Saint Johns, Ariz., 69, 79

Salt River, 11, 215

Salt River Project, 21, 132, 147, 218

Salt River Valley: agriculture in, 197; air pollution in, 220, 238; aviation in, 56; demographic and economic growth of, 21, 54, 59, 67, 72, 132, 202, 239–40; Mexican-American presence in, 152; political perspectives in, 83, 89, 216; and tourism, 18; views of, 25, 204; and water, 21, 194. *See also* Maricopa County

San Angelo, Tex., *Evening Standard*, 85

San Diego, Calif., 28, 49, 85

San Francisco, Calif.: and Goldwater family, 3–4; population of, 62; as site of Goldwater speech, 109; as site of 1960 Republican

convention, 96, 112–14; and support for Rockefeller, 111
San Francisco Chronicle, 81
San Francisco Peaks, 42
San Jose, Calif., 61
Santa Barbara, Calif., 24, 111
Santa Cruz County, Ariz., 89
Santa Fe Railway, 7, 21, 43, 152
Santa Monica, Calif., 7
Saturday Evening Post, 86
Saufley, Opal, 28
Saufley, William, 28–29, 35
Scenic Airways, 50
Schulz, William, 144–48, 230
Scott, Hugh, 137
Scottsdale, Ariz., 62, 140–41, 154, 202, 236
Scranton, William, 106, 112–13, 121, 126
Seattle, Wash., 62
Sedona, Ariz., 42, 190, 220, 238
Select Committee on Intelligence, 228
Separation Canyon, 39
Sevareid, Eric, 125
Shadegg, John, 78
Shadegg, Stephen: and *The Conscience of a Conservative*, 93; and correspondence with Goldwater, 140, 219; and Goldwater campaigns, 121, 146–47; and Goldwater newspaper column, 94
Show Low, Ariz., 87
Sidney, Ivan, 185
Sierra Club, 199, 214, 238
Sierra Vista, Ariz., 190
"Sixty Minutes," 143
Sky Harbor Airport, 17, 50, 56–57, 236
Slide Mountain, 213
Smith, Karen, 193
Snell, Frank, 59–60
Snowflake, Ariz., 42

Social Security, 58, 109, 111
Sockdolager Rapid, 37
Sonora, Calif., 3–4
South, U.S.: and Democratic Party, 85; and Goldwater appeal, 105; Goldwater vote totals in, 123; growth of Republican Party in, 121–22, 127
South Mountain Park, 17, 205
South Rim (Grand Canyon), 38, 40
Sparkes, Grace, 163
Sperling, Godfrey, Jr., 135
Sperry Rand, 59
Spivak, Lawrence, 84
Stalin, Joseph, 90
Stapleton, Ben, 61
Stassen, Harold, 98, 230
Staunton Military Academy, 12, 14, 204
Stegner, Wallace, 199
Steiner, Wesley, 218
Stevenson, Adlai, 81, 138–39
Sullivan, Thomas, 147–50
Sun City, Ariz., 145
Sun Devil Stadium, 190
Supai, Ariz., 213
Super Bowl, 190, 234
Symington, J. Fife, 208, 240
Symphony Hall (Phoenix), 190

Tabor, Gail, 239
Taft, Robert, 76
Taft, William Howard, 15, 21
Taos Pueblo, 161–62
Teapot Dome, 135
Television: distinction between TVA and, 110; Goldwater appearances on, 84, 97, 211; and 1980 campaign, 148; and 1960 presidential campaign, 107; and 1964 presidential campaign, 118–19; and 1964 presidential election results, 126

Tempe, Ariz.: growth of, 17, 54, 62; as home of Hayden family, 128; as site of artificial lake, 192; as site of Goldwater speech, 198. *See also* Arizona State University

Tempe Daily News, 198

Tempe Tribune, 239

Tenderfoot Plateau, 213

Tennessee Valley Authority (TVA), 110

Texas, 105, 107, 123, 125, 139–40

Thatcher, Ariz., 67

Thompson, Twinkle, 133, 185

Thornburgh, Jack, 49

Thurmond, Strom, 75, 226

Time, 86, 102

Tombstone, Ariz., 130

Tonalea, Ariz., 168

Tootsie, Oneita, 186

Topocoba Hilltop, 213

Toroweap Valley, 213

Tourism: and Arizona economy, 18–19, 21–23, 35, 46; and Grand Canyon, 211; and Indians, 22–23, 158; and Lake Powell, 199–200; promotion of, 18–19, 21–23, 35, 41, 241; and Rainbow Bridge, 169; and Smoki, 163–64

Tower, John, 139–40

Trading posts, 29, 168–70, 182–83

Trobham, Walter, 98

Truman, Harry, 78, 85, 141

Tuckup Point, 213

Tucson, 67, 73, 110, 237; former mayor of, 209; growth of, 57, 64, 190, 240–41; image of, 42, 190; newspaper criticism of Goldwater, 89; newspaper praise for Goldwater, 201; as site of Davis-Monthan Field, 56; television coverage of 1980 senate election results, 148. *See also* Pima County; University of Arizona

Tucson Audubon Society, 214

Tucson Daily Citizen, 89

Tully, Duke, 185

Tumber, Rosemary, 162

Tuna Creek Rapid, 38

Turley, Keith, 216

Turning Right in the Sixties (Brennan), 119

Tusayan, 157

Udall, Jesse A., 67

Udall, Morris K.: as cosponsor of Grand Canyon bill, 212; and decision in 1974 not to run for senate, 142; and depiction of Goldwater, 133, 143; as member of pioneer family, 133; praised by Goldwater, 99, 232; Washington, D.C., office of, 133

Udall, Nicholas, 69–71

Udall, Stewart, 85, 153, 209–10

Udall family, 152

United Auto Workers, 86

United Farm Workers, 153

United Indian Traders Association, 182

United States Military Academy, 14, 146. *See also* West Point

U.S. News and World Report, 126

U.S. West, 191

University of Arizona, 14–15, 25, 48, 67, 100, 104

Upchurch, Bonnie, 206

Utah, 228; and border with Arizona, 29; and Colorado River, 194, 198, 200; and Navajo reservation, 175

Valley Beautiful Citizens Council, 205–206

Valley National Bank, 59

Valley of the Sun, 18, 208. *See also* Salt River Valley

Vasey's Paradise, 36
Verde River, 215
Verde Valley, 51
Verkamp's store, 22–23
Veterans Administration, 64
Victor Publishing Company, 93
Vietnam, 109–10, 125

Waddell Dam, 218
Wallace, Norman G., 24
Wallop, Malcolm, 228
Wall Street Journal, 88
Wal-Mart, 191
Walters, Charles N., 68
Warm Creek Canyon, 32
Warner, Carolyn, 23
Washington Post, 96, 104, 134–35, 227
Watergate, 134–36, 139
Waters, Frank, 175
Watt, James, 218
Wead, Douglas, 232
Wechsler, Susan. *See* Susan Wechsler
    Goldwater
Weld, Stephen, 126
Wellton, Ariz., 67
Weston, Edward, 26
West Point, 14, 144. *See also* U.S.
    Military Academy
Westward Ho Hotel (Phoenix), 58,
    198
Wetherill, John, 29
White, Clifton, 108, 112, 120–21
White, Richard, 63–64
White, Theodore, 108, 113, 122
Whitehead, Ennis, 51
White Mountain Eagle (Show
    Low), 87
White Mountains, 42, 152, 240
Wickenberg, Ariz., 28, 142
Wickham, John A., Jr., 224
Wilderness Society, 199
Will, George, 229
Williams, Jack, 154, 181, 200–201

Williams, Josephine. *See* Josephine
    Williams Goldwater
Williams Field, 56
Wills, Garry, 138–39
Wilson, Katherine, 169, 172
Wilson, Maggie, 165
Wilson, Ray, 70
Wilson, Sam, 15, 17
Wilson, William W. (Billy), 169–70,
    172
Winslow, Ariz., 43
Wirthlin, Richard, 147
With No Apologies (Goldwater), 48
Women's Wear Daily, 15
Woolsey, Louise, 206
World War I, 47
World War II, 17, 28, 41, 51, 56, 62,
    72, 104, 167, 170, 172, 178, 196,
    202, 219
Wright, Barton, 172–75
Wynn, Bernie, 138–39
Wyoming, 29, 194, 198, 228

Yampa River, 198
Yarnell, Ariz., 28
Yavapai County, Ariz., 89, 114–15,
    148, 163–64. *See also* Prescott
Yavapai County Chamber of Com-
    merce, 163–64
Yavapai County Messenger
    (Prescott), 79
Yavapais, 186, 202, 215–19
Yellowstone National Park, 29, 132
Yosemite National Park, 199
Yuma, Ariz., 73, 90, 190
Yuma Air Base, 52, 54
Yuma County, Ariz., 89
Yuma Daily Sun, 89, 146

Zah, Peterson, 185
Zahniser, Howard, 199
Zuni Heaven, 162, 187
Zunis, 161–62, 187